In: Criminal Justice, Law Enforcement and Corrections

Batterer Intervention: Program Approaches and Criminal Justice Strategies

CRIMINAL JUSTICE, LAW ENFORCEMENT AND CORRECTIONS

Homicide Investigations
Allan B. Smythe
2009 ISBN 978-1-60692-258-3

Mass Incarceration and Offender Registry in the United States
Russell D. Javitze
2009 ISBN 978-1-60692-657-4

Batterer Intervention:
Program Approaches and Criminal Justice Strategies
Kerry Healey, Christine Smith and Chris O'Sullivan
2009 ISBN 978-1-60692-934-6

In: Criminal Justice, Law Enforcement and Corrections

Batterer Intervention: Program Approaches and Criminal Justice Strategies

Kerry Healey,
Christine Smith
and
Chris O'Sullivan

Nova Science Publishers, Inc.
New York

For permission to use material from this book please contact us:
Telephone 631-231-7269; Fax 631-231-8175
Web Site: http://www.novapublishers.com

LIBRARY OF CONGRESS CATALOGING-IN-PUBLICATION DATA

Available upon request
ISBN: 978-1-60692-934-6

Published by Nova Science Publishers, Inc. ✦ New York

CONTENTS

PREFACE

Batterer intervention programs are an integral part of any comprehensive approach to domestic violence. However, because intervention programs are relatively new, there is a need for increased communication between programming providers and criminal justice professionals. The latest publication in NIJ's Issues and Practices series, Batterer Intervention: Program Approaches and Criminal Justice Strategies provides judges, prosecutors, and probation officers with the information they need to better understand batterer intervention and make appropriate decisions regarding programming.

FOREWORD

In the late 1970's, activists working with battered women realized that, although they might help individual victims, no real progress could be made against the problem of domestic violence unless actions were taken to reform perpetrators and challenge the cultural and legal supports for battering. Batterer intervention was initiated as a first step toward changing batterers and raising cultural awareness of the problem. Criminal justice agencies have responded by referring an increasing number of batterers to interventions via pretrial or diversion programs or as part of sentencing. Among the programs contacted for this book, court-mandated batterers accounted for approximately 80 percent of all batterers attending programs.

To be effective, an integrated criminal justice response to battering must include all branches of the criminal justice system, frompolicetopretrial screeners,prosecutors,judges, victim advocates, and probation officers. This book provides information that these professionals need to work effectively and knowledgeably with batterer intervention staff and to make informed choices about program referral. Program staff will find information on the responsibilities and concerns of criminal justice personnel who prosecute, sentence, and supervise batterers. The primary goal of the book is to improve the working relationship and mutual understanding between criminal justice personnel and batterer program staff. A secondary goal of the book is to expand the debate about innovative batterer intervention approaches to include criminal justice personnel who work with batterers daily and criminal justice policymakers who are concerned with domestic violence.

Jeremy Travis
Director
National Institute of Justice

ACKNOWLEDGEMENTS

We wish to thank the many individuals in the study sites who laid aside their pressing and important work to share with us their considerable knowledge about batterer intervention. In particular, we wish to thank the batterer intervention program directors who welcomed us: Meg Crager of Family Services of Seattle; Joan Zegree of Zegree, Ellner and Berrysmith, Seattle; Dr. Ann Ganley, Seattle V.A. Medical Center; Dr. Roland Maiuro, Harborview Medical Center of Seattle; Roxanne Roos Finney, Ina Maka, Seattle; Anna Meyer, Seattle Counseling Service for Sexual Minorities; Buruch Giday, Refugee Women's Alliance of Seattle; Dr. David Adams of EMERGE, Cambridge; Dale Chell, Domestic Abuse Intervention Service (DAIS), Des Moines; Robert Gallup of AMEND, Denver; Robert McBride, The Third Path, Denver; Dr. Steven Stosny, Compassion Workshop, Montgomery County, Maryland; Wil Avery, House of Ruth, Baltimore; and Jonathan Cohen, Batterers Intervention Project, New York City. A number of other program directors shared their experiences with us by phone; in particular we would like to thank Terrence P. Crowley of Men Stopping Violence, Atlanta, and Sunya Faloyan of the Empowerment Project, Charlotte. We also thank the numerous criminal justice professionals, victim advocates, and policymakers who helped us with our site visits, including: Judith Shoshana, Hon. Helen Halpert, Sheila Hargesheimer, Sid Hoover, and Lynne Gordon in Seattle; Dr. Andrew Klein and Beth Ledoux in Cambridge; Hon. Carol S. Egly, Hon. Cynthia Moisan, and Joe Quinn in Des Moines; Suzanne Sigona, Linda Foote Smith, Dexter Shipman, Dr. Frank Robinson, Amy Houghton, Debbie Buckmaster, Mark Barnes, and Linda Ferry in Denver; and Roni Young, W. Roland Knapp, L. Tracy Brown, Rachel Wohl, and Peggy Araya in Baltimore.

Advisory board members, Robert Foster, Dr. Adele Harrell, Dr. Daniel Saunders, Dr. Richard Tolman, and Dr. Oliver Williams, were especially responsive and involved in guiding this book to completion. We are very grateful for their advice and insights. Dr. Edward Gondolf also provided important suggestions and information throughout the research process.

Carolyn Peake, program manager for the project at the National Institute of Justice (NIJ), took an active interest in the development of the book, including attending site visits to Seattle and Montgomery County, Maryland, and provided valuable support throughout the project. Cheryl Crawford, the contracting officer's technical representative at NIJ, and Virginia Baldau, former Director of NIJ' s Office of Development and Dissemination, both provided helpful suggestions that improved the book. Peter Finn of Abt Associates substantially improved drafts with his careful editing. Jocelyn Page of Abt Associates ably assisted with the compilation and analysis of State standards and guidelines for batterer intervention. Karen Minich, Angela Allegro, Sherri Brooks, Patricia Harmon, and Mary-Ellen Perry patiently coordinated the production of the book and the final desktop publication.

Kerry Murphy Healey,
Ph.D. Consultant to Abt Associates Inc.
Cambridge, Massachusetts

Christine Smith
Abt Associates Inc.
Cambridge, Massachusetts
Chris O'Sullivan, Ph.D. Victim Services Research New York, New York

Executive Summary

Requiring batterers to attend intervention programming as a condition of probation or component of pretrial diversion is fast becoming an integral part of many jurisdictions' response to domestic violence, yet many judges and probation officers lack basic information about the goals of and methods used by local batterer programs. The diversity of available programming and the emotionally charged ideological subtext to program choice make understanding and working with program providers potentially difficult for criminal justice professionals. This book is intended to meet the need for increased information exchange between criminal justice professionals and batterer treatment providers. Specifically, this book will help criminal justice personnel—including prosecutors, judges, probation officers, and victim advocates—better understand the issues surrounding batterer intervention and enable them to make appropriate referrals to programs and to communicate effectively with program providers. Program staff will find the book helpful in their efforts to understand the constraints faced by the criminal justice agencies that refer and monitor batterers as well as the underlying goals of the criminal justice system—to protect victims and to deter reoffense— and thus be able to align program practices with criminal justice expectations.

The Nature of the Problem

The legal definition of battering varies from State to State. As defined by many intervention providers, battering is a constellation of physical, sexual, and psychological abuses that may include physical violence, intimidation, threats, emotional abuse, isolation, sexual abuse, manipulation, the using of children, economic coercion, and the assertion of male privilege (such as making all major family decisions, or expecting the woman to perform all household duties). Only some of these behaviors—most commonly assault and sexual assault—are illegal. The majority of batterers arrested are heterosexual men; however, between 5 and 15 percent of those arrested for battering are women. Among females arrested for battering, many are thought to be "self- defending victims" who have been mistakenly arrested as primary or mutual aggressors. A small percentage of those arrested for battering are gay or lesbian. According to the 1992 National Crime Victimization Survey (NCVS), over 1,000,000 women were victimized by intimates (boyfriend, girlfriend, spouse or ex-spouse) compared to 143,000 men. In murders where the relationship between the victim and the offender was known, 26 percent of female murder victims were killed by intimates while 3 percent of male murder victims were killed by wives or girlfriends. (For the purposes of this book, the term "batterer" is given a masculine pronoun unless female batterers are being discussed.)

The cost of domestic violence to society and to the victims of battering is immense. Battering results in physical and psychological damage to victims, deaths, increased health care costs, prenatal injury to infants, increased homelessness of women and children, physical and psychological damage to children exposed to violence in their homes, and corresponding increases in demand for social, medical, and criminal justice services.

The Causes of Domestic Violence

Three theoretical approaches dominate the field of batterer intervention; however, in practice, most interventions draw on several explanations for domestic violence in their work. Each theory of domestic violence locates the cause of the violence differently.

- *Social and cultural theories* attribute domestic violence to social structures—such as patriarchy—and cultural values that legitimate male control and dominance over their domestic partners. *Feminist* (or "profeminist") batterer interventions are based on women's experience of these social and cultural factors, and use education and skills-building to resocialize batterers, emphasizing equality in intimate relationships.
- *Family-based theories* blame violent behaviors on the structure of the family and family interactions rather than on an individual within a family. *Family systems interventions* emphasize building communications skills and may involve the use of couples counseling with the aim of family

preservation. Family systems interventions are less common than other types of interventions because many practitioners object to treatments that do not assign blame to the batterer and identify a victim, and because this intervention approach may transfer some responsibility for the battering to the victim or endanger the victim if not performed conscientiously. As of 1996, 20 States had standards or guidelines that prohibit the use of couples counseling in batterer treatment.

- *Individual-based theories* attribute domestic violence to psychological problems such as personality disorders, the batterer' s childhood experiences, or biological disposition. *Psychotherapeutic, cognitive-behavioral, and attachment abuse* interventions are based on this theory.

Pioneers in Batterer Intervention: Program Models

Most pioneers in batterer intervention established programs based on a feminist educational model. The Duluth model is an example of a feminist educational curriculum. The EMERGE model blends feminist educational approaches with more intensive group work concerning relationships. At AMEND, feminist educational topics are used as a basis for an in-depth intervention addressing batterer psychology and moral development. All program models for batterer intervention discussed in chapter 3 are structurally similar; each proceeds from intake to assessment, victim contact, orientation, group treatment, completion or termination, and follow-up.

Current Trends in Batterer Intervention

A "one-size-fits-all" approach to batterer intervention cannot accommodate the diverse population of batterers entering the criminal justice system. Two new trends reflect the belief that more specialized approaches are needed:

- interventions tailored to a specific type of batterer (based on psychological factors, risk assessment, or substance abuse history); and
- interventions designed to enhance program retention and efficacy with specific populations (based on sociocultural differences such as poverty, literacy, race, ethnicity, nationality, gender, or sexual orientation).

Criminal Justice Response

Batterer intervention programs cannot be expected to deter domestic violence in isolation: a strong, coordinated criminal justice response is also needed. The combined impact of arrest, incarceration, adjudication, and intensive probation supervision may send as strong—or even stronger—message to batterers about their responsibility for their abusive behavior as batterer programs can. As key actions the criminal justice system can:

- *Expedite Domestic Violence Cases.* Adopt policies to expedite batterers' trial dates, sentencing, probation contact, and batterer program intake.
- *Use Specialized Units and Centralized Dockets.* Specialized domestic violence prosecution and probation units, and centralized court dockets for battering cases and restraining orders improve services to victims and better coordinate batterer prosecution, sentencing, and supervision.
- *Gather Broad-based Offender Information Quickly.* Create a system to gather complete defendant information for prosecutors and judges, including previous arrests and convictions (for both domestic violence and other crimes), substance abuse, child welfare contacts, and victim information.
- *Take Advantage of Culturally Competent or Specialized Interventions.* Maximize effective use of batterer programming by seeking appropriate interventions for batterers who are indigent, high risk, female, mentally ill, or incarcerated.
- *Coordinate Batterer Intervention with Substance Abuse Treatment.* In cases where the batterer has an alcohol or drug abuse problem, courts should mandate treatment as well as batterer intervention. Probation officers should intensively monitor batterers' compliance with substance abuse treatment through weekly urine testing.
- *Be Alert to the Risks to Children in Domestically Abusive Households.* Judges and probation officers should be alert to the danger posed by domestic violence to children (even to children who are not themselves physically abused) and coordinate with child protective services and programs that specialize in domestically abusive families to insure that batterers' children are safe and are receiving appropriate services.
- *Create a Continuum of Supports and Protection for Victims.* Victim advocates should be provided to monitor victim safety and to assist victims with the criminal justice system from the time of the assault through trial and/or probation. Victim advocates attached to probation

units are particularly important in monitoring the safety of women whose batterers are sentenced to a batterer program.

- *Encourage Interagency Cooperation.* Organize formal coordinating committees of probation officers, prosecutors, battered women's advocates, child protection workers, and batterer intervention providers to discuss batterer referral and monitoring policies regularly.

Conscientious supervision by criminal justice agencies (including monitoring by pretrial services, the judiciary, and probation officers) is central to criminal justice policy concerning battering and successful cooperation with batterer interventions.

Sources of Help and Information

There are numerous sources of additional information on batterer intervention, including State and national organizations, reference services, research literature and program manuals, and individuals who are willing to share their expertise with others in the field.

Chapter 1

INTRODUCTION

KEY POINTS

- The connection between the criminal justice system and batterer interventions is increasing: on average, 80 percent of clients in batterer programs are referred by probation officers or by court mandate.
- Judges, probation officers, criminal justice policymakers, and victim advocates need to understand the issues surrounding batterer intervention so they can make responsible referrals and communicate effectively with program providers.
- Batterer program providers need to understand the constraints faced by criminal justice agencies that refer and monitor batterers, as well as the goals of the criminal justice system.
- Battering—or domestic violence—may be defined as a constellation of physical, sexual, and psychological abuses that may include: physical violence, intimidation, threats, isolation, emotional abuse, sexual abuse, manipulation using children, total economic control, and assertion of male privilege (such as making all major family decisions and expecting the woman to perform all household duties).

- The majority of batterers are heterosexual men. Heterosexual women offenders constitute between 5 and 15 percent of those arrested for battering, and a small percentage of arrestees are gay or lesbian.
- Victims of battering come from all races, ethnicities, and socioeconomic groups; however, women with lower socioeconomic status may be at greater risk for abuse.
- Domestic violence inflicts immense damage to society in terms of physical and psychological injury to victims, deaths, health care costs, prenatal damage to infants, and physical and psychological damage to children exposed to violence in their homes.
- Evaluations of batterer interventions often raise methodological concerns and have yielded few generalizable conclusions.
- A broader, systemic examination of batterer intervention that focuses on the criminal justice response as well as program characteristics is needed.

The field of batterer intervention and the criminal justice system are becoming increasingly intertwined. On average, batterer intervention programs surveyed for this book estimated that 80 percent of their referrals were court-mandated. As a result, criminal justice personnel and victim advocates need reliable information about the nature and effectiveness of local interventions, while intervention providers need to understand the procedures used and constraints faced by criminal justice agencies that refer and monitor batterers. Obtaining current and accurate information on batterer interventions is challenging for criminal justice practitioners because programs are extremely diverse in approach and reflect a broad—and often contradictory—range of beliefs about explanations for battering as well as appropriate modes of intervention. In addition, the field is growing and diversifying in terms of the number of programs being offered, staff qualifications, and techniques used. Service providers, criminaljustice professionals, mental health workers, and researchers in the field of batterer intervention often have deeply held beliefs concerning "what works" with batterers and what best serves the needs of the victim and the criminal justice system. As a result, debates about batterer intervention may be contentious and personal, grounded in a mix of social philosophy, research findings, personal experience, and self-interest.

To assist courts and probation officers in selecting suitable batterer interventions—that is, programs that emphasize victim safety and have goals consistent with those of the criminal justice system—27 States and the District of Columbia had mandated or supported the development of State-level standards or guidelines for batterer programs, and another 13 States were in the process of developing standards by 1997 (see chapter 5, "Criminal Justice Response," and appendix A, "State Standards Matrix"). However, even in States where guidelines or standards are in place, community domestic violence coalitions, the judiciary, probation officers, and other criminal justice professionals often retain considerable discretion over program accreditation and referral. Because of the complexity of the field—and the seriousness of the ongoing threat posed to battered women when offenders are mishandled—criminal justice professionals who handle domestic violence cases have increased responsibility to be knowledgeable about the content and structure of batterer programs in their jurisdictions in order to make informed choices among the interventions being offered.

The Nature of the Problem

Domestic violence intersects with the criminaljustice system in the form of a number of criminal behaviors: assault and battery, harassment, breaking and entering, telephone misuse, violation of an ex parte or protection order, malicious destruction of property, sexual assault, and stalking as well as a number of other offenses that may not be immediately recognizable as domestic in origin (such as arson, fraud, or embezzlement). The classification of a crime as domestic violence may result in a less serious charge for the batterer despite evidence that "injuries that battered women receive are at least as serious as injuries suffered in 90 percent of violent felony crimes."[2] For this reason, judges, prosecutors, and probation officers need a clear sense of what behaviors constitute battering, who batters, who the victims of domestic violence are, and how they may appear in the criminal justice system.

About this Publication

The primary audiences for this book are judges handling and prosecutors trying domestic violence cases, probation officers supervising batterers, victim advocates, and batterer intervention providers. The book will also be useful to State and local domestic violence policy planners, domestic violence coordinating committees, and departments of public health and child welfare.

Goals of the Book

The primary goals of the book are to:

- provide current and objective information concerning the range of batterer interventions currently in operation throughout the country;
- review the most critical issues being debated by criminal justice professionals, academics, and service providers in the field;
- review promising criminal justice practices related to batterer intervention; and
- provide examples of coordinated criminal justice responses to battering that include referral to batterer intervention programs. Program enrollment, completion, and success rates were provided by the programs described in this book. No independent evaluations of the programs were undertaken for the book. However, selected evaluation literature is listed in chapter 6, "Sources of Help and Information," and evaluation outcomes are discussed briefly in this chapter. The book's focus is batterer interventions and their links to the criminal justice system. Because law enforcement commonly has little or no direct contact with batterer interventions, the book does not discuss police responses to domestic violence (e.g., the impact of mandatory arrest or the effectiveness of restraining orders).[1]

What Is Domestic Violence?

While the origins of domestic violence remain controversial (see chapter 2, "The Causes of Domestic Violence"), the majority of intervention directors interviewed for this book defined domestic violence as *a constellation of physical, sexual, and psychological abuses*.

Anne Ganley, one of the first mental health providers to establish a batterer treatment program in the late 1970's, defines domestic violence in terms of 1) the relationship of parties to the violence, 2) the perpetrator's behaviors, and 3) the function these behaviors serve.

Domestic violence is a pattern of assaultive and coercive behaviors, including physical, sexual, and psychological attacks, as well as economic coercion, that adults or adolescents use against their intimate partners.[3]

Programs reflecting a feminist perspective define domestic violence as coercive behavior aimed at gaining power and control within a relationship (see the discussion of the feminist model in chapter 2). This definition, pioneered by Ellen Pence of Duluth, Minnesota, is summarized in exhibit 1-1, "The Power and Control Wheel" of the Duluth model.[4]

Several Behaviors Batterers Use

Ganley' s and Pence's work points to the following common abusive behaviors:

- *Physical violence.* Physical abuse may include any unwanted physical behavior against a partner, such as pushing or shoving, throwing objects, hitting or beating, choking, burning, using a weapon, or restraining the partner from leaving. Physical abuse may also include refusing to get help for a partner if he or she is sick or injured. Physical abuse acts as a deterrent to independent action by the victim, including attempts to end a relationship or cooperate with the criminal justice system. Women are in the most severe danger of physical violence when they try to leave an abusive relationship: 75 percent of emergency room visits and calls to the police by battered women occur after separation.[5] Half the homicides resulting from domestic violence occur after separation.[6]
- *Intimidation.* Intimidation includes looks, gestures, and actions that remind the victim of the abuser's potential for physical violence, such as smashing things, destroying her property, abusing pets, or displaying weapons. Intimidation may also include abandoning a partner in a dangerous place.
- *Threats.* Abusers may threaten to hurt the victim, her family, her children, or her pets. They may also threaten to commit suicide or to cause trouble for the victim with government authorities, employers, family, or friends. Whether credible or not, threats can be as effective as taking action in deterring the victim from seeking help.
- *Isolation.* Isolation includes controlling what the victim does or whom she sees or contacts. The abuser may hold the victim against her will, deny access to a car or telephone, deter her from working or attending school, or alienate her from her family and friends. Isolating the victim

destroys the support networks a victim usually needs to end an abusive relationship and makes her more vulnerable to the batterer' s coercion.

- *Emotional abuse.* Verbal insults serve to undermine the victim's self-confidence, thereby discouraging her from ending the relationship. The abuser may strive to convince the victim that she is unattractive, a bad parent or wife, stupid, unemployable, crazy, incompetent, promiscuous, and the cause of the batterer's abuse.
- *Sexual abuse.* Between 33 and 46 percent of battered women are subjected to sexual abuse,[7] such as rape (especially following other physical violence),unwanted sexual practices, sexual mutilation, or forced or coerced prostitution. Other practices that some programs consider sexual abuse include not disclosing a sexually transmitted disease, making degrading sexual statements, accusing the woman of having affairs or attempting to attract other men, forcing her to imitate pornography or pose for pornographic photographs,and comparing her body and sexual behavior to that of other women.[8]
- *Using the children.* A recent study of batterers in Dade County, Florida, found that between 30 and 50 percent of the batterers and victims shared children.[9] The abuser can control the victim by threats or violence against the children, criticism of her parenting skills, and threats related to child custody. By providing for ongoing contact, joint custody enables the batterer to continue to intimidate or attack the victim, the children, or both. Some State statutes now prohibit joint custody in the event of domestic violence convictions, and recent research suggests that witnessing domestic violence has a serious long-term psychological impact on children, including increasing the child' sown propensity for violence and delinquency.[10]
- *Using economic control.* The batterer might keep control over all of the family's resources, including the victim's own income if she works, giving her an allowance or forcing her to ask for money for basic necessities. He might keep some sources of family income secret. As a result, many victims of domestic abuse have to live in a shelter or become homeless if they leave the relationship.
- *Using male privilege.* Batterers use "male privilege"— acting like the "master of the castle," making all important family decisions, expecting the woman to perform all the household duties and to wait on him—to legitimize their control over the victim by placing their own behavior in the context of common sexist norms.

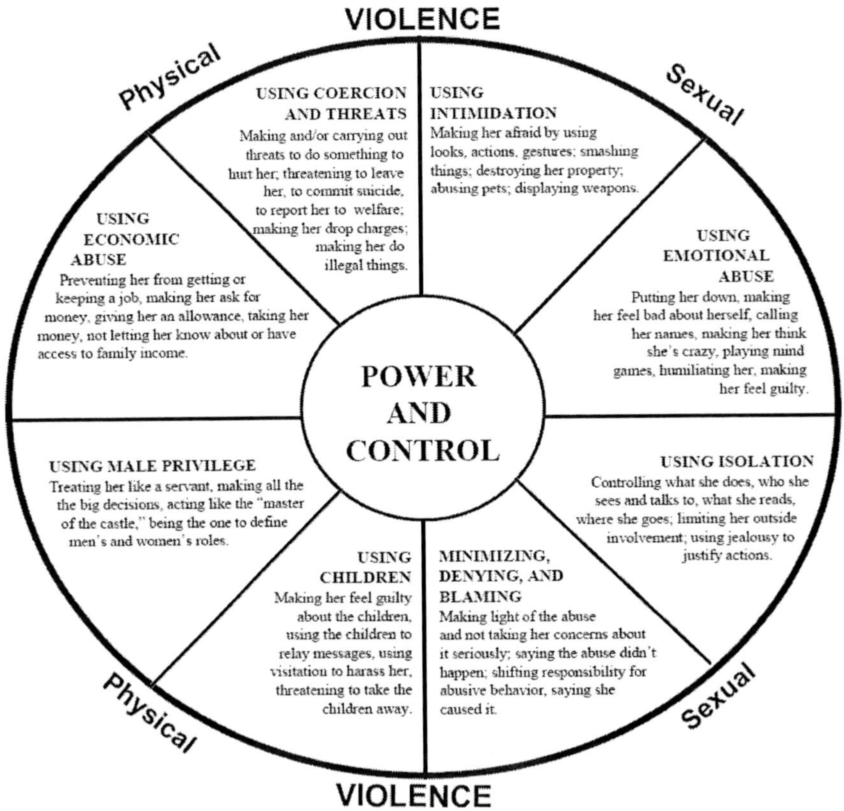

* Developed by Minnesota Program Development, Inc. Reproduced with the permission of the Domestic Abuse Intervention Project, 206 West Fourth Street, Duluth, Minnesota (218) 722-4134.

Exhibit 1-1. The Power and Control Wheel.

Not all of these abusive behaviors are illegal. However, from the standpoint of many batterer interventions, *all* abusive behaviors must be changed to correct the *pattern* of abuse (see chapter 2, "The Causes of Domestic Violence"). David Adams, program director of EMERGE in Cambridge, Massachusetts, speaks of the need to "hold convictedbatterers to a higher standard" than the legal standard because, in the context of a formerly abusive relationship, a perfectly legal shout or insult recalls for the victim her partner's earlier abuse, the mere recollection of which can revive her terror. Officers point out, however, that legal coercion cannot be used to enforce a standard not specified in the batterer' s sentence. For example, a probationer sentenced to attend a batterer program once a week is not in violation of his probation if program counselors recommend that he attend additional sessions and the batterer does not comply.

Sources of Information for This Book

The information in this book comes from the following sources:

- structured telephone interviews with program directors at 22 programs across the country;
- on-site interviews at 13 programs with more than 60 criminal justice professionals, batterer program directors and service providers, battered women's advocates and domestic violence policymakers in Cambridge and Quincy, Massachusetts; Des Moines, Iowa; Baltimore, Maryland; Denver, Colorado; and Seattle, Washington;
- interviews with academics in the field of batterer treatment and intervention, including Donald Dutton, University of British Columbia; Edward Gondolf, Research Director of the Mid-Atlantic Addiction Training Institute; Kevin Hamberger, Medical College of Wisconsin; Daniel Saunders, University of Michigan; Richard Tolman, University of Michigan; and Oliver Williams, University of Minnesota; and
- a review of books, reports, and journal articles, program evaluations, program materials, and State and local criminal justice protocols. Site work also included observations: a four-day batterer treatment training program sponsored by EMERGE of Cambridge, Massachusetts; a twoday seminar on intervention with high-risk batterers given by Michael Lindsey, founder of The Third Path and AMEND, for Iowa criminal justice professionals; a domestic violence court docket in Seattle; and State and local coalition meetings concerning batterer intervention and batterer classes and groups. Appendix B lists the names and affiliations of the individuals contacted at each site. Selection criteria for programs are discussed in chapter 3, "Pioneers in Batterer Intervention: Program Models." Chapter 6, "Sources of Help and Information," provides a selected bibliography.

Who Batters?

The majority of arrested batterers are heterosexual men. While the 1985 National Family Violence Resurvey found that a similar number of men and women (11.6 percent and 12.4 percent, respectively) admitted engaging in "any violence" against their partner during the previous year, authors of the survey point out that the superior physical strength and greater aggressiveness of men is more likely to result in serious injury to the woman, and that women's violence is often in retaliation or self-defense.[11] A recent study of defendants in domestic violence cases in one jurisdiction found that men were respondents in 90 percent of misdemeanor cases, 85 percent of felony cases, and 75 percent of civil actions.[12] Among the smaller percentage of batterers who are female, four distinct types of offenders are identified by program directors, probation officers, and victim advocates. They are lesbian batterers, so-called "female defendants" (battered women arrested for violent acts of self-defense), angry victims who have resorted to violence to preempt further abuse, and a small proportion of women batterers who have been the primary aggressors in an abusive relationship. Researchers have found that the genuinely violent woman is usually a former victim of some type of violence—child abuse, domestic violence, or sexual crimes—and often engages in violent behavior in order to deter future victimization.[13] (See chapter 4, "Current Trends in Batterer Intervention," for a discussion of issues surrounding batterer intervention with female offenders. Programs contacted for this book estimate that approximately 5 percent of batterers referred to them by the courts were female. Because the majority of interventions discussed in this book are designedfor male batterers, the term "batterer" will be given a male pronoun unless female offenders are being specifically discussed.) Although there are no reliable estimates of prevalence, some gay men also batter their intimate partners and are arrested.[14]

According to the 1992 National Crime Victimization Survey (the Victimization Survey), 51 percent of domestic violence victims were attacked by a boyfriend or girlfriend, 34 percent by a spouse, and 15 percent by a former spouse.[15] The backgrounds of incarcerated batterers—the most serious offenders—are similar to those of offenders convicted of assaults against strangers and acquaintances: half grew up living with both parents; 12 percent had lived in a foster home; 22 percent had been physically or sexually abused; 31 percent were the children of substance abusers; and 35 percent had a family member who had been incarcerated.[16] Less is known about the demographic characteristics of low- risk or "typical" batterers, but program staff and probation officers emphasized the cultural and economic diversity of these offenders.

Efforts to identify key demographic, psychological, and criminal characteristics of men who batter have led some researchers to propose batterer profiles or "typologies" to aid criminal justice professionals and batterer interventions in predicting batterers' dangerousness and potential for reoffending, as well as to match batterers with specialized forms of intervention[17] (see chapter 4, "Current Trends in Batterer Intervention"). Preliminary results from a four-site study directed by Edward Gondolf have yielded a few clues to batterer psychological characteristics; for example, 25 percent were found to have major or severe psychological syndromes, including paranoia, borderline tendencies, thought disorders, and major depression. In terms of personality traits,

- 25 percent had elevated narcissism scores;
- 15 percent were antisocial; and
- 10 percent were clinically compulsive.

The other 50 percent fell into a broad array of personality types. Gondolf emphasized that no "uniform or simplistic typologies" were emerging from his data.[18]

More promising from a criminal justice perspective are typologies based on simple demographic data, criminal records, and substance abuse data. One study by Goldkamp suggests that offenders with prior arrests involving the same victim, prior domestic violence or assault and battery arrests, and drug involvement may be at highest risk for reoffending.[19] Gondolf found that batterers who were drunk once a month reoffended at three times the rate of others in the study.[20]

The significant role of alcohol and drug abuse in domestic violence—especially in those cases coming to the attention of the criminal justice system—is often downplayed by program staff because they wish to keep their intervention focused on the voluntary nature of domestic abuse and not excuse the batterer' s behavior on the basis of a medical model of addiction. Nonetheless, analyses of domestic abuse cases and restraining orders suggest that between 71 and 85 percent of domestic violence cases involve batterers who are substance abusers.[21] According to Peter Kosciusko, a substance abuse counselor at the Dudley, Massachusetts, District Court, "While I can't say drinking is the cause of domestic abuse, it definitely pours gasoline on the fire. If we can get them sober, we have a good chance of not seeing them again."[22]

"While I can't say drinking is the cause of domestic abuse, it definitely pours gasoline on the fire. If we can get them sober, we have a good chance of not seeing them again."

—Peter Kosciusko, Substance Abuse Counselor,
Dudley, Massachusetts, District Court

While research findings and most programs contacted for this study agree that there is no "typical" batterer, the National Domestic Violence Hotline cautions victims to be aware of the potential for danger when a partner manifests several key behaviors together:

- demonstrating extreme jealousy or possessiveness;
- switching from charm to anger without warning;
- blaming others for his own negative actions;
- withdrawing love, money, or approval as punishment;
- undermining his partner's feelings and accomplishments;
- isolating his partner from friends and family; and
- exhibiting problems with drugs or alcohol.[23]

Who Are the Victims?

According to the Victimization Survey in 1992, more than 1,000,000 women and 143,000 men were violently victimized by intimates.[24] Twenty-six percent of female murder victims and 3 percent of male murder victims were killed by intimates (where the relationship between the victim and the offender is known). Victimizationbyintimates does not vary significantly by race, ethnicity, or geography. However, some victims of domestic violence are more vulnerable to abuse because of age or economic, educational, or marital status. The Victimization Survey found that the women who are most likely to be victims of domestic violence were between 20 and 34 years of age, had not graduated from college, had annual family incomes under $10,000, and were divorced or separated.[25] A recent analysis of homicide data in New York City revealed that women in the poorest boroughs (the Bronx and Brooklyn) comprised two-thirds of the victims killed by their partners and that 75 percent of women killed by husbands or boyfriends were African-American or Hispanic.[26] According to Jeff Fagan, Director of the Center for Violence Research and Prevention, "The myth of the classlessness of domestic violence is one that has persisted since the 1960's. The truth is, it is a problem of poverty, associated with other characteristics like low marriage rates, high unemployment and social problems."[27] Experts on battering emphasize that teenagers and young women in dating relationships are also at risk for violence and that battering outside cohabiting relationships should not be minimized or ignored.[28]

Intervention providers interviewed for this book had the impression that another group of women may be at unusually high risk: women in cross-cultural relationships. Men and women from different cultural backgrounds may have very different expectations about sex roles, acceptable behaviors, and the use of violence within a relationship, and men may use these different perceptions to justify battering. Immigrant women are also especially vulnerable to abuse. Language barriers may prevent these women from seeking assistance from police or victim advocates; their culture may discourage them from asserting their legal rights; and, in the case of undocumented female immigrants, maintaining the relationship with their abuser may be the only way they can gain citizenship or avoid deportation.[29]

While women from all professions and socioeconomic classes—including businesswomen, lawyers, doctors, and judges—are victims of domestic violence, women with higher incomes and status in the community often have the resources to deal with domestic violence privately without involving the criminal justice system (e.g., by using hotels or private psychological counseling). Women with limited employment options or little economic independence must often rely exclusively on the criminal justice system for protection.[30] According to Linda Ferry, who supervises domestic violence prosecutions in the Denver City Attorney's Office: "Wealthy people have other resources. That victim is not necessarily going to call the police unless she believes her life is in danger. She may, after the battering episode, go to her family, or a hotel, or a private physician who may or may not comply with the law and report it . . . . Somebody from a *poorer* neighborhood will probably end up in Denver General, where physicians *will* report it."[31]

> "Wealthy people have other resources. That victim is not necessarily going to call the police unless she believes her life is in danger. She may, after the battering episode, go to her family, or a hotel, or a private physician who may or may not comply with the law and report it . . . . Somebody from a poorer neighborhood will probably end up in Denver General, where physicians will report it."
>
> - Linda Ferry, Domestic Violence Unit, Denver City Attorney's Office

Another study found that of 11,218 women presenting at a metropolitan emergency department with injuries suffered in domestic violence, 28 percent required admission to the hospital from injuries and 13 percent required major medical treatment. Forty percent had previously required medical care for abuse.[32]

THE IMPACT OF BATTERING ON VICTIMS AND SOCIETY

The prevalence, impact, and expense of domestic abuse in terms of injuries and fatalities, medical care, and harm to children is extensive.

- In a 1993 national survey, 7 percent of women in the United States (3.9 million) reported physical abuse by their spouse or partner in the previous year.[33]
- Another 1993 study found that 14 percent of women reported having been violently abused by a spouse or boyfriend at some time in their lives.[34]
- From 1988 to 1991, 42 percent of murdered women had been killed by their partners.[35] A study of New York City homicides from 1990 to 1994 found that 49 percent of murdered women had been killed by husbands or boyfriends.[36]
- In 1994, 250,000 people were treated in emergency rooms for injuries inflicted by an intimate partner—18 percent of all victims of violence admitted to hospital emergency rooms that year.[37] In 1989, a study of one emergency ward found that 30 percent of women needing attention were victims of battering.[38]
- Between 8 and 26 percent of pregnant women in public and private clinics are victims of domestic violence.[39] Between 25 and 45 percent of battered women experience abuse during pregnancy.[40]
- In 1992, the cost of medical services to battered women, children, and elderly in Chicago was $1,633 per person.[41]

These statistics reflect only domestic violence cases identified by researchers, reported to the police, or brought to the attention of medical workers; some researchers estimate that as many as six out of seven domestic assaults go unreported.[42] A 1986 Bureau of Justice Statistics study found that 48 percent of domestic violence incidents reported in the National Crime Victimization Survey had not been reported to the police.[43] Furthermore, females victimized by intimates were six times more likely not to report the crime for fear of reprisal than female victims of violent crimes committed by strangers.[44] Researchers point out that the National Crime Victimization Survey is likely to record only the most egregious acts of domestic violence because violence not resulting in serious injury or police intervention may not be regarded by the survey respondents as a "crime."

Finally, children exposed to domestic violence are at greater risk for behavioral and developmental problems, substance abuse, juvenile delinquency, and suicide. Witnessing domestic violence as a child probably contributes to the cycle of violence: many adult batterers witnessed domestic violence in their homes as children.[45]

The severe personal and social costs of domestic violence make helping the victim and her children a moral imperative. However, there can be no lasting progress against domestic violence without deterring and rehabilitating the batterer himself.

What Works: Do Interventions Stop Battering?

While numerous evaluations of batterer interventions have been conducted, domestic violence researchers concur that findings from the majority of these studies are inconclusive because of methodological problems, such as small samples, lack of random assignment or control groups, high attrition rates, short or unrepresentative program curriculums, short follow-up periods, or unreliable or inadequate sources of follow-up data (e.g., only arrest data, only self-reported data, or only data from the original victim).[46] Among evaluations considered methodologically sound, the majority have found modest but statistically significant reductions in recidivism among men participating in batterer interventions. (See exhibit 1-2, "Selected Treatment Outcomes.") A notable exception is Adele Harrell' s 1991 methodologically rigorous quasi-experimental evaluation of batterer interven-tionsinBaltimore, conducted for the Urban Institute. Harrell's study raised particular concern in the field by its unexpected findings that participants in all three batterer interventions recidivated at a higher rate than those in the control group.[47] Preliminary results from Gondolf's four-site study sponsored by the Centers for Disease Control are inconclusive: at 12 months, reoffense rates for program graduates are similar to those for batterers who dropped out at intake, and no significant variations exist in outcomes for batterers in programs of varied length and curriculum (although a three- month, pretrial, educational program has shown slightly better outcomes when socioeconomic factors are taken into account).[48]

Frustration with the lack of empirical evidence favoring one curriculum or length of treatment has led some researchers increasingly to look at batterers as a diverse group for whom specially tailored interventions may be the only effective approach. As a result, current research is shifting toward studying which subgroups of batterers respond to which specialized interventions (see chapter 4, "Current Trends in Batterer Intervention").

Quasi-Experiments	Recidivism		Effect Size
	Treated (%)	Untreated (%)	
Dutton (1986)[a]	4	40	0.946
Chen et al. (1989)[b]	5	10	0.193
Dobash et al. (1996)[c]	7	10	0.108
Average			0.416

True Experiments	Recidivism		Effect Size
	Treated (%)	Untreated (%)	
Palmer et al. (1992)[d]	10	31	0.537
Davis and Taylor (1997)[e]	5	13	0.287
Average			0.412

Source: Davis, R.C. and B.G. Taylor, "Does Batterer Treatment Reduce Violence? A Synthesis of the Literature," Victim Services Research, New York, NY, Unpublished Manuscript, July 1997. (Table 6: Treatment Effect Sizes for Quasi and True Experiments: Comparing Treatment and No Treatment.)

[a] Dutton, D.G., "The Outcome of Court-Mandated Treatment for Wife Assault: A Quasi-Experimental Evaluation," Violence and Victims, 1(3) (1986): 163–175.

[b] Chen, H., C. Bersani, S.C. Myers, and R. Denton, "Evaluating the Effectiveness of a Court-Sponsored Abuser Treatment Program," Journal of Family Violence, 4 (1989): 309–322.

[c] Dobash, R., R.E. Dobash, K. Cavanagh, and R. Lewis, "Re-education Programs for Violent Men—An Evaluation," Research Findings, 46 (1996): 1–4.

[d] Palmer, S.E., R.A. Brown, and M.E. Barrera, "Group Treatment Program for Abusive Husbands: Longterm Evaluation," American Journal of Orthopsychiatry, 62(2) (1992): 276–283.

[e] Davis, R.C. and B.G. Taylor, "A Proactive Response to Family Violence: The Results of a Randomized Experiment," Criminology, 35 (2) (1997): 307–333.

Exhibit 1-2. Selected Treatment Outcomes.

At the same time, the question of how to evaluate batterer interventions may need to be reframed to include the broader context of criminal justice support. For example, research suggests that arrest alone is not as effective in reducing recidivism as is arrest as part of a coordinated multiagency response to domestic violence.[49] These findings point to the need for a broader, systemic examination of the efficacy of batterer intervention. It seems likely that even if research identifies the perfect matches between interventions and offenders, criminal justice and community support for the interventions will have a crucial impact on the effort's success. Andrew Klein, chief probation officer of the Quincy, Massachusetts, District Court Model Domestic Abuse Program, observed, "You can't separate batterer treatment from its [criminal justice system] context. You can't study the effectiveness of treatment without studying the quality of force which supports it." Research supports this view: "[P]olice visits to the home, combined with an eventual arrest of the perpetrator, which was also followed by court-mandated treatment, were significantly more likely than other combinations of criminal justice actions to end repeat incidents of violence."[50] Gondolf's research also points to the importance of systemwide assessments of batterer intervention. In particular, Gondolf is concerned about the often long delay between arrest and program enrollment: "The lag may be so long that the program may be addressing men about a former life."[51] Systemwide evaluation could answer the important question of whether the speed of criminal justice response and program enrollment is more important than either program content or length.

In conclusion, Andrew Klein emphasizes that, at a minimum, every intervention must be effective in *monitoring abusive behavior* during the program because victims are more likely to stay with batterers who are in an intervention. In Klein's opinion, "[B]atterer intervention is a public safety program, not treatment; you must keep the focus on victim safety. Otherwise, the criminal justice system is only offering the batterer a safe haven to escape the consequences of his offense."

> "Batterer intervention is a public safety program, not treatment; you must keep the focus on victim safety. Otherwise, the criminal justice system is only offering the batterer a safe haven to escape the consequences of his offense."
>
> - Andrew Klein, Chief Probation Officer, Quincy, Massachusetts, District Court Model Domestic Abuse Program

CONCLUSION

While the criminal justice system is devoting increased attention to domestic violence, many mechanisms and protocols for dealing with batterers are new and still being refined. A number of States are still in the process of writing standards or guidelines for batterer programs. In the absence of conclusive research findings, practitioners and academics continue to debate the appropriate content of batterer interventions. In this dynamic environment, judges who adjudicate and prosecutors who try domestic violence cases, probation officers who supervise batterers, and advocates who serve victims of domestic violence all need to keep informed about new developments in the field of batterer intervention in order to perform their jobs effectively. The remainder of the book provides information on the theoretical debate surrounding domestic violence and batterer intervention (chapter 2); batterer program operation (chapter 3); current trends and refinements of practice in batterer intervention (chapter 4); criminal justice responses to batterer interventions, including community and interagency cooperation (chapter 5); and national and local sources of help and information (chapter 6).

REFERENCES

[1] For a comprehensive treatment of law enforcement issues, see Buzawa, E. and C. Buzawa, *Do Arrests and Restraining Orders Work?* Thousand Oaks, CA: Sage Publications, 1996.

[2] See Zorza, Joan, "The Gender Bias Committee's Domestic Violence Study: Important Recommendations and First Steps," 33 *Boston Bar* J.4, 13 (July/August 1989); and Langan, P.A. and C.A. Innes, *Preventing Domestic Violence Against Women*, Washington, DC: U.S. Department of Justice, Bureau of Justice Statistics, August 1986: 3.

[3] Ganley, A., "Understanding Domestic Violence," in *Improving the Health Care Response to Domestic Violence: A Resource Manual for Health Care Providers*, Harrisburg, PA: Family Violence Prevention Fund and the Pennsylvania Coalition Against Domestic Violence, n.d.

[4] For an overview of Pence's philosophy and the Duluth program model (which is also discussed in chapter 3, "Pioneers in Batterer Intervention"), see Pence, E., "Batterers' Programs: Shifting from Community Collusion to Community Confrontation," February 1988, available from the Domestic

Abuse Intervention Project (see chapter 6, "Sources of Help and Information").

[5] Stark, E. and A. Flitcraft, "Spouse Abuse, Surgeon General's Workshop on Violence and Public Health Sourcebook," presented at the Surgeon General's Workshop on Violence and Public Health, Leesburg, Virginia, October 1985, cited in National Clearing House for the Defense of Battered Women, *Statistics Packet, 3d ed.,* Philadelphia: February 1994.

[6] Langhan and Innes, Preventing Domestic Violence Against Women.

[7] Frieze, I. H. and A. Browne, "Violence in Marriage," in Family Violence: Crime and Justice, n.d., cited in State of Iowa, Final Report of the Supreme Court Task Force on Courts' and Communities' Response to Domestic Abuse, submitted to the Supreme Court of Iowa, August 1994:10.

[8] Material provided by House of Ruth, Baltimore.

[9] Goldkamp, J. S., The Role of Drug and Alcohol Abuse in Domestic Violence and Its Treatment: Dade County's Domestic Violence Court Experiment, Final Report, Philadelphia: Crime and Justice Research Institute, June 1996: Executive Summary, viii.

[10] A number of child welfare departments, notably the Department of Social Services in Massachusetts, have

[11] developed protocols and interventions for children who have witnessed domestic violence. Research citing the harmful impact of domestic violence on children include: Widom, C.S., "The Cycle of Violence," *Research in Brief*, Washington, DC: U.S. Department of Justice, National Institute of Justice, October 1992: 3; Thornberry, T.P., "Violent Families and Youth Violence," *Office of Juvenile Justice and Delinquency Prevention (OJJDP) Fact Sheet #21*, Washington, DC: OJJDP, December 1994; Straus, M.A., F.J. Gelles, and S. Steinmetz, *Behind Closed Doors*, Garden City, NY: Anchor/Doubleday, 1980; Peled, I., P.G. Jaffe, and J.L. Edelson, eds., *Breaking the Cycle of Violence: Community Responses to Children of Battered Women*, Thousand Oaks, CA: Sage Publications, 1995; Miller, G., "Violence By and Against America's Children," *Journal of Juvenile Justice Digest*, 17(12) (1989): 6; Carlson, B .E.,"Children's Observations of Interparental Violence" in *Battered Women and Their Families*, ed. A.R. Edwards, New York: Springer, 1984: 147–167.

[12] Straus, M.A. and R.J. Gelles, eds., *Physical Violence in American Families: Risk Factors and Adaptations to Violence in 8,145 Families*, New Brunswick, NJ: Transaction Publishers, 1990: 96–98. See also Straus, M.A., "Physical Assaults by Wives: A Major Social Problem," in *Current Controversies on Family Violence*, ed. R.J. Gelles and D.R. Loseke,

Newbury Park, CA: Sage Publications, 1993: 67–87. This article raises questions about the nature and prevalence of violence by women against their partners.

[13] Ibid.

[14] Recent research on the sequelae of child abuse and neglect, including child sexual abuse and witnessing domestic violence as a child, suggest a link between child victimization and later involvement in domestic violence for men as well. See Straus, Gelles, and Steinmetz, *Behind Closed Doors*.

[15] Island, D. and P. Letellier, *Men Who Beat the Men Who Love Them: Battered Gay Men and Domestic Violence*, New York: Harrington Park Press, n.d.: 12–14.

[16] Bureau of Justice Statistics, *Domestic Violence: Violence Between Intimates,* Selected Findings, Washington, DC: U.S. Department of Justice, November 1994: 1. (NCJ-149259)

[17] Ibid.

[18] Edward Gondolf, Associate Director of Research, Mid- Atlantic Training Institute, is conducting a quasi-experimental evaluation of four model batterer intervention programs. This study, when concluded, is expected to advance knowledge of batterer typologies. Daniel Saunders has analyzed interview data that compares treatment outcomes of graduates from a cognitive behavioral group to batterers who received process-psychodynamic group therapy. See Saunders, D., "Interventions for Men Who Batter: Do We Know What Works?" *In Session: Psychotherapy in Practice*, 2(3) (1996): 81–93. See also Saunders, D., "Husbands Who Assault: Multiple Profiles Requiring Multiple Responses," in *Legal Responses to Wife Assault*, ed. N.Z. Hilton, Newbury Park, CA: Sage Publications, 1993; Saunders, D., "A Typology of Men Who Batter: Three Types Derived from a Cluster Analysis," *American Journal ofOrthopsychiatry*, 62(2) (1992); and Goldkamp, *The Role of Drug and Alcohol Abuse,* 191ff.

[19] Interview with Edward Gondolf, October 22, 1996.

[20] Goldkamp, The Role of Drug and Alcohol Abuse, 197.

[21] Interview with Edward Gondolf, October 22, 1996.

[22] Doherty, W.F., "Cases Spur Debate on Alcohol's Link to Domestic Violence," *Boston Globe*, July 21, 1997, B2.

[23] Ibid.

[24] National Domestic Violence Hotline, quoted in program materials provided by the House of Ruth, Baltimore.

[25] Bureau of Justice Statistics, *Violence Between Intimates*.

[26] Ibid.

[27] Belleck, Pam, "A Woman's Killer Is Likely to Be Her Partner, A New Study in New York Finds," *New York Times*, March 31, 1997, A16NE.
[28] Ibid.
[29] See Sousa, C., L. Bancroft, and T. German, "Preventing Teen Dating Violence: A Three Session Curriculum for Teaching Adolescents," produced by the Dating Violence Intervention Project, Cambridge, MA (see chapter 6, "Sources of Help and Information").
[30] See Lin, M.W.L. and C.I. Tan, "Holding Up More Than Half the Heavens: Domestic Violence in Our Communities, A Call for Justice," in K. Aguilar-San Juan, ed., *The State of Asian America: Activism and Resistance in the 1990s*, Boston: South End Press, n.d.: 321.
[31] See Butler, C., "Myths About Woman Abuse," in *For Shelter and Beyond*, 2d ed., Boston: Massachusetts Coalition of Battered Women's Groups, n.d., 21.
[32] Not all States require physicians to report cases involving domestic violence.
[33] Berrios, D.C. and D. Grady, "Domestic Violence: Risk Factors and Outcomes," *The Western Journal of Medicine*, 155(2) (August 1991) cited in Family Violence Prevention Fund, "The Healthcare Response to Domestic Violence Fact Sheet," San Francisco, n.d.
[34] The Commonwealth Fund, "First Comprehensive National Survey of American Women Finds Them at Significant Risk " (news release), New York: July 14, 1993.
[35] FamilyViolencePreventionFund, *MenBeating Women: Ending Domestic Violence, A Qualitative and Quantitative Study of Public Attitudes on Violence Against Women*, New York: conducted by EDK Associates, 1993, cited in "The Health Care Response to Domestic Violence Fact Sheet."
[36] Analysis by the Center for the Study and Prevention of Violence, Institute for Behavioral Science, University of Colorado at Boulder, cited in "The Health Care Response to Domestic Violence Fact Sheet."
[37] Belleck, "A Woman's Killer Is Likely to Be Her Partner."
[38] "Abuse High, Survey Finds," *Boston Globe*, August 25, 1997.
[39] McLeer, S. and R. Anwar, "A Study of Battered Women Presenting in an Emergency Department," *American Journal of Public Health*, 79(1) (January 1989), cited in "The Health Care Response to Domestic Violence Fact Sheet."
[40] Berrios, D.C. and D. Grady, "Domestic Violence: Risk Factors and Outcomes."
[41] State of Iowa, Final Report of the Supreme Court Task Force, 17.

[42] Meyer, H., “The Billion Dollar Epidemic,” *American Medical News*, January 6, 1992, cited in "The Health Care Response to Domestic Violence Fact Sheet.”

[43] National Clearinghouse for the Defense of Battered Women, *Statistics Packet, 3d ed.,* Philadelphia, February 1994.

[44] Langhan and Innes, Preventing Domestic Violence Against Women.

[45] Bureau of Justice Statistics, Domestic Violence: Violence Between Intimates, 5.

[46] Roberts, L. and R. Burger, “Child Abuse,” in *For Shelter and Beyond: Ending Violence Against Women and Their Children,* 2d ed., Boston: Massachusetts Coalition of Battered Women Service Groups, n.d.: 107; see also note 10.

[47] For a critique of major batterer intervention evaluations, see Davis, R.C. and B.G. Taylor, “Does Batterer Treatment Reduce Violence? A Synthesis of the Literature,” Victim Services Research, New York, NY, July 1997; Tolman, R. and J. Edelson, “Interventions for Men Who Batter: A Review of Research” in *Understanding Partner Violence: Prevalence, Causes, Consequences, and Solutions*, Minneapolis: National Council on Family Relations, 1995: 262–273; Saunders, D., “Interventions for Men Who Batter: Do We Know What Works?” *In Session: Psychotherapy in Practice*, 2(3) (1996): 81– 93; and Gondolf, E., “Batterer Intervention: What We Know and What We Need to Know,” Paper presented at the Violence Against Women Strategic Planning Meeting, sponsored by the National Institute of Justice, Washington, DC, March 31, 1995.

[48] Harrell, A., *Evaluation of Court Ordered Treatment for Domestic Violence Offenders,* Final Report, Washington, DC: The Urban Institute, October 1991.

[49] Interview with Edward Gondolf, October 22, 1996. Similarly, Davis and Taylor's study reported positive outcomes for short-term, intensive programs.

[50] See Rebovich, D.J., “Prosecution Responses to Domestic Violence: Results of a Survey of Large Jurisdictions,” in *Do Arrests and Restraining Orders Work?,* ed. BuzawaandBuzawa, 176–191; and Schmidt, J. and L. Sherman, “Does Arrest Deter Domestic Violence,” in *Do Arrests and Restraining Orders Work?,* ed. Buzawa and Buzawa, 43–53.

[51] Tolman and Edelson, p. 264, citing Syers, M. and J. Edelson, “The Combined Effects of Coordinated Criminal Justice Intervention in Women Abuse,” *Journal of Interpersonal Violence*, 7: 490-502.

[52] Interview with Edward Gondolf, October 22, 1996.

Chapter 2

THE CAUSES OF DOMESTIC VIOLENCE: FROM THEORY TO INTERVENTION

KEY POINTS

- Most interventions employ a mixture of theories in their curriculums, the most common of which is a psychoeducational model that encourages profeminist attitude change while building interpersonal skills using cognitive-behavioral techniques.
- Three categories of theories of domestic violence dominate the field. Each locates the cause of domestic violence differently, and each theory leads practitioners to employ different approaches to batterer intervention:

— *Society and Culture.* Social and cultural theories attribute the problem to social structure and cultural norms and values that endorse or tolerate the use of violence by men against women partners. The *feminist* model of intervention educates men concerning the impact of these social and cultural norms and attempts to resocialize them emphasizing nonviolence and equality in relationships.

— *The Family.* Family-based theories of domestic violence focus on the structure of the family, interpersonal interactions within the family, and the social isolation of families. The *family systems* model of intervention focuses on developing healthy communication skills with a goal of family preservation and may use couples therapy, a treatment approach prohibited by 20 State standards and guidelines regulating batterer intervention (to protect the safety of the victim).

— *The Individual.* Psychological theories attribute domestic violence to personality disorders, the batterer's social environment during childhood, biological disposition, or attachment disorders. *Psychotherapeutic* interventions target individual problems and/or build cognitive skills to help the batterer control violent behaviors.

Both feminist educational and cognitive-behavioral interventions can be compatible with the goals of the criminal justice system—protecting the victim as well as rehabilitating the offender. However, feminist educational programs offer some advantages. By contrast, family systems interventions conflict with criminal justice goals by failing to identify a victim and a perpetrator, an identification the law requires.

The origins of domestic violence are the subject of active debate among victim advocates, social workers, researchers, and psychologists concerned with batterer intervention. More than in most fields, the theoretical debate affects practice. Over the last two decades, a number of practitioners representing divergent theoretical camps have begun to move toward a more integrated "multidimensional" model of batterer intervention in order to better address the complexity of a problem that has psychological, interpersonal, social, cultural, and legal aspects. Two practitioners who advocate an eclectic approach to batterer intervention describe the dilemma of practitioners looking for a single explanation for battering as follows:

During a recent conversation, a respected colleague of ours suggested that marital aggression was rooted in a need for control. "Men," he said, "use aggression to control their female partners." We agreed. Control is certainly an important factor in the dynamics of marital violence. His treatment approach, well known and effective, focused on helping abusers relinquish control and share power with their spouses. Several weeks later, we discussed the same topic with the director of a treatment program for wife abusers, who stated that "poor impulse control" and "defective self-concept" were the critical factors. We agreed. Abusers are certainly impulsive and often have poor self- esteem. Her treatment program, which focused on these factors was, she claimed, very successful. Sometime later, one of our graduate students, well aware of these previous conversations, reported on a workshop she had attended. The model presented at the workshop conceptualized marital violence as a couples' problem and suggested that communication between spouses was the critical factor. Conjoint couples' counseling was suggested as an effective intervention for violent couples. Again, we could agree. The safest conclusion would appear to be that there are numerous routes by which husbands come to be wife abusers and a multitude of variables that increase the likelihood of violence.[1]

In practice, few batterer programs represent a "pure" expression of one theory of domestic violence; the majority of programs contacted for this book combine elements of different theoretical models. As a result, when discussing program theory with batterer intervention providers, criminal justice professionals need to understand not only the primary theory the program espouses but also the program's content, because programs may identify with one theory but draw on or two more theories in their work. Experts caution criminal justice agencies against accepting an eclectic curriculum uncritically: program components borrowed from different theoretical perspectives should be thoughtfully chosen to create a coherent approach, not a scattershot attempt hoping to hit some technique that works.

Criminal justice professionals are likely to encounter programs based on one or more of the following theories of domestic violence. Each theory locates the cause of the violence differently:

- *Society and culture*—Social theories of domestic violence attribute the problem to social structures and cultural norms and values that endorse or tolerate the use of violence by men against women partners. For example, the *feminist model* of intervention educates men concerning the impact of these social and cultural norms and attempts to resocialize them emphasizing nonviolence and equality in relationships.
- *The family*—Some sociologists locate the cause of domestic violence in the structure of the family, the interpersonal interactions of families, and the social isolation of families. For example, *family systems theory* attributes the cause to communication problems and conflict within intimate relationships and teaches communication skills to help partners avoid violence. As noted below, couples counseling, an intervention based on family systems theory, is controversial because of its failure to assign blame for the abuse to one person and to identify a victim. Couples counseling is also considered dangerous to the victim because it

encourages the victim to discuss openly issues that may spark later retaliation by the batterer.

- *The individual—Psychological theories* attribute domestic violence to the individual batterer's predispositions and experiences. Battering may be attributed to personality disorders and biological dispositions to violence or, as *social learning theory* suggests, to the role of the batterer' s social environment during childhood. *Attachment theory,* a form of social learning theory, focuses on the interaction of caregivers with their children and the impact of that first attachment on an individual's ability to establish safe and healthy relationships later in life. Batterer interventions based on this theory attempt to facilitate secure attachments between batterers and loved ones (intimate partners, children, and parents). Psychodynamic approaches target the underlying psychological cause of the violence, while cognitive behavioral approaches teach batterers new patterns of nonviolent thinking and behavior.

It is important for criminal justice professionals to understand the assumptions and goals of service providers whose interventions have divergent theoretical bases, because not all intervention approaches employ techniques that are equally compatible with the goals of the criminal justice system—protecting the victim as well as rehabilitating the offender.

The Language of Batterer Intervention

The shift in providers of help to batterers and their partners from psychotherapists to feminist social activists to professional mental health providers has created tensions in the field that are exhibited in the language of batterer interventions. Criminal justice professionals need to be aware of the connotations of various terms so that they can communicate effectively with service providers.

For example, the term "domestic violence" itself has a gender-neutral connotation. A number of feminists, seeing a link with other violence against women and noting the severity of injuries inflicted on women by male partners, prefer such terms as "wife abuse" and "woman abuse."[2] Programs based on feminist theories of battering are often described as "profeminist," indicating male support for feminist goals. Mental health professionals may talk about "counselors" or "therapists" providing "treatment" to "clients," while profeminist "facilitators" or "teachers" provide an "intervention" to "batterers" using a didactic format described as "classes." Feminist-based programs object especially to the word "treatment" and may not consider rehabilitation the program's primary goal, as Red Crowley of Atlanta's Men Stopping Violence program explains:

> Let's start with the word *treatment*. We do not see our work as therapy. Battering is the natural outgrowth of patriarchal values. We want to change those values. Batterers' intervention classes serve a number of purposes: they, like shelters, make visible what has been systematically concealed, that is, the horrendous problem of violence against women; create an opportunity to engage the community and the criminal justice system in the effort to stop the violence; and contribute to research. Giving men who want to change the opportunity to do so is just one purpose of the intervention.

The three most widely used intervention approaches—"educational" or "psychoeducational classes," "couples therapy," and "group process"—are each associated with a theory of the cause of domestic violence. Thus, "educational programs" are most often based on feminist theory; "couples therapy" may suggest a link with family systems theory; and "group process" programs base their work on either psychodynamic or cognitive behavioral theories. Some practitioners—especially those with eclectic programming—may use terms interchangeably; others harbor strong objections to mislabeling their approach and consider some terms to have great symbolic meaning. Criminal justice professionals need to be sensitive to the language used by intervention providers and to ask practitioners to explain the importance of unfamiliar terminology.

OVERVIEW OF THEORIES AND RELATED INTERVENTIONS

Feminist (or profeminist; see box, "The Language ofBatterer Intervention"), family systems, and psychotherapeutic theories of domestic violence offer divergent explanations of the root causes of battering and lead to distinct intervention models. The following section outlines the basic tenets of each theory, illustrates how these assumptions influence the choice of intervention strategies, and notes the advantages and disadvantages of each theoretical and treatment approach. As noted previously, however, examples of programming based exclusively on one theory are becoming increasingly rare.

Feminist Approaches: The Social Problem Approach

Batterer intervention programs originated in the early 1970's, as feminists and others brought to public attention the victimization of women and spawned grass roots services such as rape hot lines and battered women's shelters.[3] According to Anne Ganley of Seattle's Veteran Administration Medical Center and David Adams of EMERGE in Boston, providers of services to battered women felt that victims who had received services either returned home to face the same destructive environment or left the relationship—and the batterer found a new victim. To help victims, advocates realized, it was also necessary to address the root cause of their problems—the perpetrators of violence. Profeminist men concerned with sexism in themselves and society felt a particular responsibility for working with male abusers. As a result, some of the first systematic interventions for batterers developed from a profeminist perspective.

What Is a Feminist Model of Battering?

Central to the feminist perspective on battering is a gender analysis of power.[4] According to this view, domestic violence in intimate relationships mirrors the patriarchal organization of society in which men play a dominant role in most social institutions. Along with verbal, emotional, and economic abuse, violence is a means of maintaining male power in the family when men feel their dominance is being threatened. Economic roles have left women dependent on men and unable to escape abusive situations.[5] Men's superior physical strength may enable them to dominate women through violence.

Feminists argue that a consequence of the social arrangement in which men hold the positions of respect and power is that men and women alike devalue the feminine and overvalue the masculine. To the batterer, women are childlike and incompetent. It is not uncommon for batterers to convince their wives that they are not capable of adult activities, such as driving a car or holding a job.[6] For example, a former victim reported that her husband had convinced her that she could not turn on the washing machine without breaking it, so she had to wait until he returned from work before she could do the laundry for their seven children. Similarly, in disputed custody cases when a batterer and partner separate, the husband often contends that his wife is incapable of taking care of the children.[7]

In the feminist view, batterers feel that they should be in charge of the family: making decisions, laying down rules, disciplining disobedient wives and children, and correcting unsatisfactory performance of duties.[8] Batterers may typically exercise control over the family in nonviolent, coercive ways and only sometimes resort to violence. As men, batterers feel entitled to gender-based respect and obedience; therefore, what they perceive to be disrespect and disobedience infuriates them. Batterers often rationalize their violence on the grounds that it was necessitated by their partner's actions: she provoked or caused it, and they simply reacted as any man would.

Feminist programs attempt to raise consciousness about sex role conditioning and how it constrains men's emotions and behavior (through education around sexism, male privilege, male socialization). Programs with a feminist philosophy present a model of egalitarian relationships along with the benefits of nonviolence and of building relationships based on trust instead of fear (see exhibit 2-1, "Equality Wheel"). Most feminist approaches support *confronting* men over their power and control tactics in all domains of the relationship, including verbal and psychological abuse, social isolation, the undermining of the victim's self-confidence, and sexual coercion (see exhibit 1-1, "The Power and Control Wheel"). A particular concern of profeminist male group facilitators is the constant risk and temptation of colluding with batterers. For example, a male facilitator at Family Services of Seattle reported that when his female cofacilitator was absent at one session, the men in the group expected him to drop his profeminist "guise" and participate in or agree with their negative characterizations of women.

Advantages and Criticisms of the Feminist Model

Perhaps because work with batterers was originated by battered women's advocates and feminists, the feminist perspective has influenced most programs. A national survey conducted in 1986 found that 80 percent of programs attempt to change sex role attitudes, stop violence, and increase self-esteem.[9] Even programs adopting a family systems model (see below) may advocate an egalitarian and democratic relationship to couples in treatment. Support for the feminist analysis of the role of power in domestic violence comes from the observation that most batterers are able to control their anger and avoid resorting to violence when "provoked" by someone more powerful than they, such as their work supervisors, police officers, or judges. Further support for the feminist analysis comes from research showing that batterers are less secure in their masculinity than nonbatterers[10]—the theory being that men who do not feel masculine will need to assert their masculinity more forcefully to compensate for their sense of inadequacy. Other studies have documented the sense of *entitlement* batterers feel in controlling their partners' behavior and in justifying violence if these women deviate from the female sex role.[11]

Critics have claimed that the feminist perspective overemphasizes sociocultural factors, such as patriarchal values, to the exclusion of individual factors like growing up abused.[12] Men's behavior in intimate relationships varies across individuals, and broad cultural factors cannot explain this variability. Feminist theory predicts that *all* men in our society will be abusive, claim its critics, adding that besides being untrue, this theory makes it impossible to predict *which* men will be violent. To make individual predictions, a model must assign a role to other factors including, but not limited to, psychological deviance.

Other criticisms center not on the validity of feminist explanations of battering but on the translation of that theory into programming. For example, some observers argue that feminist educational interventions are too confrontational in tone and, as a result, are ultimately self-defeating, alienating batterers, increasing their hostility, and making them less likely to become engaged in treatment. It is possible that the goal of the feminist model—to rebuild the batterer' s belief system in order to achieve nonviolence—may be unnecessarily ambitious and adversarial. Batterers' existing value systems may be more easily fine-tuned to emphasize nonviolence (e.g., building on religious convictions or humanism) without a feminist overlay.

Another concern is that educational programs may effectively transmit information without deterring violent behavior. A 1991 evaluation of three short-term psychoeducational batterer programs in Baltimore found that while batterers considered the curriculum helpful, they recidivated at a higher rate than batterers who did not receive treatment.[13] A study of graduates of Duluth's Domestic Abuse Intervention Project found that completion of the feminist educational intervention had no impact on recidivism after five years.[14] Outcomes such as these point to the need for broader evaluations that examine the impact of systemic factors—arrest and prosecution policies, court procedures, and probation supervision—on intervention effectiveness, as well as a clarification of the goals of feminist-based interventions. If deterrence is not a likely outcome of an intervention, other goals, such as punishment, education, behavioral monitoring, or social change, must be explicitly advanced. (A few practitioners are in fact shifting their primary focus away from individual change in batterers in favor of social change through a coordinated community response. See chapter 5, "Criminal Justice Response").

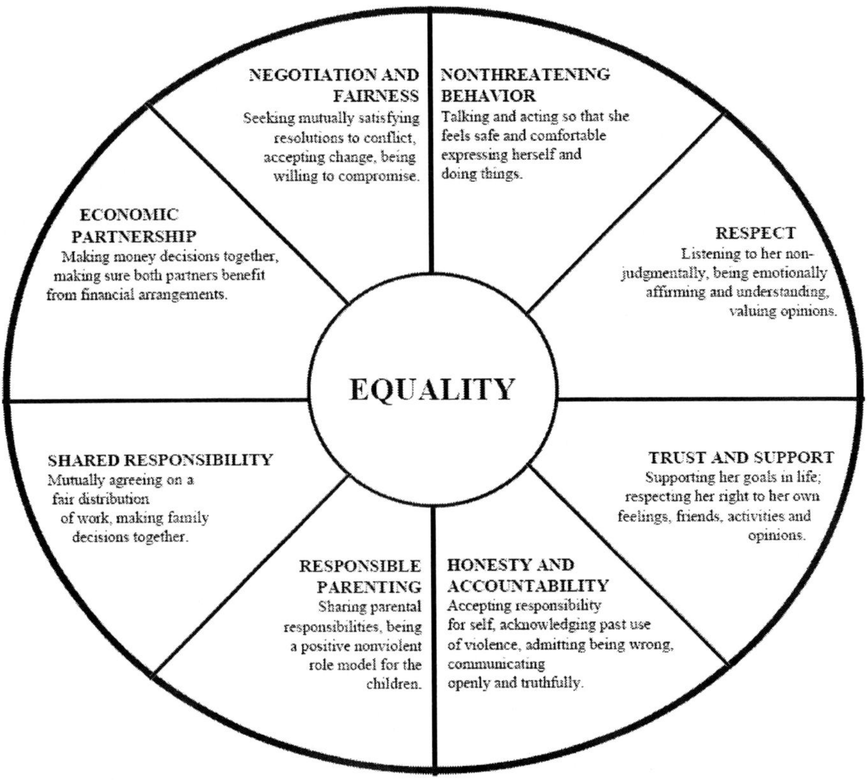

* Reproduced with the permission of the Domestic Abuse Intervention Project, 206 West Fourth Street, Duluth, Minnesota, (218) 722-4134.

Exhibit 2-1. Equality Wheel.

The Family Systems Model

The family systems model regards individual problem behaviors as a manifestation of a dysfunctional family unit, with each family member contributing to the problem. Rather than identifying one individual as the cause of the violence and removing that person from the home or singling that person out for treatment, the model advocates working with the family or couple together, providing support with the goal of keeping the family intact.

According to the family systems (or "interactional") model,[15] both partners may contribute to the escalation of conflict, with each striving to dominate the other. Family systems theorists believe that most abuse is verbal and emotional, but as the conflict escalates, either partner may resort to violence. Because, from this perspective, *interactions* produce violence, no one is considered to be the perpetrator or victim, even if only one person is physically violent. Family systems theory also suggests that interactions may permit or facilitate abusive behaviors in one person, such as a nonabusive parent's failure to intervene in child abuse or a family member's failure to establish appropriate personal boundaries, thus setting the stage for their own victimization. Family systems therapists criticize psychological approaches that focus on individual deficits (low self-esteem, dependence, anger) while neglecting to teach interpersonal skills that could promote safety. Family systems theory leads to treatment that involves improving communication and conflict resolution skills. Both members of the couple can develop these skills through "solution-focused brief therapy" that:

- locates the problem in the interaction rather than in the pathology of one individual;
- focuses on solving the problem, rather than looking for causes; and
- accentuates the positive—for example, examining occasions when the couple avoided violence.

Advantages and Criticisms of the Family Systems Model

Advocates of the family systems approach note that many violent couples would like to remain together and that there may be positive aspects to the relationship that counseling can build on. However, while some observers report that over half of domestic violence couples remain together,[16] a study of abused wives whose husbands did become nonviolent found that most of the women subsequently terminated the marriage because of other marital problems that became apparent after the violence ended.[17]

Both feminist and cognitive-behavioral approaches agree that partner abuse does not involve shared responsibility. Both approaches firmly hold that batterers bear full responsibility for the violence, victims play no causal role, and no one incites violence. Of particular concern to both feminist and cognitive-behavioral proponents is the format of couples counseling: encouraging each partner to discuss problems openly with the other partner can put the victim at risk after the session if the woman expresses complaints. Furthermore, no frank exchange between counselor and victim concerning the abuse is likely to be possible in the presence of the batterer. Moreover, the format is conducive to victim- blaming. Finally, if the court prohibits the batterer from contacting the victim, the family systems approach will violate the court order. For these reasons, couples counseling is expressly prohibited in 20 State standards and guidelines (see box, "Controversial Approaches to Batterer Intervention" and appendix A.3). Judges involved with partner abuse cases that also involve child abuse need to pay particular attention to safety issues raised by family systems interventions, which may be the treatment approach recommended by child welfare workers who are working toward a goal of family reunification. In such cases, issues of victim and child safety must be weighed carefully, and if a family systems approach is chosen, close monitoring is needed.

Psychological Approaches: A Focus on Individual Problems

Psychological perspectives hold that personality disorders or early experiences of trauma predispose some individuals to violence.[18] Being physically abusive is seen as a symptom of an underlying emotional problem.[19] Parental abuse, rejection, and failure to meet a child's dependence needs can be the psychological source of battering. People with these underlying problems may choose partners with whom they can reenact the dysfunctional relationship they had with their parents. Two forms of batterer intervention have evolved from this perspective: individual and group psychodynamic therapy and cognitive-behavioral group therapy.

Individual and Group Psychodynamic Counseling

Psychoanalysis can be undertaken not only in individual counseling but also in unstructured batterer groups that allow members to explore their life experiences. Psychodynamic therapies involve uncovering the batterer' s unconscious problem and resolving it consciously. Proponents of psychodynamic therapy for batterers believe that other interventions are superficial: since other therapies are unable to eliminate the abuser's deep-rooted and unconscious *motive* for aggression, they cannot end violence but only suppress it temporarily. Long-term change requires exposing and resolving the root cause of the violent behavior.

Advantages and Criticisms of Psychodynamic Approaches

Browne and Saunders recently conducted a study comparing a "process psychodynamic treatment model" with a feminist/cognitive-behavioral intervention and found no difference in recidivism rates based on partners' reports. Nevertheless, they argue:

> [T]here were two advantages to the process-psychodynamic model. It retained a significantly higher percentage of men in treatment and it was more successful with men who had dependent personality disorders. Regardless of the treatment approach used, more self-disclosure and less lecturing were related to greater group cohesion, which in turn was related to lower recidivism rates.[20] (Emphasis added)

Critics argue that psychodynamic therapy merely assigns a psychiatric label to people who batter (e.g., insecure, narcissistic, dependent, compulsive, or suffering from intermittent explosive disorder) without explaining how they got that way or what can be done about it.[21] The psychodynamic approach has also been criticized for allowing batterers to continue the behavior until the underlying psychological problem is resolved.[22] David Adams, director of EMERGE, gives the example of a batterer mandated to treatment who had already learned in individual psychotherapy that he battered because he was insecure. At the intake interview for the batterer program, the counselor asked the man whether he was going to continue to choose to be violent until he resolved his insecurity. The man said that he had never thought of battering as a choice, but now he would reconsider the notion.[23] Feminists argue that labeling batterers as having psychological problems not only exonerates them in their own eyes but also ignores the cultural acceptability of male dominance in the family and how it serves to keep the batterer in control of his partner. The approach pays attention to *internal* psychological functions of abuse for the batterer but ignores the *interpersonal* function of controlling the other person's behavior.

In practice, many psychologically oriented programs have moved away from the original stance that battering is caused primarily by psychological disorder and always indicates an emotional problem. Instead, they have integrated social explanations with psychological explanations. For example, some psychologically oriented theorists propose that it is the combination of a man's low self-esteem and a cultural expectation that men should be dominant and successful that produces a batterer.

Cognitive-Behavioral Model of Change

Cognitive-behavioral therapy is used in the treatment of violent offenders. Whereas the psychoanalytic tradition focuses on psychological disorders based in the unconscious and early childhood experiences, the cognitive-behavioral model focuses on conscious material in the present: therapy is intended to help individuals function better by modifying how they think and behave in current situations. The theory behind cognitive-behavioral batterer interventions maintains that behaviors are learned as a result of positive and negative reinforcements (rewards and punishments) for engaging in particular behaviors under particular circumstances (e.g., parental pride or praise for aggressive behavior). Behavior is also influenced by how people mentally construct and interpret their environment and experiences—that is, the way they think about themselves, other people, and their relationships. The cognitive- behavioral theory postulates that men batter because:

- they are imitating examples of abuse they have witnessed during childhood or in the media;
- abuse is rewarded;
- it enables the batterer to get what he wants; and
- abuse is reinforced through victim compliance and submission.

Cognitive-behavioral interventions focus on "cognitive restructuring" and skill building. Counselors focus on identifying the chain of events that lead each batterer to violence, starting with beliefs and "self-talk"—the way we talk to ourselves in our minds (see exhibit 2-2, "A Cognitive Model of Woman Abuse"). For example, a batterer whose partner is ten minutes late may tell himself, "She's out with her boyfriend" or "She can't be trusted." The programs attempt to restructure the beliefs and "self-talk" that lead to violence; for example, "I don't know why she's late, but I'm sure she's trying to get here." The programs help batterers to analyze the thought patterns underlying violent reactions (e.g., "Dinner isn't ready because my wife doesn't respect me") and learn new ways of understanding situations that trigger violence (e.g., "Dinner isn't ready because my wife had a busy day"). The program teaches nonviolent alternative behaviors, such as conflict-resolution tactics, relaxation techniques, and communication skills.[24]

Advantages and Criticism of the Cognitive-Behavioral Models

One advantage of the cognitive-behavioral model is that its analysis of battering and its intervention strategy are compatible with a criminal justice response to domestic violence. The approach holds the batterer fully responsible for his violence and fully responsible for learning and adopting nonviolent alternatives. Without trying to solve larger issues of social inequality on the one hand, or delving into deep-seated psychological issues on the other, the cognitive-behavioral approach simply focuses on the violent acts themselves and attempts to change them. The model also offers a straightforward intervention that can be implemented in a limited period of time.

The feminist perspective criticizes the cognitive-behavioral approach for failing to explain why many men with thought patterns or skills deficits that allegedly explain their domestic violence are not violent in other relationships, how culture or subcultures influence patterns of violence, and why some men continue to abuse women even when the behavior is not rewarded.[33] These criticisms are usually moot because most cognitive-behavioral programs integrate the feminist analysis of domestic violence, both in the cognitive component (for example, by examining thoughts that encourage wife-beating, such as "She should obey me. I'm the man of the household.") and the social learning aspects (for example, by discussing how sexism in the media and in society provides models of social support for abusing and degrading women). (See exhibit 2-3, "Example of an Integrated Feminist/Cognitive-Behavioral Strategy.")

ATTACHMENT ABUSE

A small number of practitioners base batterer interventions on psychological theories of attachment, affect, and individuation. These interventions consider battering to be "attachment abuse"—that is, abusive behaviors toward intimates arising from the individual's insecure attachment to his or her caregivers as a child. Attachment theory describes two broad categories of attachment relationships: secure attachments that result from the caregiver's responsiveness to the child's emotional and physical needs, and a range of insecure attachment patterns that may develop if a child's emotional and physical needs are not met by caregivers. Insecure attachments in childhood may lead, in adult relationships, to emotional distress, anxiety, anger, depression, and emotional detachment when the specter of loss or separation arises in an intimate relationship. These feelings may lead to attachment abuse.

Batterer interventions based on theories of attachment, such as the Compassion Workshop (see chapter 4), seek to enhance the batterers' ability to regulate their own emotions and to stimulate a sense of "compassion" for both themselves and their intimates (partners, children, and elders) using cognitive behavior techniques that are designed to interrupt the batterers' violent emotional response to guilt, shame, and fear of abandonment.

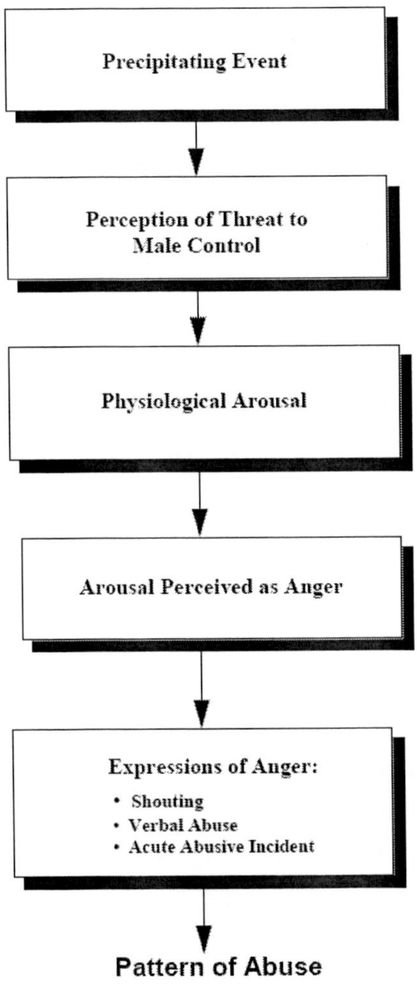

* Adapted from Donald Dutton, "An Ecological Nested Theory," in *Feminist Psychology in Transition*, ed. P. Caplan, 1984.

Exhibit 2-2. A Cognitive Model of Woman Abuse.

Controversial Approaches to Batterer Intervention

The following approaches, although commonly used, are controversial. Criminal justice professionals referring batterers to programs that feature these techniques must be careful to learn how these approaches are being integrated into the programs and be wary of programs using these methods as their primary intervention.

Anger Management

While some researchers have suggested that a small percentage of battering may be attributable to a psychological disorder involving uncontrollable rage,[25] the "anger management" model attributes battering to out-of-control (rather than uncontrollable) anger. Anger management programs offer a short-term intervention that teaches batterers to recognize the physiological signs of anger and to then implement relaxation techniques to defuse the anger.[26] The intervention may also teach stress management and communication skills.[27] Many batterer treatment providers disavow the single-focus "anger management" treatment, instead incorporating anger management as one component of their intervention, sometimes under another name.

Critics have raised several concerns about the anger management approach—even as a component of more comprehensive treatment:

- Anger management programs address a single cause of battering, ignoring other, perhaps more profound, causes.[28]
- According to the feminist model, although they may claim to feel out of control, batterers are *not* out of control: battering is a decision, a choice. The social learning model adds that batterers choose to use or threaten violence because of its effectiveness in controlling their partners. The violence persists because it is rewarded.

- Anger management programs teach batterers nonviolent ways to control their partners. If the underlying issue of batterer control of the victim is not addressed, critics maintain, men will misuse the techniques used to "control" anger—stress management and communication skills—to continue to control the victim. For example, a batterer could refuse his childcare responsibilities on the grounds that it is stressful.
- According to "misattribution of arousal" theory, men learn to label all strong emotional states as anger when they are, in fact, experiencing feelings of betrayal or hurt.
- Interventions therefore need to focus on identifying the underlying emotion men are feeling in situations in which they batter rather than on means of controlling the mislabeled anger.[29]
- Two studies of anger management interventions that were parts of comprehensive batterer treatment programs found that men who completed the programs but whose violence continued reported that they had used anger management techniques to attempt to control their violence, whereas men who were successful in avoiding violence after the program said they ended their abuse through empathy, a redefinition of manhood, and cooperative decisionmaking.[30]

Finally, some practitioners are concerned that any short-term, single-focus approach can be dangerous because it gives victims, judges, and batterers the illusion that the problem has been solved. Some practitioners feel that the availability of brief, inexpensive anger management programs even undermines the credibility of the more difficult, lengthy, and expensive treatments other programs provide. One-time "Saturday Afternoon Special"-style anger management programs arouse particular concern among practitioners who feel that such short-term programs trivialize the severity of the problem in the eyes of the batterer and are unlikely to have any deterrent effect.

Individual and Couples Counseling

Many practitioners disapprove of—and at least 20 State standards and guidelines expressly prohibit— couples counseling for batterers. In addition, a number of program directors disapprove of individual counseling as the sole intervention for battering. Group work is considered important in helping abusers to overcome their denial by hearing other men acknowledge and deal with their behavior, and to break the isolation that is considered part of the syndrome of abuse.

Although systematic research comparing couples and group interventions has not been conducted,[31] anecdotal evidence and the beliefs of providers (many of whom serve on committees to draft or approve State standards or guidelines) have limited the utilization of couples therapy for domestic violence. The practitioners' disapproval is based on a belief that victims of abuse are intimidated and cannot fully participate in therapy in the presence of their abusers. If victims do reveal the batterer's violence or disclose other problems, they face the threat of reprisal. Restrictions on couples therapy and individual psychotherapy for battering are a point of contention between feminist-oriented batterer intervention providers and mental health providers in many communities.

Self-Help Groups: Batterers Anonymous

Self-help batterer groups are modeled on Alcoholics Anonymous and Parents Anonymous. Member-run support groups are facilitated by former batterers who have been nonviolent for at least a year.[32] Although there are some ground rules and facilitators may introduce specific topics, the approach is unstructured, with members setting the agenda, usually addressing their personal concerns.

Self-help or support groups are an accepted model of follow-up for batterers who have completed a program and want continued support to prevent relapse, to continue the change process, or to have a place to address ongoing problems. Self-help groups are controversial as an initial intervention, however, because it is questionable whether former batterers—especially those who have been nonviolent for only a year—are qualified to conduct groups, unless they have been extensively involved with a program, have been trained, and are supervised. In addition, facilitators tend to use an aggressive, even belligerent, style of confrontation that more traditional programs view as inappropriate modeling of antagonistic behavior that borders on abuse. By contrast, other professionals are concerned that support groups run by former batterers may be insufficiently confrontational about members' excuses for violence and too supportive of batterers' hostility toward women.

Compatibility of the Models with Criminal Justice Goals

The feminist educational approach to batterer intervention is theoretically more compatible with a criminal justice perspective than either the family systems or psychotherapeutic approaches in several respects.[34]

- The feminist educational view of domestic violence is that the behavior is criminal, not just the result of faulty couple interactions or mental illness.
- The feminist educational view is that consequences are appropriate. By contrast, the psychotherapeutic explanation results in a treatment approach that is designed to modify the inner emotional life of the batterer through insight and possibly medication. Changing the inner person and prescribing medication to alter behavior may be considered by some to be beyond the scope of a criminal justice intervention.
- The primary goal of feminist educational programs is to hold batterers responsible for their violence. While most psychological programs also make this claim, feminists believe that the psychotherapeutic view of batterers as victims of childhood trauma or other mistreatment undercuts a program's ability to hold batterers responsible. The family systems approach—unlike the criminal justice system—holds the victim as well as the batterer accountable.

- The explicit goal of feminist educational approaches is to end the abusive behavior rather than to heal the batterer (the psychotherapeutic goal) or to improve relationships (the family systems goal).

A case can be made, however, that psychological interventions can also meet the needs of the criminal justice system. The aim of the criminal justice system in sending men to batterer programs is to reduce recidivism; for this to happen, the intervention has to be effective. While advocates of the feminist educational model criticize the psychotherapeutic model for failing to hold batterers responsible for their behavior, advocates of the psychotherapeutic approach respond that educational interventions are not successful in deterring or rehabilitating batterers because they are too short and superficial and do not address the needs of batterers with severe mental illness, who may comprise up to 25 percent of all batterers.[35] Indeed, the "confrontational" and didactic process of the feminist model—as well as the feminist rhetoric in which it is framed—may alienate the batterer and increase his hostility and resistance. For example, an assistant group facilitator for the Compassion Workshop in Silver Spring, Maryland, reported that, when he was in treatment, feminist interventions had only increased his anger and denial, while subsequent, nonconfrontational, compassion-based treatment had helped him become nonviolent. His wife, a cofacilitator of the group whose role was to give the perspective of the victim, agreed that the feminist education model had exacerbated her husband's abuse but that after psychologically oriented counseling, he was now violence free.

While the narrow treatment goals of the strictly educational feminist programs are compatible with the criminal justice view—simply stopping the abusive behavior as expeditiously as possible and holding the batterer responsible—the feminist theory of domestic violence also has broad social goals that may be seen as going beyond the purview of the criminal justice system. Because feminist theory locates the cause of domestic violence in social structures and the organization of society, social change may be seen as the ultimate goal of the curriculums. In a sense, though, even this broad goal is consistent with a criminal justice agenda in that it suggests that broad-based community education and a coordinated community response are necessary for preventing domestic violence. In contrast, it is difficult to identify a broad prevention strategy that follows from either the individualistic psychotherapeutic theory of domestic violence or the family systems model.

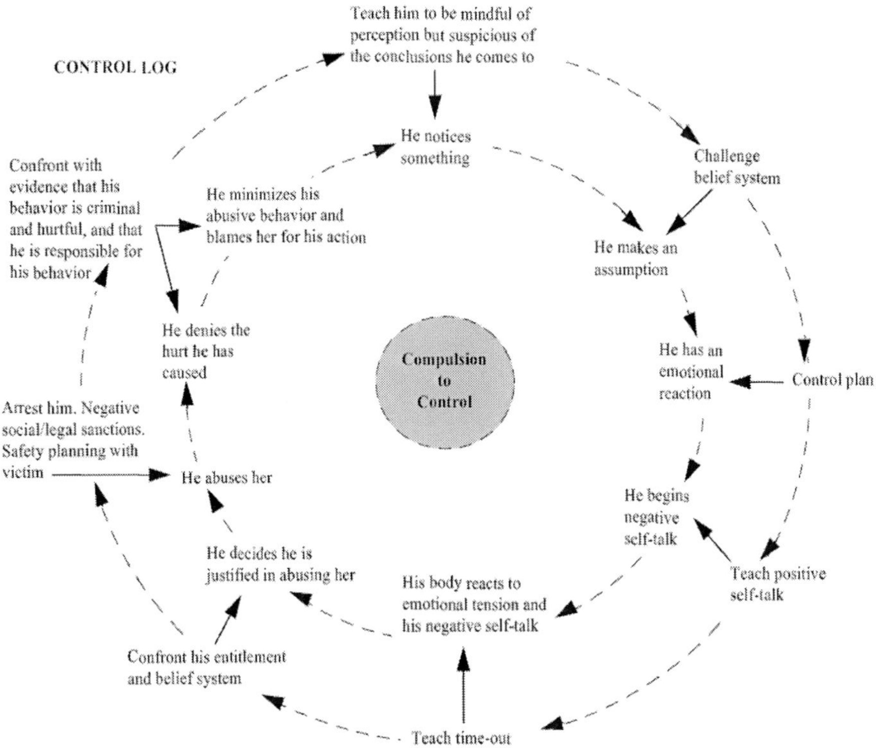

Source: Wil Avery, House of Ruth, Baltimore, Maryland.

Exhibit 2-3. Example of an Integrated Feminist/Cognitive-Behavioral Strategy.

Finally, some practitioners and criminal justice professionals are beginning to regard any form of batterer intervention as a proxy for intensive probation. While the curriculum may not deter reoffenses over time, at least during program participation batterers are being monitored closely, and their victims are receiving at least minimal attention and referrals. This heightened vigilance with regard to the batterer's behavior and the victim's welfare is compatible with criminal justice goals.

As will be seen in the following chapters, however, theoretical compatibility with the criminal justice system is not the only important factor in selecting a batterer intervention. On a practical level, interventions must be able to retain batterers in treatment and address any obstacles to program participation.

Conclusion: Multidimensional Models Dominate the Field

Many practitioners accept that there are compelling features in more than one theoretical model. In practice, regardless of their primary perspective, most programs have adopted some tenets of the feminist model. For example, they view sexual inequality and masculine role expectations of dominance as core issues to address—along with cognitive- behavioral techniques for modifying behavior—and they teach batterers to use "time-outs" (a behavioral technique for controlling emotional outbursts). Longer-term programs may progress through the feminist and cognitive models in stages, and some even progress to a psychotherapeutic group process model for aftercare. These programs have a brief initial phase using a feminist educational model to tackle denial of responsibility, a longer second phase teaching cognitive-behavioral techniques for skill-building, and a third phase delving into individual psychological issues in an unstructured format for those men identified as having psychological problems contributing to battering. (See chapter 3, "Pioneers in Batterer Intervention: Program Models," for a detailed description of various program models.) Other programs blend treatment modalities and approaches by combining individual, group, and couples treatment sequentially over an extended period of two to three years.

Programs may also use different models or materials to accommodate the special needs of specific types of batterers, most commonly substance abusers, African Americans, Asians, Latinos, recent immigrants, female offenders, gay and lesbian batterers, or batterers with poor literacy skills. (See chapter 4, "Current Trends in Batterer Intervention," for a discussion of culturally specific interventions.)

Some practitioners may resist incorporating consideration of individual psychology and cultural differences in interventions because they are concerned that the individual approach will eclipse consideration of the sociological factors emphasized by the prevailing feminist model. However, the critical issue from a criminal justice perspective is simply "what works"; if mixed-model interventions that incorporate psychotherapeutic elements or cultural competence are shown to be more effective in retaining and engaging batterers in treatment, questions of theory are likely to become secondary.

Discussions such as these are rapidly being translated into experiments in practice. Chapter 4, "Current Trends in Batterer Intervention," discusses a range of innovations in batterer treatment that attempt to link individual characteristics of batterers to specific interventions or combinations of interventions in order to increase program retention and effectiveness.

References

[1] Rosenbaum, A. and R.D. Maiuro, "Eclectic Approaches in Working With Men Who Batter," in Treating Men Who Batter: Theory, Practice, and Programs, ed. P.L. Caesar and K.L. Hamberger, New York: Springer, 1989: 65–195.

[2] Mary Russell, for example, justifies her use of the expression "wife assault" on the grounds that "domestic violence" and "family violence" ignore the "male to female direction" of most violence between partners. See Russell, M., "Wife Assault Theory, Research, and Treatment: A Literature Review," Journal of Family Violence, 3 (3) (1988): 193–208.

[3] Schechter, S., Women and Male Violence: The Visions and Struggles of the Battered Women's Movement, Boston: South End Press, 1982.

[4] Pence, E. and M. Paymar, Education Groups for Men Who Batter: The Duluth Model, New York: Springer, 1993.

[5] In support of the point that women may remain with men who abuse them because of economic dependence, Ida Johnson found in a study of 426 battered women leaving a Central Florida battered women's shelter that a woman was more likely to return home if the batterer had a high income and the woman was unemployed; if she had an independent income and his income was insufficient to support a family, the woman was unlikely to return home. Johnson, I. M., "Economic, Situational, and Psychological Correlates of the Decision-making Process of Battered Women," Families in Society: The Journal of Contemporary Human Services, (March 1992): 168–176.

[6] There is disagreement over whether batterers actually believe that women are incompetent or whether promoting that notion merely serves their needs to control their wives in order to restrict their activities. Rusbult and Martz, in a study of women leaving a domestic violence shelter in Lexington, Kentucky, found that the strongest predictor of whether women would return to the batterer was whether they had a driver's license and access to a car. Rusbult, C.E. and J. M. Martz, "Remaining in an Abusive Relationship: An Investment Model Analysis of Nonvoluntary Dependence," Personality and Social Psychology Bulletin, 21 (1995): 558–571.

[7] O'Sullivan, C. and B. Birns, Contested Custody Cases When Violent Marriages End, Paper presented at the First National Conference on Children Exposed to Family Violence, Austin, Texas, June 1996.

[8] Browne, K., D.G. Saunders, and K.M. Staecker, "Process-Psychodynamic Groups for Men Who Batter: Description of a Brief Treatment Model," University of Michigan, January 26, 1996.

[9] Gondolf, E. W. and J. Hanneken, "The Gender Warrior: Reformed Batterers on Abuse, Treatment, and Change," Journal of Family Violence, 2 (2) (1987): 177–191.

[10] Gondolf and Hanneken, "The Gender Warrior." The measure is Bem's Sex Role Inventory.

[11] Browne, Saunders, and Staecker, "Process-Psychodynamic Groups for Men Who Batter."

[12] Dutton, D., "Patriarchy and Wife Assault: The Ecological Fallacy," Violence and Victims, 9 (2) (1994): 167– 182.

[13] Harrell, A., "Evaluation of Court Ordered Treatment for Domestic Violence Offenders," Final Report, Washington, DC: The Urban Institute, 1991.

[14] A 1990 evaluation of the Duluth Domestic Abuse Intervention Project (DAIP) found that program participation had no impact on recidivism. Shepard, M., "Predicting Batterer Recidivism Five Years After Community Intervention," Report, Duluth, Minnesota, 1990.

[15] Giles-Sims, J., Wife-battering: A Systems Theory Approach, New York: Guilford, 1983.

[16] While it is true that many victims who seek services want to maintain the relationship while eliminating the abuse, and that most programs report that 30 to 40 percent of the men in treatment are separated, no long-term data show what percent of relationships in which there has been battery last. See Sirles, E.A., S. Lipchik, andK. Kowalski, "A Consumer's Perspective on Domestic Violence Interventions," Journal of Family Violence, 8 (3) (1993): 267.

[17] Bowker, L., Ending the Violence: A Guidebook Based on the Experience of 1,000 Battered Wives, Holmes Beach, FL: Learning Publications, 1986.

[18] Russell, "Wife Assault Theory."

[19] Specific disorders that have been found in batterers are post-traumatic stress disorder (probably due to childhood trauma), depression, low self-esteem, and personality disorders. Personality disorders usually mentioned by therapists who work with batterers are antisocial personality disorder, narcissism, and borderline personality disorder. In addition, passive-aggression, paranoia, obsessive-compulsive disorder, and intermittent

explosive disorder have been said to foster aggression. A psychotherapeutic reference describes the personality disorders as follows: People with antisocial personality disorder are irresponsible, irritable, and aggressive; they are not sadistic but are reckless and have no remorse; they are unable to maintain friendships or romantic relationships. Narcissists are hypersensitive but lack empathy; they have difficulty with relationships because they expect others to meet their special needs. Borderline personalities are characterized by instability of identity, self-image, and relationships; they want to be alone but fear abandonment; they are often moody and depressed and, in severe cases, self-destructive and suicidal. Reid, W.H. and M.G. Weise, The DSM-III-R Training Guide, New York: Brunner/Mazel, 1989. See also Dutton, D., "Trauma Symptoms and PTSD-like Profiles in Perpetrators of Intimate Abuse," Journal of Traumatic Stress, 8 (2)(1995): 299–316; and Maiuro, R., T.S. Cahn, P.P. Vitaliano, B.C. Wagner, and J.B. Zegree, "Anger, Hostility, and Depression in Domestically Violent Versus Generally Assaultive and Nonviolent Control Subjects," Journal of Consulting and Clinical Psychology, 56 (1) (1988): 17–23.

[20] Browne, Saunders, and Straecker, "Process-Psychodynamic Groups for Men Who Batter."

[21] See Dutton, "Patriarchy and Wife Assault."

[22] Adams, D., "Treatment Models for Men Who Batter: A Profeminist Analysis," in Feminist Perspectives on Wife Abuse, ed. K. Yllo and M. Bograd, Newbury Park, CA: Sage Publications, 1988: 176–199.

[23] Adams, "Treatment Models for Men Who Batter," 176– 177.

[24] Hamberger, K.L. and J. E. Hastings, "Recidivism Following Spouse Abuse Abatement Counseling: Treatment Program Implications," Violence and Victims, 5 (3) (1990): 160.

[25] Information provided by Roland Mauiro.

[26] Hamberger, K.L. and J. E. Hastings, "Court-Mandated Treatment of Men Who Assault Their Partner: Issues, Controversies, and Outcomes," in Legal Responses to Wife Assault, ed. Z. Hilton, Newbury Park, CA: Sage Publications, 1993: 188–229.

[27] Tolman, R. M. and D. G. Saunders, "The Case for the Cautious Use of Anger Control With Men Who Batter," Response, 11 (2) (1988): 15–20.

[28] Tolman and Saunders articulate this concern, while accepting anger management as part of a cognitive- behavioral intervention: "The use of anger control techniques with batterers is problematic when battering is framed exclusively as an anger problem, when the issues of dominance and

control of women by men are ignored in treatment, and when practitioners fail to address societal reinforcements for battering." Tolman and Saunders, "The Case for the Cautious Use of Anger Control With Men Who Batter," 19. See also Ptacek, J., "The Clinical Literature on Men Who Batter, A Review and Critiques," in Family Abuse and Its Consequences: New Directions in Research, ed. B.T. Hotaling, D. Finkelhor, J.T. Kirkpatrick, and M.A. Straus, Newbury Park, CA: Sage Publications, 1986: 149–162.

[29] Dutton, D., The Domestic Assault of Women: Psychological and Criminal Justice Perspectives (revised), Vancouver: University of British Columbia, 1995.

[30] Two studies showing a recurrence of violence among program participants who said they used anger management to reduce their violence are: Gondolf, E., "Men Who Batter: How They Stop Their Abuse," Paper presented at the Second National Conference for Family Violence Researchers, Durham, NC, 1984; and Kelso, D. and L. Personette, Domestic Violence and Treatment Services for Victims and Abusers, Anchorage: Altam, 1985.

[31] Daniel O'Leary' s studies comparing single-sex group and couples-group interventions were unable to retain couples when the batterer had a history of severe violence. Rosenbaum, A. and K. D. O'Leary, "The Treatment of Marital Violence," in Clinical Handbook of Marital Therapy, ed. N.S. Jacobsen and A.S. Gurman, New York: Guilford, 1986. Gondolf studied 12 men who had been through a men's group program and were deemed to be fully reformed (versus 38 who were not). Several of these highly motivated men had sought professional help before coming to the batterer program but they had found no improvement after individual or couples therapy. According to their self-reports, the batterer group they subsequently attended gave them what they needed to stop battering. Gondolf and Hanneken, "The Gender Warrior."

[32] Edelson, J. L. and M. Syers, "Relative Effectiveness of Group Treatments for Men Who Batter," Social Work Research and Abstracts, (June 1990): 10–17.

[33] According to social learning theory, a retaliatory attack should decrease future abuse. However, two national surveys found that when women resist violently, the batterer' s violence usually increases in severity. This result is consistent with the feminist view that the intent of physical abuse is to punish resistance and disobedience. Bowker, L., Ending the Violence: A Guidebook Based on the Experience of1, 000 Battered Wives, Holmes Beach, FL: Learning Publications, 1986; Feld, S. L. and M.A. Straus,

"Escalation and Desistance From Wife Assault in Marriage," in Physical Violence in American Families, ed. M.A. Straus, and R.J. Gelles, New Brunswick, NJ: Transaction, 1990: 489–505.

[34] Edelson and Syers, "Relative Effectiveness of Group Treatments for Men Who Batter." This article reports an experiment in which all comers to a program were assigned to a brief or intense intervention and to one of three models: the Duluth "educational" model, a self- help group, and a combined group process-educational model. The results showed no difference between the brief and intense programs, except for the few men of color who were less likely to recidivate if they completed the long program; the structured feminist educational model was found to be most effective.

[35] Gondolf, E., "Multi-Site Evaluation of Batterer Intervention Systems: A Summary of Preliminary Findings," Working Paper, Mid-Atlantic Addiction Training Institute, October 24, 1996.

Chapter 3

PIONEERS IN BATTERER INTERVENTION: PROGRAM MODELS

KEY POINTS

- This chapter describes program services in the larger, more well-established programs visited for this book.
- Specialized innovative programming is discussed in chapter 4, "Current Trends in Batterer Intervention."
- Common mainstream program procedures include:

— *Intake:* First contact with batterer referred by the criminal justice system.

— *Assessment:* Client agrees with terms of program and is assessed for dangerousness, extent of abuse, substance abuse, mental illness, illiteracy, or other obstacles to treatment.

— *Victim Contact:* Partners may be notified about batterer's status in the program and any imminent danger, and referred to victim services.

— *Orientation:* An initial phase of group intervention that may be more didactic than later meetings.

— *Group Treatment:* May involve a set educational curriculum or less structured discussions about relationships, anger-management skills, or group psychotherapy.

— *Leaving the Program:* Batterers may complete the program, be terminated for noncompliance, or be asked to restart the program.

— *Follow-up:* May consist of informal self-help groups of program graduates or less frequent group meetings.

- Program content varies, but all the well-established programs discussed in this chapter include feminist educational approaches that may be combined with cognitive-behavioral or psychotherapeutic approaches.

This chapter provides an overview of program services and procedures in five communities visited for this book. The chapter's primary focus is on larger mainstream batterer interventions. The following chapter, "Current Trends in Batterer Intervention," discusses smaller specialized interventions in detail (see box, "Selection of Programs Studied," and appendix B, a listing of individuals interviewed at each site).

No mainstream program approach or curriculum has yet been proven to be more effective in reducing recidivism than any other.[1] As a result, many program directors and criminal justice professionals stress structure over content; they believe that regardless of a program's philosophy or methods, any responsible intervention that requires weekly contact can help contain batterers' abuse through close monitoring of their behavior (see chapter 5, "Criminal Justice Response").[2] According to Andrew Klein, chief probation officer for the Quincy, Massachusetts, District Court, "If only appropriate clients are referred—people who know they did wrong, have some motivation to change, are under external pressure to change, and are sober—if the program monitors behavior, not attitude, and if the program lasts long enough, then the content doesn't matter. . . . To be considered effective, the program must stop the battering and keep offenders from battering again for at least one year."

> "If only appropriate clients are referred—people who know they did wrong, have some motivation to change, are under external pressure to change, and are sober—if the program monitors behavior, not attitude, and if the program lasts long enough, then the content doesn't matter. . . . To be considered effective, the program must stop the battering and keep offenders from battering again for at least one year."
>
> —Andrew Klein, Chief Probation Officer, Quincy, Massachusetts, District Court Model Domestic Abuse Program

PROGRAM PROCEDURES

The following discussion draws on program practices at the five sites with special emphasis on issues of common concern.

Intake and Assessment

The batterer' s first contact with the program occurs when he arranges for an intake interview. At this time, the client signs release forms that give the program permission to contact his probation officer and his partner. The program then notifies the probation office that the client has chosen it for treatment. (See appendix D for sample intake and assessment forms.)

The first step of the intervention is the intake assessment, a process that can span one to eight weekly sessions.[3] The initial session may be done as an individual interview or as part of a group orientation. Intake sessions serve several purposes:

- to get the client to agree with the terms and conditions of treatment and to sign the program contract;
- to begin to assess the nature and extent of the batterer' s abusive behavior; and
- to screen for other problems such as substance abuse, mental illness, and illiteracy.

In addition to specific questions about domestic violence, the assessment typically includes questions about the batterer's family history, propensity for violence outside the family, and substance abuse. Ideally, the session begins to foster rapport between the clinician and the batterer, in addition to initiating the actual intervention. For example, details about the nature of the abuse are often gleaned through questions regarding the first, the most recent, and the most severe battering incidents. Describing this behavior in detail can increase the batterer' s awareness of the extent of his violence, and this can form a foundation for later, more in-depth discussions of the abuse and its consequences. Similarly, programs usually ask about a range of behaviors that are psychologically or sexually abusive. This questioning helps the batterer broaden his definition of abuse.

Programs vary in how clinical their assessments are and to what extent they measure the batterer' s psychological makeup in an effort to identify other problems that could interfere with the intervention. Some programs screen for possible problems by using simple checklists and then referring the client for formal psychological evaluation if a substance abuse or mental health problem is suspected. Other programs, such as AMEND and The Third Path, use standardized instruments like the Millon Clinical Multiaxial Inventory (MCMI) to do clinical assessments themselves. The director of one of the AMEND programs[4] explains, "We use the MCMI both as a diagnostic tool and a treatment planning tool, and to start thinking about the majority of our clients who have personality disturbances as falling along a continuum from mild personality dysfunction to more pronounced conditions."

Selection of Programs Studied

Thirteen programs in five communities were selected to represent a range of approaches to batterer intervention.

- Two of the largest and most established programs in the country—EMERGE in Quincy, Massachusetts, and AMEND in Denver—were chosen to represent pioneers that continue to modify their models in keeping with the most recent trends in batterer intervention.
- The Domestic Abuse Intervention Services (DAIS) of Des Moines represents one of the many programs that use the "Duluth model," a popular curriculum developed by the Domestic Abuse Intervention Project of Duluth, Minnesota.
- Family Services of Seattle, a subsidized provider of batterer intervention to low-income clients, was founded as an anger management program but shifted its emphasis to follow the Duluth model.
- The Harborview Medical Center in Seattle, Washington, was chosen to represent a public health model of batterer intervention. The center runs a self-styled "eclectic" program for batterers as outpatients in a private hospital setting that emphasizes psychotherapy.
- House of Ruth, in Baltimore, another Duluth-based intervention, was chosen to represent programs that prefer "colorblind" interracial groups in contrast to the current trend toward specialized single-race or culture interventions that take into account the racial and cultural context of the violence (see chapter 4, "Current Trends in Batterer Intervention").
- Colorado's The Third Path, founded by Michael Lindsey, was included for its innovative use of psychological treatment and batterer typology, as well as its focus on high-risk offenders.
- The Compassion Workshop of Silver Spring, Maryland, was chosen for its innovative approach to batterer intervention, which uses cognitive restructuring techniques to prevent violent responses to emotional pain and to cultivate compassionate, nonviolent relationships.

A number of smaller programs that serve specialized populations were observed in Seattle. Zegree, Ellner and Berrysmith conducts two therapy groups for batterers as part of its mental health practice. Anne Ganley, a pioneer in batterer treatment, directs a program for veterans that utilizes the Duluth curriculum at the Mental Health Clinic of the Seattle Veterans Administration Medical Center. Ina Maka, a Native American-operated intervention, uses the context of Native American cultural lore as part of a family-preservationist model of batterer intervention. Sexual Minorities Counseling Services targets gay and lesbian batterers. Women's Refugee Alliance sponsors individual and group batterer counseling for recent Southeast Asian immigrants. These specialized programs are discussed in chapter 4, "Current Trends in Batterer Intervention."

> "We use the MCMI both as a diagnostic tool and a treatment planning tool, and to start thinking about the majority of our clients who have personality disturbances as falling along a continuum from mild personality dysfunction to more pronounced conditions."
>
> —Gary Gibbens, Director of Arapahoe County, Colorado, Chapter of AMEND

Programs may refer batterers who are found to have other psychological problems, like clinical depression, elsewhere for psychiatric treatment or individual counseling. However, referrals are not considered a substitute for the batterer intervention program. Rather, psychotherapy is delivered concurrently with the batterer intervention, as is also typically the case when substance abuse is the problem. Programs try not to screen out batterers with multiple problems as long as they comply with the concurrent treatment. For example, batterers who are clinically depressed may continue in the program as long as they take their psychiatric medication, while batterers with substance abuse problems must remain sober and submit to random urine screenings or breathalizer tests. In the Quincy, Massachusetts, District Court, for example, batterers must take weekly urine tests. The batterer pays $5 per test, but the probation office will pay if the offender cannot.

Many programs do deny services to certain batterers. One of the most common reasons for turning batterers away at intake is if they are part of a cultural or language group that another program can serve better. While established programs are striving to develop the culturally sensitive methods discussed in chapter 4, "Current Trends in Batterer Intervention," other programs have chosen to develop alliances with grassroots organizations serving specific cultural communities, such as non-English-speaking immigrants. Family Services of Seattle, for example, refers Spanish- speaking batterers to a local organization formed to serve Hispanic immigrants, and it refers batterers in same-sex relationships to a local gay and lesbian counseling agency. EMERGE, on the other hand, offers special in-house groups for African American male batterers and for lesbian batterers, and it has Latino and Asian American counselors on staff to serve batterers from these cultural groups.

Another common reason for rejecting clients at intake is unwillingness or inability to pay. Intake fees may be $50 or more. Rather than pay, many clients prefer to return to probation or the court to request a change in their conditions. To get batterers past this initial barrier to treatment, Sid Hoover, supervisor of Seattle's Municipal Probation Domestic Violence Unit, offers "especially worthy" batterers a limited-time discount coupon to reduce the cost of intake from $45 to $25. Family Services of Seattle, one of several local interventions that receive city funds to reduce the cost of providing services to indigent clients, allows the probation office to designate which clients will be offered reduced-rate intake. (See chapter 4, "Current Trends in Batterer Intervention," for a discussion of program fees and indigence.) According to Hoover, "Getting people into intake is half the hurdle; if you can get them into the intake, their fear about the whole enterprise starts to decline. Their comfort level goes up because they've been in there. They've seen the people, they realize that it's relatively painless, and the program people aren't dehumanizing them."

> "Getting people into intake is half the hurdle; if you can get them into the intake, their fear about the whole enterprise starts to decline. Their comfort level goes up because they've been in there. They've seen the people, they realize that it's relatively painless, and the program people aren't dehumanizing them."
>
> —Sid Hoover, Supervisor, Domestic Violence Probation Unit, Seattle

Some programs consider a batterer inappropriate for treatment if he unequivocally denies that he committed any violence. A probation officer in Seattle noted batterers' difficulty in adjusting to their new roles as court-mandated clients: "We're kind of breaking the news to them—you're going to a DV treatment program—so they can start to turn themselves from defendants into health care consumers. They've got to switch hats from fighting the system to taking responsibility for their life." At intake, the batterer has just been referred from the criminal justice system where, in the role of defendant, he was expected to insist on his innocence. Now that he has agreed to a plea bargain, it is no longer appropriate for him to deny his guilt. The batterer may not have much time to make this adjustment—some courts give the defendant less than a week to make contact with the program. The lack of time to change his mindset, combined with the batterer's tendency to minimize and deny his violence, forms the first obstacle to treatment. Apart from information gathering and initial indoctrination to program rules, overcoming this obstacle is the primary task of the intake session. In Des Moines, the intake counselor uses the police report to confront the batterer with the facts of the case. Other programs postpone confronting batterers until treatment begins.

> "We're kind of breaking the news to them— you're going to a DV treatment program—so they can start to turn themselves from defendants into health care consumers. They've got to switch hats from fighting the system to taking responsibility for their life."
>
> —Sid Hoover, Supervisor, Domestic Violence Probation Unit, Seattle

Victim Contacts

A number of States require that batterer programs contact partners (see appendix A, "State Standards Matrix"). At a minimum, partner notification is needed at four points:

- when the batterer begins attending the program;
- if and when he has been terminated from treatment for noncompliance;
- when he has completed the program; and
- if an imminent threat to victim safety arises (see below).

Programs with a strong advocacy policy will typically contact the partner every two to three months as long as the batterer remains in the program.

Since batterers typically minimize or deny their abusive behavior, assessments and ongoing monitoring often involve separate interviews with the victim to gain additional information about the relationship. As part of the client contract, batterers may therefore be required to sign releases that permit counselors to contact current and past partners. (Some States, like Iowa, avoid the need for consent by exempting counselors from ordinary client confidentiality requirements when it comes to victim contacts.) A trained victim liaison usually interviews victims by telephone for reasons of safety and efficiency. The liaison assures the victim of absolute confidentiality; nothing she says will be repeated to her partner or his counselor without her consent. At EMERGE, the victim liaisons make it clear to victims that the program's primary concern is the safety of victims and their children. If the victim is willing to discuss the abuse, the advocate may also ask about the duration, frequency, and severity of the abuse in order to assist in the batterer' s treatment. However, liaisons make clear that furthering the batterer's treatment is only a secondary goal of the victim contact. A victim liaison from AMEND expressed a similar view:

> When I first started working here, we were getting more background on the batterer from his partner, such as what his childhood was like. That was

helpful for the therapist in treating him, but at the same time I don't think it was so helpful for her to have to dredge up all that information about him. So we've moved away from that in our conversation and started talking more about the victim and her plans and trying to educate her about domestic violence.

The Impact of State Standards on Intervention Strategies

Each of the five communities visited for this book developed its own response to domestic violence. The responses were influenced in part by the statutory standards of care in each State.

The State standards in Iowa, for example, require that the Duluth curriculum be used in all batterer interventions. As a result, the probation office in Des Moines finds it easiest to ensure that the Duluth model is being followed by referring all batterers to a single provider, the Domestic Abuse Intervention Services (DAIS) program of Des Moines. In constrast, Washington and Colorado allow providersto implement a variety of treatment approaches as long as they follow specified procedures related to intake assessment, frequency of victim contacts, and duration of program participation. This flexibility allows more than a dozen programs of varying sizes and theoretical approaches to provide services to cities like Seattle and Denver. Some of Seattle's programs serve distinct populations using curriculums designed especially for Asians, veterans, Latinos, Native Americans, gays and lesbians, or recent immigrants (see chapter 4, "Current Trends in Batterer Intervention"). By contrast, EMERGE, one of two programs that receive referrals from Quincy, Massachusetts, District Court, provides services to diverse populations under one umbrella agency. Finally, in Baltimore, where State standards are still being debated, an established Duluth-style program currently receiving the bulk of referrals will soon compete with a controversial new program for court referrals.

In addition to helping with safety planning, the victim liaison can describe to the victim the basic features of the batterer intervention program as well as its limitations (see below).

Victim liaisons (many of whom are called "advocates") interviewed for this book expressed surprise that most of the partners they contact have never sought services from a battered women's agency. These victims come to light only as a result of legal intervention with their abusers; they may not even be aware that services are available to them. Contacting the partner when the batterer enters the program therefore offers the opportunity to raise the victim's awareness of her situation and to begin to help her think about her own and her children's safety. As the director of battered women's services in Des Moines added, "For every batterer who gets arrested, his victim will have some sort of contact from battered women's services, whether it's legal advocacy, like warning of his release from jail or explaining pretrial hearings, or basic safety planning."

> "For every batterer who gets arrested, his victim will have some sort of contact from battered women's services, whether it's legal advocacy, like warning of his release from jail or explaining pretrial hearings, or basic safety planning."
>
> —Director of a battered women's shelter, Des Moines

Because this contact may be the first chance the victim has ever had to tell her story to a helping professional, it is crucial that the contact be handled sensitively by another woman who has experience working with battered women. The EMERGE partner pamphlet lists the following examples of questions to ask the victim:

- Are you always trying to second-guess your partner to avoid an argument?
- What does your partner do when he loses his temper?
- Do you have holes in your walls or broken possessions from times when your partner lost his temper?
- Has he ever hurt you physically or threatened you?
- What would it take for you to get away?
- Do you know that there are many other women who have experienced what you are going through and that help is available?

The House of Ruth in Baltimore invites victims to a separate open house to discuss the program's goals and methods and to provide an opportunity for victims to learn more about the House of Ruth's victim and children's services, including legal counseling and referral to other service agencies. The following two sections highlight program techniques for working with victims.

Raising Victim Awareness

In order to develop rapport with the victim, the victim liaison must affirm the victim's experiences and communicate respect for the victim's right to make her own decisions. The victim liaison shows concern for the victim's safety by speaking to her when the batterer is not present and assuring her complete confidentiality. Victim advocacy starts by offering support, assuring the victim that other women have also faced similar circumstances. "Mainly we try to focus the conversations on her, try to reach her that way," one liaison said. "We ask her what she'd like us to address— whether it's the kids, or continued abuse, or drug and alcohol issues." The victim liaison makes sure that the victim knows that services are available to her and tells her how she can contact the local battered women's shelter and support group. While stressing that the interview is voluntary, the liaison asks if the victim is willing to describe the incident that resulted in her partner's entering the program. The victim liaison tries to learn all she can not only about the extent of the physical violence but also about any emotional and sexual abuse. Just as the intake worker tries to broaden the batterer' s definition of abuse, the victim liaison attempts to help the victim become aware of the broader context of the abuse. She lets her know that other victims have reported similar experiences of being humiliated, berated, threatened, or intimidated into complying with their partner's wishes.

> "Mainly we try to focus the conversations on her, try to reach her that way. We ask her what she'd like us to address—whether it's the kids, or continuedabuse, or drug andalcohol issues."
>
> —Victim Liaison, AMEND

Some program group leaders have difficulty convincing some victims from other cultures that they have a right to live without violence and to be treated as their husband's equal. An Asian counselor described the dilemma of being an Asian immigrant and a victim: "For Asians, the family is the most important thing, not the individual, as it is for most Americans. The Asian culture believes that talking to someone outside the family about private matters shames the family." For those coming from countries with strong patriarchal values that completely disempower women, programs take pains to educate the victim about American laws and cultural norms.

Another important reason to contact the victim when the batterer enters treatment is to guard against false hopes that the program can make him change. The program stresses that it is up to the batterer to take responsibility for his violent and controlling behaviors, and acknowledges that many batterers are not willing to stop being abusive. The liaison tells the victims (just as counselors tell the batterer) that there is no quick fix—change takes a long time and requires a genuine commitment by the batterer. Victim liaisons assure the partner that she is in no way responsible for making him stop and that the responsibility to change is the batterer' s and his alone.

Making independent contact with the victim also ensures that she gets accurate information about the program's goals and methods. Particularly during the first few weeks of treatment, batterers often use the program to manipulate the victim, distorting what has been said in group to blame her for the abuse. For example, one victim liaison from AMEND recalls, "The therapist got into describing what bipolar is. Then these guys go home and say to the victim 'My therapist said you're manic depressive,' allowing the focus to shift to the victim rather than remain on his behavior." In explaining the general goals of the intervention and the standard techniques the batterer will be taught, the liaison can circumvent the batterer' s distortions beforehand. Victim liaisons also warn the victim that batterers often use their entry into treatment as a justification for pressuring their partners to stay in the relationship and that such pressure is another sign of continuing nonphysical abuse.

Ongoing Advocacy and Safety Planning

The victim liaison has the difficult task of balancing cautions against false hopes with respect for the victim's right to make her own decisions. Should the victim decide that she wants to remain with the batterer, the liaison needs to respect that choice but still help her plan for her safety. One victim liaison usually tells the victim, "Well, you know we can't guarantee he's going to change. . . . So what are you going to do just in case he doesn't change?" The liaison advises the victim to identify the absolutely essential items she would need if she suddenly had to leave home. Then the liaison helps her develop a plan to have these things available, preferably through a trusted neighbor, relative, or friend. For instance, the victim might plan to give someone an extra set of her car keys, copies of her and her children's birth certificates, and the originals of other important documents and prescriptions.

> "I usually tell the victim, 'Well, you know we can't guarantee he's going to change. . . . So what are you going to do just in case he doesn't change?'"
>
> —Victim Liaison, AMEND

Safety planning can also be more long term. Victim liaisons may continue to support the victim over the course of the batterer' s treatment, and this support may help her to prepare to leave him. On the advice of the victim liaison, programs like EMERGE, AMEND, Family Services of Seattle, and Zegree, Ellner and Berrysmith all agree that they sometimes maintain a noncompliant batterer in treatment in order to give the victim extra time to leave safely. In addition, batterers are also occasionally retained in treatment as a form of supervision and monitoring intended to increase victim safety. For example, a liaison at AMEND noted, "There are cases we have kept on that we felt we could have terminated because we knew that there was going to be no success in rehabilitating the batterer. But it was better—for victim safety—for us to have some containment, because at least we knew then what was going on with them."

> "[T]he 'victim informant' position is difficult for victims. If the victim gives [the program] information about the batterer's abuse or other lapses, the batterer may retaliate against her. Her abuser may then see it as her fault—not his—that he has to keep going to the program."
>
> —Lucinda Cervantez, Community Advocate, New Beginnings, Seattle

While all the programs visited for this book had some form of contact with victims over the course of the batterer' s treatment, some victim liaisons oppose this blending of batterer and victim services. A battered women's advocate in Seattle suggested that "the 'victim informant' position is difficult for victims. If the victim gives [the program] information about the batterer's abuse or other lapses, the batterer may retaliate against her. Her abuser may then see it as her fault—not his—that he has to keep going to the program." Other victim advocates and liaisons agree that contacting victims can be a delicate matter, as an AMEND liaison explained:

A lot of times we get information that we can't confront him on—for example, the victim will call and say, "He's been drinking, but I don't want you to confront him on it. I just wanted you to know." So then we tell the therapist, and the therapist tries to figure out how he can incorporate this information into the guy's treatment without violating her confidentiality and safety. And some therapists can do that better than others, finding a back way of confronting him and getting it to come out another way.

Because of these concerns for the victim, some State standards prohibit or discourage batterer programs from contacting the victim directly.

Orientation

Established programs have adapted their interventions over the years to continue the assessment process during the initial phase of group intervention. New clients meet together for one or more orientation sessions during which the reeducation process begins; at the same time, counselors use the sessions to make a more accurate appraisal of the extent of the batterer' s violence and substance abuse than may have been possible during intake.[5] For example, the Arapahoe County, Colorado, chapter of AMEND requires that its clients be alcohol- and drug-free during the entire six-week orientation period as a test of their sobriety. Batterers who do not comply with the abstinence rule are placed in special groups for substance-abusing batterers. The group leaders, certified both as batterer group leaders and chemical dependency counselors, provide drug counseling, such as relapse prevention techniques, in combination with the standard AMEND intervention. The program typically requires random urine screens and the use of Antabuse.

AMEND also added alcohol education to its orientation curriculum because some clients have drinking problems that neither their probation officers nor the intake assessment has brought to light. As one of AMEND's co-directors explains, "Because a lot of our people have alcohol and drug problems, we'll go through a basic kind of alcohol education [during everyone's orientation]. . . . One of our goals that first four to six weeks is to find out who has a problem and get them dried out."

> "Because a lot of our people have alcohol and drug problems, we'll go through a basic kind of alcohol education [during everyone's orientation]. . . . One of our goals in that first four to six weeks is to find out who has a problem and get them dried out."
>
> —Gary Gibbens, Director of Arapahoe County, Colorado, Chapter of AMEND

Besides improving the program's ability to assess the client, the orientation serves to establish rapport between participants and counselors. Staff who conduct orientation seek to reduce the batterers' initial defensiveness. As one program director put it, "We try to reassure them that we're here to help them, not to beat them up. We try to form an alliance with each person . . . suggesting that maybe there are things he can learn here to improve his relationships with his partner and kids."

> " We try to reassure them that we're here to help them, not to beat them up. We try to form an alliance with each person . . . suggesting that maybe there are things he can learn here to improve his relationships with his partner and kids."
>
> —Meg Craeger, Former Director, Family Services, Seattle

The session then turns to the program goals and the rules for participating in the group. Some of the rules relate to attendance, punctuality, and payment of fees; others are related specifically to the group process, such as confidentiality, abstaining from alcohol and other drugs 24 hours before each group session, and participating constructively in group discussions. Other rules may prohibit sexist or degrading language and insulting or intimidating counselors or other group members, and require waiting in turn to speak. Finally, the program explicitly states the expectation that batterers will refrain from all violent, intimidating, or threatening behavior toward their partners.

ONGOING LETHALITY ASSESSMENT

Victim liaisons and batterer counselors routinely inform clients that all staff have an ethical and legal duty to warn the victim if they believe she is in imminent danger of further abuse. While they cannot predict dangerousness, practitioners are told to watch for signs that a batterer intends to harm someone. Some of these signs may be revealed during the intake assessment and the initial partner contact. When either the batterer or his partner indicates that these signs are present, the counselor must warn the batterer's partner and probation officer about the potential danger.[6] Warning signs based on the batterers' previous behavior include:

- the severity of previous injuries to the partner;
- incidents of forced sex with the partner;
- prior threats to kill, especially those involving the brandishing of a gun or other weapon;
- history of alcohol or drug abuse, or a major mental illness such as schizophrenia, manic depression, or personality disorder;
- obsessive jealousy or possessiveness, or stalking behaviors like spying on the victim; and
- suicide threats, especially if the batterer has attempted suicide in the past.

In addition to considering indicators based on past history, practitioners also conduct ongoing risk assessments during the intervention, looking, for example, for any recent escalation of violence or victim expressions of fear for her life. If, during the course of treatment, the batterer reveals he has or is developing a plan (as opposed to a fantasy) to harm his partner, the practitioner has an ethical and legal duty to warn—and even take steps to protect—the potential victim.[7] The batterer can be said to have a plan, as distinguished from a fantasy, if he has expressed an intention to take concrete steps to carry out violence (e.g., purchase a weapon, save money toward the objective) or has actually carried out one or more steps. Counselors' legal duty to protect potential victims varies by State law and, in some cases, by State batterer intervention standards or protocols.

In Tarasoff v. The Regents of the University of California,[8] the U.S. Supreme Court ruled that therapists who have determined—or should have determined—that a client is a threat have a duty to use reasonable care to protect an intended victim by, for example, warning the victim, hospitalizing the client, and warning police. In the case of batterer program staff, duty to warn may include the victim, her victim advocate, the batterer's probation officer, the courts, or police.

Subsequent Federal cases have set even stricter standards.[9] Identifying a potential threat to the victim allows law enforcement authorities to conduct a risk assessment, evaluate the situation, and develop a case management plan to preempt the threat by vigorous prosecution of existing offenses or engaging the assistance of other mental health or social services staff.[10]

In addition to indoctrinating new members about program rules, orientation sessions are used to teach batterers the underlying assumptions of the program.

- Counselors establish a broad definition of abuse that includes psychological and sexual abuse.
- To motivate batterers to change, counselors highlight the consequences of the batterer' s abusive behavior for his children—often the best motivation to change.
- Counselors also begin to build empathy for their partners among batterers by discussing the consequences of abuse for the victim.
- Depending on the treatment approach, these sessions may also cover societal beliefs and norms that support violence, place physical abuse along a continuum of other controlling behaviors, or focus on the batterer' s typical thought patterns preceding an abusive incident.

Two of the eight beginner classes, as they are called, of EMERGE are devoted to demonstrating that there is no "quick fix" to domestic violence. Batterers learn to acknowledge the long-term effects of their abuse on their partners and the strategies they have used to keep her in the relationship. The codirector of EMERGE notes that group members can readily list such quick-fix strategies as apologizing, buying her gifts, and even enrolling in a treatment program, but they are less able to offer longer-term solutions that require them to take responsibility for their own violence and respect their partner's wishes.[11]

Orientation sessions tend to be more like didactic classes than later sessions, which may take on a more therapeutic tone. One reason for the lecture-type format is to maintain order among new members who would sidetrack group discussions by turning attention away from their own behavior with complaints about their partner or the criminal justice system. Another, more subtle, reason for the structured format is to firmly establish norms for how to participate in group discussions before members graduate to more informal groups. The sessions also set a tone of active participation, making clear that clients will not be allowed to attend class without really participating in group discussions.

Finally, the orientation phase—especially if it is extended over a number of weeks—can also serve as a screening device for the more therapeutic ongoing groups. By requiring attendance at six to eight intake group sessions as a prerequisite for continued participation, programs like Family Services of Seattle and EMERGE of Quincy weed out more disruptive clients, who would eventually drop out regardless of the intervention. Remaining in the orientation sessions demonstrates a commitment to a long-term solution to their pattern of abuse.

Most of the programs visited require that each batterer admit to his violence by describing to the group the abusive incident that led to his enrollment. As one program director explains, "If a man insists that he has been falsely charged, I will send him away saying, 'If you haven't done anything wrong, you need a lawyer, not a batterers program. This program is for men who have a violence problem, not a legal problem.' "

> "If a man insists that he has been falsely charged, I will send him away saying, 'If you haven't done anything wrong, youneeda lawyer, notabatterers program. This program is for men who have a violence problem, not a legal problem.' "
>
> —Antonio Ramirez, ManAlive, San Francisco

If the batterer refuses to admit wrongdoing, or shows patterns of disruptive or resistant behavior during class, he is usually dropped from the program at that point. The requirement that he admit to his violence, combined with mandatory attendance at multiple orientation sessions, sets a minimum standard that all participants must meet in order to continue in the program as a member of an ongoing group.

Leaving the Program

Batterers may leave programs because they are requested to terminate program attendance due to noncooperation, violence, nonpayment of program fees, or other failure to follow program rules; because their probation has been revoked; or because they have met the program's completion criteria. Some programs offer aftercare for program graduates.

Penalties for Noncompliance

Clients can fail a program in a number of ways. The most common is a failure to attend group regularly. Another is by violating crucial program rules—like being disruptive or aggressive in group or coming to group under the influence of alcohol. If the client was identified in the assessment as having a substance abuse problem, failure to follow through on a referral for alcohol or other drug treatment (or continued use of substances) would be another serious infraction. Of course, violating a restraining order or repeating any form of violence could also be grounds for termination. (For a full discussion of program communication with probation officers and the courts, see chapter 4, "Current Trends in Batterer Intervention.")

Programs may take a range of actions against a client who has failed. Before resorting to terminating the client, the program may issue a warning or require the batterer to begin the program again. For the majority of clients whose treatment is court-ordered, the program reports failure to attend or a resumption of violence to their probation officer. For batterers with a substance abuse problem, another reportable violation condition may be failure to maintain sobriety. For these clients, AMEND staff report directly to the probation officer any indications of any use, whether from random urine testing or the client's or victim's reports. With the cooperation of probation and the courts, the client's time in treatment may be extended.

A victim advocate from AMEND emphasized the importance of support from the probation officer in court-mandated cases: "When we want to restart them, sometimes [probation officers] aren't real supportive of that, and that really hampers our decision-making process a lot. Or, I know that this probation officer may not be able to extend treatment because the judge isn't going to back up the probation officer, so we have to terminate the batterer." By contrast, when batterers reoffend in Massachusetts, State standards require a six-month extension of treatment. Even if the infraction is less serious than repeated abuse, the violation can be used to restart the treatment clock. A court- ordered client of the Des Moines DAIS program who has too many absences (missing 4 sessions in a 12-week period) is required to start the program over again.

> "When we want to restart them, sometimes [probation officers] aren't real supportive of that, and that really hampers our decision-making process a lot. Or, I know that this probation officer may not be able to extend treatment because the judge isn't going to back up the probation officer, so we have to terminate the batterer."
>
> —Victim Advocate, AMEND

Programs are cautious about terminating a batterer because of the danger it may pose to the victim. However, they must send a clear message that clients are required to make constructive use of treatment in order to remain.[12] Program staff are also concerned that the victim not be lulled into a false sense of security if the batterer attends groups but does not try to change. Nonetheless, programs ideally consult with the victim before terminating a client. Programs may also need to terminate a batterer who poses a threat to staff.

At AMEND, one batterer (who had been arrested for holding his wife hostage and attempted murder) turned his threats and anger on program staff and the victim liaison when his wife informed him that she had reported continued physical and sexual abuse to an AMEND victim advocate. The batterer was terminated, and program staff helped the victim to move out-of-state.

Completion

While some programs use attendance as the sole criterion for successful completion, Washington State requires that each program have specific exit criteria. Family Services' exit criteria require the batterer to write a "responsibility letter" and an "empathy letter."

- The batterer pretends he is writing the responsibility letter to his partner and children (if any), accepting full responsibility for his abusive behavior and identifying and acknowledging the painful consequences to them.
- In the empathy letter, the batterer writes as though he were the victim, describing his feelings (as the victim) about the abuse.
- The batterer then reads the letters aloud to the group, although he decides whether to share them with his family.

AMEND also makes a distinction between having completed treatment by attendance only and a more successful discharge. If a batterer has attended a minimum of 36 weekly sessions, he has fulfilled his sentence and is dismissed with an "administrative" discharge. If, however, he has accomplished his treatment goals, remained sober, and respected his partner's wishes for no contact, if applicable, the client receives a successful or "clinical" discharge. While either way the court-mandated client is no longer required to attend further treatment, the program's final report to probation will indicate whether or not the therapist believes the client has worked successfully with the program. If the client receives only an administrative discharge and later reoffends, the court may sentence him to jail rather than allow him to enter treatment again.

Follow-up

Some programs offer follow-up or aftercare in the form of ongoing support groups for clients who complete the program successfully. Washington State standards require a full year of contact with the program, but only 26 weekly sessions, so that programs offer monthly meetings as a separate follow-up phase to the standard treatment. Although not required to by State standards, the Des Moines DAIS program offers a weekly support group for men who have successfully completed its 16- or 24-week program. The program director is committed to providing aftercare so that batterers who have completed the program have the opportunity to meet with other men who are recovering from violence, to get support for maintaining a nonviolent lifestyle, and to continue to practice the conflict resolution and anger management skills the program taught them. One program director voiced concern, however, that most men are not being trained to deal with the hypothetical "ultimate situation" that could trigger relapse for them: "Batterers need to be prepared, to know 'What would you do? Who would you call for help?' " Relapse prevention and support for former batterers is important, according to AMEND director Rob Gallup, because "often the perpetrator is as isolated as his partner."

Program Content: Established Interventions Using Weekly Groups

The group modality is the intervention of choice in dealing with batterers for several reasons.[13]

- The group combats the implicit social approval of abusive behavior that many batterers perceive from family and friends. By sending consistent messages that do not condone any form of abuse and encourage nonviolent alternatives, the group serves as a healthy support system for batterers who wish to change.
- Successful group members can serve as role models to batterers who are just beginning to confront their own violent behavior, helping to break through a new member's minimization of his abuse.
- By providing a new source of support, the group reduces the batterer's excessive dependence on his partner to meet all his emotional needs.

However, group leaders must be alert and ready to intervene when batterers try to commiserate with one another, forming unhealthy bonds that excuse abusive behavior. As one set of group leaders advised, "Be vigilant about male bonding— batterers love to stick up for each other against their partners."

> "Be vigilant about male bonding—batterers love to stick up for each other against their partners."
>
> —Group Leader, DAIS, Des Moines

Some programs are strictly structured, such as those using the Duluth curriculum (described below), prescribing the order in which topics are to be addressed. Other programs give discretion to group leaders to choose from a range of program content, while confronting batterers' behavior more directly. Program directors warned that some leaders may resort to a more flexible approach because they lack the skill to keep group discussions focused on the planned curriculum. It is important, therefore, to distinguish between a flexible curriculum and uncontrolled digressions from the set discussion schedule.

Whatever the structure or treatment approach, each group session typically begins with a round-robin style check-in, followed by the selected topic or educational piece for the meeting, ending with goal setting and check-outs. Check- ins are a way to introduce new members to the group and reinforce the program's focus on the batterer' s behavior. They can be brief (each person states his name and one of the rules of the group) or more lengthy (each member describes his most recent or severe abusive behavior). In more therapeutically oriented programs, the check-ins can lead to discussions that take up the bulk of the session. For example, the group may discuss possible solutions to conflicts recounted by group members. For more educational programs, the check-ins are followed by a more structured presentation from the curriculum. Regardless of emphasis, at the end of the session programs typically assign homework that is designed to encourage each client to apply the session's topics directly to his life. Check-outs help participants summarize what they learned and clarify their behavioral goals for the coming week.

Advantages of Open-Ended Group Interventions

For practical reasons, group membership is typically open-ended, with new clients cycling in as other clients graduate. Program administrators argue that having a new member join ongoing groups offers distinct advantages because new members:

- benefit from joining a group that has already established norms for accountability;
- serve as reminders for those who have been attending group of the consequences of violence; and
- act as mirrors to other members of how much progress they have made since they entered the program.[14]

Accountability as the Foremost Goal

Most batterers deny or avoid accepting responsibility for their actions—that is, they refuse to view battering as a choice. As a result, one of the main goals of all reputable batterer intervention programs is to get the batterer to become accountable for his abusive behavior.[15] The challenge of the intervention is to force the batterer to acknowledge his violence in terms of the full range of abusive acts he has committed, thereby broadening his understanding of what constitutes unacceptable behavior.

Program staff have divided the most common tactics batterers use to avoid accountability into three categories:

- denying the abuse ever happened ("I didn't lay a hand on her; she made the whole thing up");
- minimizing the abuse, either by downplaying the violent acts ("It was just a slap") or underestimating its effects ("She bruises easily"); and
- blaming the abuse on the victim ("She drove me crazy"), drugs or alcohol ("I was drunk, I don't remember anything"), or other life circumstances ("I was at the end of my rope 'cause I was working 16 hours a day").

Because these tactics are so common, group leaders in nearly all programs watch for them and confront batterers whenever they try to use them. For example, some facilitators will use the police report of the attack to bring the severity of the batterer' s actions into perspective. Group leaders also guard against what they call "sidetracking," referring to batterers' attempts to turn the discussion away from their behavior by complaining about their partner, the criminal justice system, or racial or social injustice (see chapter 4, "Current Trends in Batterer Intervention"). As one group leader suggested, "Don't get sucked into their stories; only give them attention when they talk about their behavior." Whatever the treatment approach, batterer interventions keep the focus on the batterer's behavior and its consequences.

> "I'd advise new group leaders: 'Don't get sucked into their stories; only give them attention when they talk about their behavior.' "
>
> —Group Leader, DAIS, Des Moines

Cognitive-Behavioral Techniques

The majority of programs visited for this book incorporated cognitive-behavioral techniques into their group interventions. As discussed in chapter 2, "The Causes of Domestic Violence," a common intervention is to offer the batterer specific tools that help him see that his acts of violence are not uncontrollable outbursts but rather foreseeable behavior patterns he can learn to interrupt. Cognitive-behavioral techniques help the batterer recognize how he stokes his own rage through irrational "self-talk," the internal dialogue that the batterer uses to build himself up to an abusive incident. [16] Examining the thoughts and feelings that precede the abuse helps the batterer to realize that he did not just "lose his temper." Rather, he felt that his partner had disappointed him in some way, began telling himself negative things about her, and then used that negativity to justify his violence. If she is ten minutes late coming home from work, for example, he may tell himself, "She is seeing another man, she is a slut, she's made a fool out of me." He may have negative thoughts about what his partner is saying or doing ("She's like a broken record") or think of ways to blame her for his violence ("She's really asking for it now"). The batterer repeats these negative thoughts to himself until he no longer thinks of her as his wife or girlfriend; she becomes an object that failed to perform as expected, and so violence becomes justified in his own mind.[17]

In brief, cognitive-behavioral techniques target three elements:

- what the batterer thinks about prior to an abusive incident;
- how the batterer feels, physically and emotionally, as a result of these thoughts;
- what the batterer does, such as yelling and throwing things, that builds up to acts of violence.[18]

The group helps members to recognize and interrupt these thought patterns and the anger associated with them. The batterer learns to use his negative thoughts and feelings as cues to prevent future violent episodes. When he notices himself beginning the pattern—thinking negatively about his partner and starting to feel angry—some programs teach him to take a "time-out." This gives him a chance to interrupt the internal dialogues and substitute reality checks and positive coping statements. At the same time, he is taught to reduce his state of physiological arousal through relaxation techniques (e.g., deep breathing exercises, biofeedback) or noncompetitive forms of physical exercise such as walking or bicycling. However, rather than use time-outs to reflect on their self-talk and reduce their anger, some batterers misuse them as an excuse to interrupt an argument. Victims advocates point out that this is a good reason to have ongoing contact with victims, to learn about and confront such distortions illustrated by a batterer who himself reported, "We have time-outs. They're going great. She sits on the couch when I tell her to." Several programs have developed rules that are also explained to the partner to make sure the batterer uses standard time-outs constructively.[19] Rules include limits on the length of the standard time-out, revisiting the issue at stake at a mutually agreeable time later, and not watching television or using alcohol or other drugs while taking a time-out.[20] At EMERGE, time-outs are not taught because, according to co-director Susan Cayouette, "Time-outs are still abusive to women— they tell her, 'If I stay with you, I will be abusive.' "

> "One batterer said, 'We have time-outs. They're going great. She sits on the couch when I tell her to.'"
>
> —Victim Advocate, AMEND

The Duluth Curriculum: Issues of Power and Control as Primary Targets

Many batterer intervention programs adhere to, or borrow from, a psychoeducational and skills-building curriculum that is a component of the Duluth model. Developed in the early 1980's by the Domestic Abuse Intervention Project (DAIP) of Duluth, Minnesota, the model emphasizes the importance of a coordinated community response to battering and places battering within a broader context of the range of controlling behaviors illustrated in the "The Power and Control Wheel" (see exhibit 1-1).[21] The wheel depicts how physical violence is connected to male power and control through a number of "spokes" or control tactics: minimizing, denying, blaming; using intimidation, emotional abuse, isolation, children, male privilege, economic abuse, and threats. According to the Duluth model, the batterer maintains control over his partner through constant acts of coercion, intimidation, and isolation punctuated by periodic acts of violence.

The curriculum is taught in classes that emphasize the development of critical thinking skills around eight themes: 1) nonviolence, 2) nonthreatening behavior, 3) respect, 4) support and trust, 5) honesty and accountability, 6) sexual respect, 7) partnership, and 8) negotiation and fairness. Depending on the total length of the program, two or three sessions are devoted to each theme. The first session of each theme begins with a video vignette that demonstrates the controlling behavior from that portion of the wheel. Discussion revolves around the actions that the batterer in the story used to control his partner; the advantages he was trying to get out of the situation; the beliefs he expressed that supported his position; the feelings he was hiding through his behavior; and the means he used to minimize, deny, or blame the victim for his actions. At the close of each session, the men are given homework: to identify these same elements in an incident when they exhibited similar controlling behaviors. During subsequent sessions devoted to the theme, each group member describes his own use of the controlling behavior, why he used it, and what its effects were. Alternative behaviors that can build a healthier, egalitarian relationship are then explored.

Putting the Duluth curriculum into practice requires considerable skill on the part of group leaders. One group observed for this book strayed dramatically from the evening's agenda, as members succeeded in sidetracking the discussion away from their behavior onto complaints about the curriculum and about their partners. Even when the agenda is adhered to, the classroom-style format can allow some members to sit back and not participate in discussions or even reflect on their behavior. Group leaders have to be vigilant against both the active and passive ways batterers avoid taking responsibility for their abuse, both inside and outside of group. Furthermore, directors of several programs noted that the tenor of the group intervention varies substantially depending on the style of the group leaders and how they view their role (e.g., as educators who teach new skills or as therapists who confront the men's inappropriate behavior).

EMERGE and AMEND: More in-Depth Group Counseling

Two other programs stand out for their longevity and model reputations, EMERGE of Quincy, Massachusetts, and AMEND of Denver, Colorado. However, unlike the Duluth model, both programs include more in-depth counseling in addition to reeducation and skills building. Similarly, the director of the DAIS program in Des Moines expresses particular concern that its Duluth-style program may not be enough to reform or deter more high-risk or chronic offenders. In fact, the Des Moines DAIS worked with the local domestic violence coalition to secure a special waiver from the State standards so that it could pilot test a more therapeutic model with high-risk offenders.[22]

The director of EMERGE argues that any treatment that fails to span at least 4 to 6 months runs the risk of never breaking through the batterer's facade of compliance.[23] Many batterers, often known for being manipulative and intelligent, can readily adapt to a short-term intervention, quickly learning to "talk the talk." If the intervention is too short, it may end during this "honeymoon" phase, leaving the provider satisfied with a job seemingly well done but with the abusive behavior fundamentally unchallenged and unchanged. As a result, the EMERGE program lasts a minimum of 48 weeks (including orientation). The founders of AMEND believe chronic offenders may require from one to five years of treatment to genuinely change the abusive behavior,[24] with their 36-week program constituting the minimum period of time necessary. However, preliminary findings from a multisite evaluation currently under way for the Centers for Disease Control (CDC) do not support the notion that longer is better: graduates from a 3-month intensive program fared as well as those who completed 9 months of treatment in terms of reoffenses at a 12-month follow-up.[25]

Program Summaries for Three Mainstream Batterer Intervention Models

Program models for the three major program approaches discussed in this chapter share many similarities, but they also have a few significant differences.

The Duluth Curriculum

Program Structure — Program length varies by local standards but generally involves 2 or 3 sessions on each of eight themes:

- nonviolence;
- nonthreatening behavior;
- respect;
- support and trust;
- honesty and accountability;
- sexual respect;
- partnership; and
- negotiation and fairness.

Approach: Each unit begins with a video illustrating the abusive behavior targeted for change. Discussion is didactic and confrontational. The Duluth model (which incorporates the curriculum) emphasizes that batterer intervention must take place in the context of a coordinated community response to domestic violence.

The EMERGE Model

Program Structure — 48-week program divided into two stages: 8 weeks of orientation, and 40 weeks of group work. EMERGE recommends additional time in the program for approximately one-third of the batterers. Orientation topics include:

- defining domestic violence;
- negative versus positive "self-talk";
- effects of violence on women—"quick fixes" (e.g., apologies, promises) versus long-term solutions (e.g., taking responsibility for their abuse, developing respect, genuine changes);
- psychological, sexual, and economic abuse;
- abusive versus respectful communication; and
- effects of partner abuse on children.

Second stage groups meet weekly for two hours. Group sessions typically include:

- a short "check-in" for old group members and a long "check-in" for any new group members. Short check-ins recount any conflicts during the week; long check-ins detail the last abusive episode and focus on batterer responsibility;
- longer discussions concerning issues raised during check-in that focus on alternatives to violence; and
- development of individualized goals based on current and past abuse.

Approach: EMERGE emphasizes the broader relationship between batterer and victim: it targets not only physical but also emotional and psychological abuse for reform. Exercises to develop respect and empathy for the victim are used. Group leaders use confrontation.

The AMEND Model

Program Structure — Period of intervention is variable, from 36 weeks (the standard period for batterers mandated to treatment) to five years for the most difficult cases. AMEND prefers a long treatment period. AMEND takes a "multimodal" approach to batterer intervention centered on group therapy, but it may also include some individual counseling or couples work.

Approach: AMEND's philosophy has seven tenets:

- belief in the feminist "power and control" theory of battering is central;
- intervention with batterers cannot be value-neutral—violence is a crime;
- violence and abuse are choices, and the victim is not responsible for the violence;
- counseling has two aims: 1) teaching behavior change to stop violence and abuse, and 2) addressing the psychological features of the batterer's problem;
- ending violence is a long-term process, from one to five years;
- ending violence is complex and requires "multimodal intervention"; and
- the treatment of batterers requires special skills and training.

The founders of both EMERGE and AMEND also argue that psychoeducational approaches alone do not address the true nature of the problem. If the batterer' s problem were simply a deficit in skills, he would be far less functional in the broader world outside the family. The director of EMERGE argues, "Batterers know how to get along with their bosses, for instance; they just don't use these same social skills in their intimate relationships."[26] Focusing solely on the batterer's thoughts, feelings, and reactions—by teaching anger management techniques, for example—can inadvertently reinforce the batterer' s egocentric view of the world. As a result, EMERGE and AMEND strive to balance cognitive-behavioral techniques with confrontational group process to force the batterer to accept responsibility for his abusive behavior and its consequences.

While it is important to give batterers specific tools to interrupt their abusive behavior patterns, they need more than new skills. Like the Duluth model, EMERGE and AMEND believe that batterers need resocialization that convinces them they do not have the right to abuse their partner, a process AMEND refers to as "habilitating" the batterer.[27] For AMEND, this means redressing batterers' maladaptive moral development. For EMERGE, as explained below, the focus is more on the abusive relationship and the emotional consequences of the abuse for the victim.

The EMERGE Approach

Batterers who successfully complete the program's orientation phase of eight didactic and skills-based sessions, and admit to at least some form of domestic violence, graduate to an ongoing group (see exhibit 3-1, "The EMERGE Model"). The groups blend cognitive-behavioral techniques with "accountability-focused group therapy," which is more flexible and interactive than programs that adhere strictly to a preset curriculum, such as the Duluth model. The ongoing groups use confrontation and feedback.

New members introduce themselves to the ongoing group through a so-called "long check-in." First, the new member describes the incident that brought him to the program, typically the most recent abuse. The batterer has to focus on his own behavior, without talking about what his partner did to supposedly provoke the abuse. One group facilitator interrupts batterers' attempts to sidetrack the issue with phrases like, "Right now, I just want to know what *you* did. . . . I'm not interested in what you think she did wrong before you hit her. . . . *Your* behavior is the reason you're here."

"Right now, I just want to know what you did. . . I'm not interested in what you think she did wrong before you hit her. . . . Your behavior is the reason you're here."
—Group Facilitator, EMERGE

Through the long check-in, which may last ten to twenty minutes, the new member has to admit to his violence in front of the group. The group facilitator asks close-ended questions to elicit details about which specific acts of violence were committed, such as:

- Did you punch her with your fist?
- Did you knock her down?
- Did you have anything in your hand when you hit her? Any kind of weapon?

Long check-ins are repeated with any member the therapist suspects of using violence again based on something the batterer has said in group or the partner has reported to the advocate. After the check-ins from new members, each ongoing group follows with short check-ins for regular members centering on their interactions during the past week, particularly situations involving conflict or tension with their past or current partners. Group therapists may probe for information regarding other controlling behaviors, verbal abuse, or alcohol and drug use, as well as any positive principles the client may have practiced. Members are reminded to concentrate on their own behavior rather than their partners'.

After check-ins are completed, a member may ask for a turn, or the group facilitator may call on a member, to follow up on something he disclosed during check-in. Typically, the person taking the turn describes the recent conflict or incident in detail, focusing on his thoughts, feelings, and actions. Other group members are taught to give appropriate feedback that avoids "quick-fix" advice. Appropriate feedback includes listening attentively, asking questions that determine the sequence of events, and confronting the person when he tries to avoid accepting responsibility for his behavior. Once the facts of the event are clear, the group turns to brainstorming alternatives to how the person behaved with his partner, and he then evaluates the usefulness of the options proposed. The turn concludes when the person practices the alternative he thinks will work best, sometimes in role-play with another group member. Each session concludes with goal setting for the coming week and check-outs.

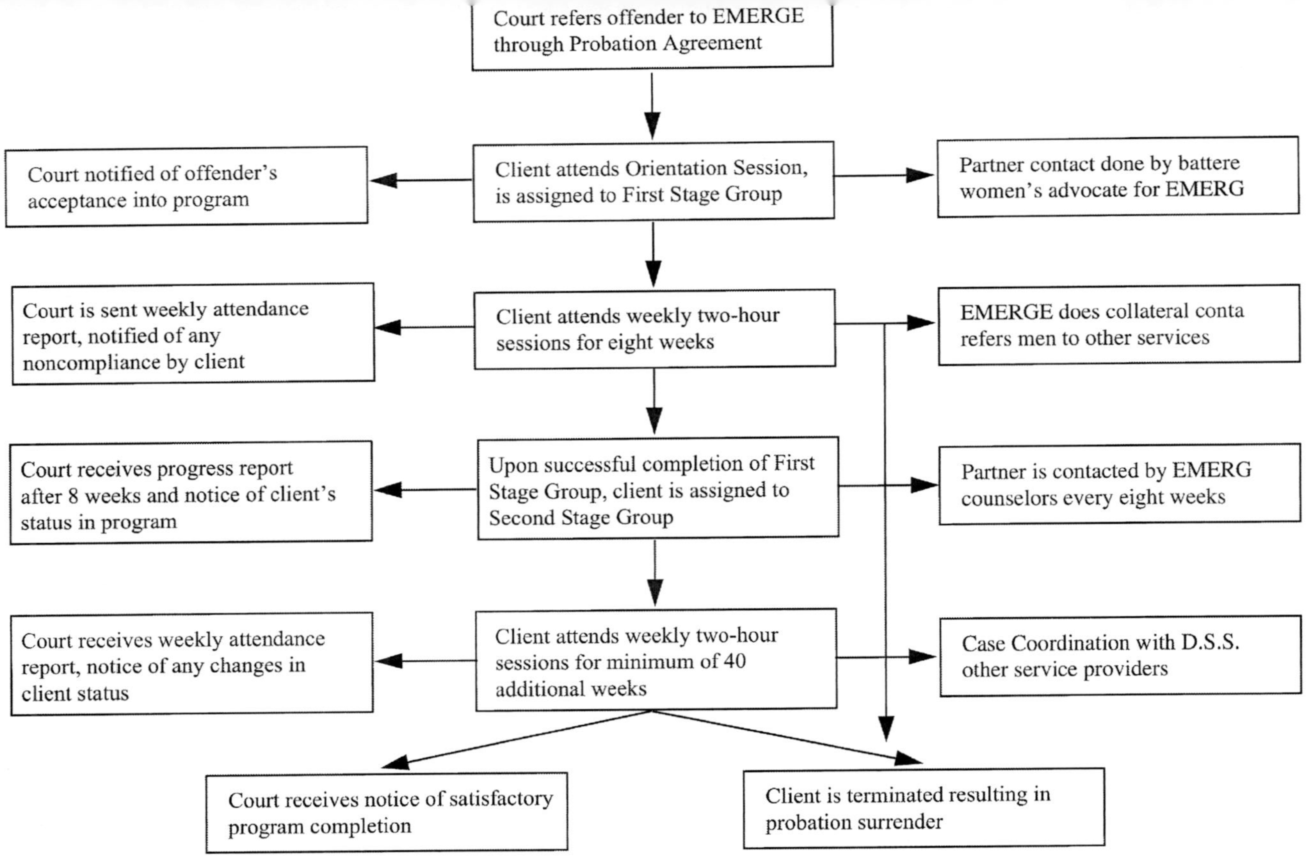

Source: EMERGE, Program Manual, First Stage Groups for Men Who Batter, Cambridge, MA, 1992.

Exhibit 3-1. The EMERGE Model.

The EMERGE approach focuses on the broader relationship between the batterer and the victim, addressing other concerns of the partner in addition to stopping the physical violence. To build empathy, the therapist may instruct the client to do a special check-in involving the narrating of an abusive incident as though he were his partner. Clients are instructed always to refer to their partner by her first name (rather than as "my wife" or "my girlfriend" or "the wife") as a reminder not to think of the women as possessions or objects. To address broader concerns in the relationship, follow-up questions in a client's turn may center on the partner's thoughts and feelings during the conflict, with the group leader balancing learning about the broader context of the conflict against being sidetracked by complaints about her behavior. To maintain this balance, the therapist asks questions about the batterer' s responsibility for his behavior and the feelings the victim has expressed about his actions.

Group therapists also incorporate the partner's concerns, as expressed to them or the victim liaison, in establishing the client's individual treatment goals. In addition to the standard goals of no physical or sexual abuse toward the victim or the children, each client develops behavioral goals that address his favorite control tactics. For instance, the partner may have expressed concerns about a client's extreme jealousy. The group would then help the client develop specific behavioral goals, such as: "I will not ask jealous questions of my partner when she gets home late," or "I will not call to check up on my partner while she is at work." The goals would also incorporate positive alternatives, such as: "The next time I catch myself thinking jealous thoughts, I will use positive self-talk," or "Instead of checking up on my partner, next time I'll take a walk." The main features of the goals are that they continue to direct attention to the client's behavior and that the partner is in agreement with them.

The AMEND Approach

The designers of AMEND share the commitment to longer- term treatment with the founders of EMERGE. AMEND also aims to establish accountability, increase awareness of the social context of battering, and build skills. Group therapists at AMEND use the Duluth "Power and Control Wheel," cognitive-behavioral techniques, and other anger management tools. However, the AMEND model uses therapeutic group process to address psychological factors. But, whereas an ordinary therapy group might try to support the client and help him express his feelings, AMEND group leaders are "moral guides" who assume more directive, value-laden positions—in particular, taking a firm stand against violence and confronting the client's behavior as unacceptable and illegal.

AMEND identifies four stages in the long-term therapeutic process of recovery from violence: crisis group, advanced group, self-help/support group, and political action group. Most men do not continue past the first two therapeutic stages.

- *Stage I (Crisis Group)*. The first 12 to 18 weeks of group therapy are devoted to breaking through the batterer' s denial. Through education and confrontation, the batterer begins to accept some responsibility for his violence.
- *Stage II (Advanced Group)*. After four or five months of group therapy, assuming the client has been actively engaged in reflecting on his patterns of abuse and in practicing anger management techniques, his cognitive distortions begin to decline and his denial breaks down. The batterer begins to recognize his own rationalizations. He will still try to minimize and deny his violence (or blame his partner for it), but when confronted in group, he will begin to admit the truth—that he chose to be violent to get what he wanted from his partner. The director of AMEND noted how often batterers might admit during this stage, "The funny thing is, I wasn't even that mad. I just wanted to show her who's boss." These periodic breakthroughs define the second stage of recovery.

> The director of AMEND noted how often batterers admit, "The funny thing is, I wasn't even that mad. I just wanted to show her who's boss."
>
> —Robert Gallup, Executive Director, AMEND

However, the work of the group does not stop there; batterers continue to vacillate between accepting and avoiding responsibility for their behavior. They may have learned to "talk the talk," but they may also continue to be manipulative or verbally abusive to their partners. They may also present a good face to the group, reporting only what went right during the week. Unless the therapist can totally break through the batterer's facade, the risk of relapse remains. This is one of the reasons ongoing partner contacts are important to the AMEND intervention. Through victim advocates, therapists can learn about verbal abuse or other intimidating or threatening behavior and then confront the batterer about these more subtle forms of abuse.

The final phase of recovery for those in the advanced group is the beginning of genuine, profound personal change. The batterer in this phase has reformed outwardly; he no longer tries to control his partner through violence or intimidation. This is a painful and frightening time for clients because they begin to feel long-suppressed emotions, such as those from childhood traumas. Group therapists at AMEND call this time "the tunnel" because clients are midway through the change process: they do not know whom they are changing into, but they do not want to return to the person they used to be. The group process shifts to a warmer and more supportive tone at this stage, more akin to conventional insight or client-centered therapy. In addition, the therapist continues to teach more sophisticated skills like relaxation techniques and ways to manage conflict.

Those who choose to continue in therapy may become overly attached to the therapist, so that setting and maintaining boundaries become especially important. (For example, one group leader mentioned that clients might want to continue the discussion after group or feel that it was appropriate to follow a facilitator home to talk further.)

As the client prepares to end therapy, he is encouraged to develop a responsibility plan that includes a support network that will help him continue to practice healthy communication skills and avoid future violence (Stage III, Self-Help/Support Group). A few men will go beyond self-help groups to become more involved in community service and political action aimed at ending domestic violence (Stage IV, Political Action Group).

Implementation Issues

The more in-depth approaches of EMERGE and AMEND require more sophisticated group therapy skills than, say, psychoeducational programs that adhere strictly to the Duluth curriculum. The designers of the EMERGE approach recommend that groups be led by a male-female team to model nonabusive interactions between the sexes and to guard against more subtle male bonding or victim blaming, which a male group leader alone might inadvertently encourage. Because batterers can be such difficult clients, the codirector of AMEND also recommends close clinical supervision of all group leaders. For example, the Arapahoe County, Colorado, chapter of AMEND devotes a two-hour staff meeting once a week to case reviews with therapists and victim advocates to ensure the quality of the intervention.

Conclusion

The programs discussed in this chapter represent mainstream approaches to batterer intervention. All the programs share a common interest in assuring the safety of the victim and stopping violent behaviors by the batterer. The question of how best to achieve nonviolence is critical from a criminal justice standpoint. While confrontational approaches are appropriate as a reminder to batterers that violent behavior is illegal and socially unacceptable, less punitive approaches, such as those advocated by psychologists, may produce greater retention in treatment and lower rates of recidivism. Until more evaluations are available, however, all batterer interventions can promote criminal justice goals by intensively monitoring the behavior of mandated batterers and reporting violations of probation conditions or any imminent threat to the victim to the proper criminal justice authorities.

REFERENCES

[1] See Browne, K., D.G. Saunders, and K.M. Staecker, "Process-Psychodynamic Groups for Men Who Batter: Description of a Brief Treatment Model," University of Michigan, January 26, 1996; and Gondolf, E., "Multi- Site Evaluation of Batterer Intervention Systems: A Summary of Preliminary Findings," Working Paper, Mid-Atlantic Addiction Training Institute, October 24, 1996.

[2] Lindsey, M., R. W. McBride, and C. Platt, *AMEND Philosophy and Curriculum for Treating Batterers*, Littleton, CO: Gylantic, 1993.

[3] Edelson, J. and R. M. Tolman, *Intervention for Men Who Batter: An Ecological Approach*, Newbury Park, CA: Sage Publications, 1992.

[4] AMEND has five sites, each with its own director.

[5] An intensive group orientation that supplements individual intake sessions has also been found to bolster program retention. Tolman, R.M. and L.W. Bennet, "A Review of Research on Men Who Batter," *Journal of Interpersonal Violence*, 5 (1990): 102.

[6] Campbell, J. C., "Prediction of Homicide of and by Battered Women," in *Assessing Dangerousness: Violence by Sexual Offenders, Batterers, and Child Abusers*, ed. J. C. Campbell, Thousand Oaks, CA: Sage Publications, 1995: 96–113; Hoffnung, P.S., "General High Risk Factors: Likelihood of Serious Harm," Quincy, MA: EMERGE, n.d.

[7] Saunders, D. G., "Woman Battering," in *Assessment of Family Violence: A Clinical and Legal Sourcebook*, ed. R.T. Ammerman and M. Hersen, New York: John Wiley & Sons, 1992: 208–235.

[8] *Tarasoff* v. *The Regents of the University of California*, 529 P2d 553 (Cal. 1974) (Tarasoff I); reargued 551 P2d 334 (Cal. 1976) (Tarasoff II).

[9] See Lipari v. Sears, Roebuck and Co., 497 F.Supp. 185 (D. Neb. 1986) and *Jablonski* v. *United States*, 712 F2d 391 (Ninth Circuit, 1983), which held that therapists may be liable even when a specific victim is not identified.

[10] See Fein, R.A., B. Vossekuil, and G.A. Holden, "Threat Assessment: An Approach to Prevent Targeted Violence," *Research in Action Series*, Washington, DC: National Institute of Justice, September 1995.

[11] Adams, D., L. Bancroft, T. German, and C. Sousa, "Program Manual: First Stage Groups for Men Who Batter," Quincy, MA: EMERGE, 1992.

[12] Adams et al., "Program Manual: First Stage Groups for Men Who Batter."

[13] Gondolf, E.W., Men Who Batter: An Integrated Approach to Stopping Wife Abuse, Holmes Beach, FL: Learning Publications, 1985.

[14] Lindsey, McBride, and Platt, AMEND Philosophy and Curriculum for Treating Batterers.

[15] Adams, D., "Treatment Models for Men Who Batter: A Profeminist Analysis," in *Feminist Perspectives on Wife Abuse*, ed. K. Yllo and M. Bograd, Newbury Park, CA: Sage Publications, 1988: 176–199; Lindsey, McBride, and Platt, *AMEND Philosophy and Curriculum for Treating Batterers*; Paymar, M., *Violent No More: Helping Men End Domestic Abuse*, Alameda, CA: Hunter House, 1993.

[16] Adams et al., "Program Manual: First Stage Groups for Men Who Batter"; Edelson and Tolman, *Intervention for Men Who Batter.*

[17] Family Services Domestic Violence Treatment Program, "Men's Domestic Violence Workbook," Seattle, WA: Family Services Domestic Violence Treatment Program, 1996.

[18] Zegree, J., S. Ellner and D. Berrysmith, "Men's Group Manual," Seattle, WA: Zegree, Ellner and Berrysmith Domestic Violence Treatment Program, 1995.

[19] Ibid., A-11.

[20] Family Services, "Men's Domestic Violence Workbook"; Lindsey, McBride, and Platt, *AMEND Philosophy and Curriculum for Treating Batterers*; Zegree, Ellner and Berrysmith, "Men's Group Manual."

[21] Paymar, *Violent No More*; and Pence, E., "Batterers' Programs: Shifting from Community Collusion to Community Confrontation," Duluth, MN: Domestic Abuse Intervention Project, 1988.

[22] The pilot is being patterned after The Third Path in-depth counseling program.

[23] Adams, D., Course on "Counseling Men Who Batter," a staff training seminar that fulfills all the requirements for accrediting batterer group facilitators in Massachusetts.

[24] Lindsey, McBride, and Platt, AMEND Philosophy and Curriculum for Treating Batterers.

[25] Interview with Edward Gondolf, October 22, 1996.

[26] Adams, Course on "Counseling Men Who Batter."

[27] Lindsey, McBride, and Platt, AMEND Philosophy and Curriculum for Treating Batterers.

Chapter 4

CURRENT TRENDS IN BATTERER INTERVENTION: INNOVATIONS FROM THE FIELD AND THE RESEARCH COMMUNITY

KEY POINTS

- Many researchers and practitioners have concluded that a "one-size-fits-all" intervention cannot accommodate the diverse population of batterers entering the criminal justice system.
- The development of more specialized approaches to batterer intervention is not in conflictwith the trend toward the development of State standards or certification criteria for batterer interventions, so long as those standards allow for a diversity of responsible programming.
- Two new trends in batterer intervention reflect the perceived need for more specialized approaches:

— interventions tailored to specific types of batterers (batterer typology), such as high-risk offenders, those with psychological problems, or substance abusers; and

— interventions with curriculums or program policies intended to accommodate sociocultural differences in batterers, such as poverty, poor literacy, race, ethnicity, nationality, gender, and sexual orientation.

- By contrast, the originator of one new cognitive-behavioral intervention argues that the problems of diverse batterers can be addressed in a "one-size-fits-all" format that treats heterosexual male and female batterers, gay and lesbian batterers, victims, and child abusers with one didactic cognitive-behavioral curriculum.

Both practitioners and academics have long been concerned that a "one-size-fits-all" intervention approach is neither effective nor appropriate for the diverse population of batterers entering the criminal justice system. Program directors and probation officers interviewed for this book frequently observed that battering was not a "monolithic" or "unitary" phenomenon, as had been argued previously by some theorists and treatment professionals: they saw no *one* type of batterer and found no *one* intervention or treatment to be effective with all batterers. In response to this diversity, two categories of program refinements are emerging from practitioner innovations and cooperative field research among practitioners, criminal justice agencies, and academics:

- interventions that are tailored to specific types of batterers ("batterer typology") based on the batterer' s psychological profile, criminal history, substance abuse history, or assessment of lethality; and
- intervention models that tailor curriculums and program policies to accommodate batterers' sociocultural differences, such as poverty, poor literacy, race, ethnicity, nationality, gender, or sexual orientation.

In addition, a new theory of the origins of battering has been advanced, together with an unconventional treatment approach. The merit of many of the models and curriculums continues to be debated. However, the need for innovation is also increasingly recognized and accepted. Researchers interviewed for this book emphasized that the development of new or the refinement of older batterer intervention models need not conflict with the adoption of State standards or certification criteria for batterer interventions. Standards need only be flexible enough to permit responsible variation among programs and to provide guidelines for the safe development of new approaches.

INTERVENTIONS BASED ON BATTERER TYPOLOGIES

Evidence that individual factors play a role in battering is easily found. Not everyone who grows up witnessing domestic violence becomes a batterer, and not all batterers grew up witnessing domestic violence; most males exposed to a "culture of violence" and male dominance do not batter. The questions remain whether and, if so, *how* the individual attributes that contribute to violence should be treated and whether programs can diversify to meet the needs of every typology.

Mounting Evidence of the Need for Typologies

Arguments that intervention should be tailored to accommodate individual psychological characteristics are not new.[1] However, research findings pointing to the need for batterer typologies have generally failed to alter treatment programs, both because feminist-based programs view the focus on psychological attributes of batterers unfavorably and because researchers do not agree on what a typology of batterers might look like.

Psychological Typologies

Unfortunately, no consensus concerning psychological categories for batterers has emerged from the research community although several overlapping typologies have been proposed. For example, Gondolf's 1988 study using 525 battered women as informants yielded three types ofbatterers: sociopathic, antisocial, and typical.[2] However, as noted in chapter 1, Gondolf' s current research on batterers—which includes psychological assessments using the Millon Clinical Multiaxial Inventory-III (MCMI), a diagnostic tool used by a number of programs—has yielded an extremely varied picture of batterer psychology that does not fit neatly with earlier research: 25 percent showed evidence of a severe mental disorder; 25 percent showed narcissistic personality traits; 24 percent showed passive-aggressive traits; and 19 percent were clinically depressed. Over half the men appeared to have abused alcohol.[3] Other researchers have arrived at the following tripartite classification scheme for batterers:[4]

- *The "Family Only" Batterer* is characterized as rigid, perfectionist, and conforming, with limited social skills. The family-only batterer did not experience much physical abuse in childhood and is mildly to moderately violent toward his family.
- *The Dysphori c/Borderline Batterer* is very emotional, experienced parental rejection and fears abandonment, and is extremely abusive psychologically but not severely violent physically.
- *The "Generally Violent/Antisocial" Batterer* tends to abuse alcohol, lacks empathy, has rigid gender role attitudes, and is narcissistic—that is, expects special treatment and deference. He was physically abused in childhood and engages in other crimes, viewing violence as the appropriate method of solving problems.

Donald Dutton has recently proposed yet another tripartite scheme that is similar, but not identical, to the others.[5] Dutton classifies batterers as emotionally volatile, psychopathic, or overcontrolled/explosive.

The Third Path and AMEND use the MCMI to produce profiles of pathology that allow for the classification of batterers to aid treatment.[6] At The Third Path, psychological traits are addressed in group, and groups are structured so that a mixture of personality types is present.

While psychological typologies are interesting from a theoretical standpoint, they offer little assistance to the criminal justice system as yet because of the in-depth assessment needed to identify these characteristics and the paucity of typology-based interventions available in the field. The criminal justice-based typologies discussed below offer a more practical frontline approach to batterer triage; nonetheless, the more subtle distinctions made possible by psychological typologies may be of great use to jurisdictions and program providers that are willing to integrate group process intervention with the educational model used by most programs (see "Typology in Action: Colorado's 18th Judicial District," p. 61). For example, in Iowa, State officials have consulted with Michael Lindsey, founder of Colorado's AMEND and The Third Path, to explore options for using batterer typology to identify high-risk offenders for private counseling, or alcohol treatment, or extended interventions that would address psychological factors as well as provide education, although Iowa State Standards mandate the use of the Duluth curriculum.

Criminal Justice-Based Typologies

While courts, probation officers, prosecutors, and program screeners in all jurisdictions routinely make decisions concerning the dangerousness of offenders and the appropriateness of various interventions for individual batterers, few jurisdictions have systematic assessment tools based on an articulated theory of batterer typology. Typical of the majority of jurisdictions visited for this book was the Quincy, Massachusetts, Court Model Domestic Abuse Program, which provides probation officers with a manual containing specific guidelines to help them assess the dangerousness of offenders and a discussion of intervention issues but no standardized diagnostic form or referral protocols. Recent research by John Goldkamp may offer a practical, more standardized approach to offender classification. Using demographic information, criminal histories, and substance abuse data from his study of the Dade County Domestic Violence Court, Goldkamp proposes several classification strategies to assist in the disposition of batterers.[7] Goldkamp's typologies focus on predicting batterer retention in treatment and the likelihood of reoffending, both with the same victim and with other women (see exhibit 4-1, "Predictive Classification of Rearrest"). Goldkamp's approach is attractive from a criminal justice perspective because, as listed below, the information necessary to predict retention in treatment and recidivism should be already available to most prosecutors, probation officers, and judges in rap sheets and probation reports without having to do a special assessment of the offender. These provide:

- *basic demographic information* concerning the offender, such as race/ethnicity, age, relationship to the victim, and victim gender;
- *a detailed criminal history*, such as current offense, any prior civil court cases, convictions, and number and types of arrests—assault and battery arrests, same- victim arrests, and domestic-violence-related arrests; and
- information about drug and alcohol involvement, including types of drugs abused.

TYPOLOGIES FOCUSING ON RAGE

Roland Maiuro, of the Harborview Medical Center in Seattle, has argued for a clinical diagnosis of "intermittent explosive disorder" for some batterers. A small proportion of batterers explode with rage. Research points to some offenders who are either generally violent toward everyone or who episodically lack impulse control toward both intimate partners and other people.

However, as a practical matter, this type of batterer frequently is already receiving specialized treatment. A number of probation departments consider batterers with extensive histories of violent criminal behavior or domestic violence inappropriate for traditional batterer programs, recommending instead incarceration, intensive probation, or very long-term, intensive interventions that incorporate psychological evaluation and counseling. Similarly, many standard programs already integrate an "anger management" component, which uses readings and cognitive- behavioral exercises designed to help men recognize the physiological signs of anger and develop skills to reduce arousal and avoid violent behavior.

Maiuro suggests that this approach may be especially helpful with batterers who are diagnosed as having intermittent explosive disorder. However, programs need to make clear to batterers with this diagnosis that what may appear to be uncontrollable anger may in fact be controllable with cognitive-behavioral techniques, so that they do not use the diagnosis as an excuse for battering (see "Prohibited Methods/Theories" in appendix A.3, "State Standards Matrix").

Goldkamp's analysis found that "[t]he probability of rearrest was far greater for persons with any prior convictions, any prior assault and battery arrests, and indications of involvement with other drugs of abuse (not alcohol)."[8]

This analysis is consistent with Gondolf' s finding that monthly drunkenness triples an offender's likelihood of rearrest.[9]

Using a matrix that categorized defendants and probationers by dropout risk on one dimension and rearrest risk with the same victim on the other, Goldkamp was able to draw some potentially useful distinctions among offenders that go beyond assessing dangerousness: "[M]ore than one-third (37 percent) of the sample would fall into the lowest dropout risk and lowest same-victim rearrest categories. (In other words, they should be great treatment prospects and pose little risk to the victim.) But some defendants who pose little threat to the victim (low risk of rearrest) are not classified as likely to stay in treatment. About seven percent of all defendants/ probationers are in the high dropout risk category, even though they are in the lowest victim risk category."[10] This sort of analysis would be extremely helpful to probation officers, prosecutors, and judges in determining sentences and assigning batterers to specialized programs. After assignment to a specific program, the batterer could then be subject to additional intake assessment, including a psychological evaluation, if the program was geared to address psychological issues.

> "The probability of rearrest was far greater for persons with any prior convictions, any prior assault and battery arrests, and indications of involvement with other drugs of abuse (not alcohol)."
>
> - John Goldkamp, Professor of Criminal Justice, Temple University

The following discussion presents an approach to batterer classification that combines both psychological and criminal justice factors to create offender profiles as an aid to sentencing and supervision.

Typology in Action: Colorado's 18th Judicial District

The 18th Judicial District Probation Department in Colorado has implemented a unique batterer assessment and intervention assignmentprocess based on Michael Lindsay's research concerning batterer typology. Frank Robinson, consultant clinical social worker to the probation office, and Michael Lindsey have collaborated on an assessment tool, the Domestic Violence Behavioral Checklist, which catalogs the batterer' s history of intimate relationships, parenting, criminality, substance abuse, and social and psychological dysfunction to assign the batterer to one of three offender groups: low, medium, or high level of risk. The one-page assessment tool includes 38 questions and requires approximately 45 minutes to administer. Probation officers or volunteers can be easily trained to implement it.

Low-risk offenders must not have caused any physical injury and must not have committed any previous violent offenses against the victim. The offender's claim that this was the first episode of violence—not merely the first episode to be *reported*—needs to be corroborated by the victim. In addition, low-risk offenders must:

- have no history of verbal or psychological abuse (as reported by the victim);
- have no history of "chaotic or dysfunctional behavior";
- not have committed the offense during a period of separation;
- have no children involved in the dispute; and
- have no more than two—of a possible seven—low-risk criteria checked (see box, "The Domestic Violence Behavioral Checklist," p. 62).

This group of offenders is likely to be offered deferred prosecution wherein they are allowed to enter a guilty plea with the understanding that if they complete an accredited batterer program and do not reoffend for three years, the plea will be withdrawn and the charges dropped. The prospect of no criminal record is often a compelling motivation for first- time batterers who are professionals or middle-class *to complete a program.*

Medium-risk offenders are those with more than two low- risk factors, or one or more medium risk factors (see above). Probation recommends that medium-risk offenders be sentenced to probation with a condition of program completion and assigns them to a probation volunteer for close tracking (see chapter 4, "Current Trends in Batterer Intervention," for a discussion of the use of volunteers for probation supervision).

High-risk offenders include any batterer with even *one* high-risk indicator (see above). For the purposes of intervention, probation divides the high-risk group into two subgroups:

- batterers who are out of control despite consequences or interventions, and
- batterers whose lives are chaotic and dysfunctional and who are obsessed with their victim.

Those in the first group are not appropriate for participation in batterer programs; probation recommends that they be incarcerated. The second group, which is supervised by a specially assigned probation officer with a reduced caseload, is recommended for both long-term (more than 36 weeks) and intensive (more than one session per week) program interventions that are structured to address the challenge of high-risk offenders. Although the court uses several programs, many of the high-risk offenders are referred to The Third Path, where

Robert McBride, program director, conducts a detailed intake assessment that identifies offenders with personality disorders so that therapists can better understand and attempt to change their behaviors.

THE DOMESTIC VIOLENCE BEHAVIORAL CHECKLIST

The Domestic Violence Behavioral Checklist, a copyrighted assessment tool developed by Michael Lindsey, founder of AMEND and The Third Path, and Frank Robinson, a consultant clinical social worker to the Department of Probation in the 18th Judicial District outside of Denver, Colorado, is a compilation of weighted psychological and criminal justice risk indicators intended to classify the batterer for the purposes of assignment to specialized or mainstream interventions (see chapter 6, "Sources of Help and Information").

- *Low-riskfactors:* a child custody dispute; multiple relationships (cohabitations/ marriages);arrests for nondomestic violence disturbance; and dysfunction in school, work, finances, or other relationships (e.g., few friends).
- *Medium-risk factors:* having lost contact with one's children; restricted visitation with one's children; multiple separations; a partner who left hurriedly with no warning; a volatile relationship; aggressive victim-blaming; arrests with an underlying domestic - violence basis; a criminal history apart from domestic violence; violation of a restraining order; no friends or an alienated family; an admitted pattern of abusive behavior; multiple charges over a short period of time; a family history of mental illness, violence, substance abuse, child abuse, or multiple living arrangements; admission of guilt to a lesser charge than the crime; or suicidal thoughts.

High-risk factors: batterers who are looking for their partners; have difficulty eating, sleeping, or working; commit offenses while separated; have other domestic-violence-related arrests; stalk their victims; were on probation at the time of arrest; are suicidal or homicidal; have a history of substance abuse or were intoxicated at the time of the offense; deny any crime; or refuse to "let their partner go."

Probation officers also note on the checklist other factors that may suggest assigning the offender to a specific intervention, such as the batterer' s gender, sexual orientation, primary language, need for substance abuse or child abuse treatment, or other special needs. In this manner, the Domestic Violence Behavioral

Checklist integrates assessment of batterer typology and lethality with assignment to culturally appropriate interventions.

Cultural Specificity: The Influence of Class, Race, and Subculture

Factors that can affect the expression of domestic violence and response to treatment include socioeconomic status, racial or ethnic identity, country of origin, and sexual orientation.

- While a national survey of a random sample of married couples found domestic violence in all social milieux, the survey revealed a higher prevalence among poorer families.[11] Low-income men may be subject to greater stress in everyday life, and their lack of economic power and possible financial dependence on female partners may threaten their sense of masculinity, perhaps increasing the motive to assert dominance and control through physical violence.
- Wealthy batterers are less visible because they enjoy greater privacy in their family lives and have more resources for dealing with problems without involving the police or social services. Should they be prosecuted, they can afford a private attorney who may get them a lighter sentence, and they can pay for private counseling or psychotherapy in lieu of a batterer group. Most men in mandated batterer programs visited for this book had relatively low levels of income and education.
- Men of color are also mandated to treatment in numbers disproportionate to their representation in the local population. Researchers attribute this overrepresentation to a correlation with low socioeconomic status, lingering discrimination in the criminal justice system, and greater exposure to violence in the community. Resistance to treatment may be higher among minority men: some African American men have attributed their being mandated to programs to racism, a charge that facilitators have had to recognize without accepting it as an excuse for battering.
- Research suggests that men of color—including African American and Latino men—have a lower program completion rate than other cultural or racial groups.[12] As a result, some researchers and practitioners have proposed that the effectiveness of interventions will be enhanced among minority men if programs are not merely culturally sensitive, but, as discussed below, culturally competent.[13] All the jurisdictions visited for this book had at least limited access to specialized treatment groups for batterers of different races, ethnicities,

and sexual orientations, and most— but not all—agreed that specialized interventions enhanced the engagement of batterers in treatment.

Adapting Interventions to Accommodate Differences in Socioeconomic Status

Although no program contacted for this book attempted to segregate its clients by socioeconomic characteristics, most programs reported concerns about client poverty and illiteracy.

Program Fees

Most programs offer a sliding scale for program fees. In some cases, "reasonable" fees and sliding fee scales are mandated by State standards for batterer programs or accrediting agencies for service providers (see appendix A). For example, Family Services of Seattle is subsidized by local government so that their intake fee can be reduced to $25, as compared with the $45 or more payment required by the majority of batterer programs in Seattle. Often, however, sliding scales and fee reductions are not enough. In Baltimore, despite a sliding scale that ranges from $5 per week for those making $198 or less per month to $65 for those making over $2,400 per month, a large number of batterers are rejected because they cannot afford to pay.

Program directors report that fees are critical to the survival of most programs, and no one claims that interventions are profitable. While few programs contacted for this book rely on a mix of public funding and grants (see appendix C), the majority rely on payments from batterers for between 40 and 100 percent of their program income. Program directors across the country also emphasized that some minimum payment for program participation is necessary so that batterers understand that treatment is valuable and thus develop a personal investment in its being successful. Nevertheless, requiring mandatory payments from unemployed or low-income batterers remains controversial. Some probation officers worry that inability to pay excludes a large number of men who would otherwise benefit from intervention. Baltimore probation officer Willie Saunders expressed concern that too many batterers were falling outside the system: "The sliding scale should go to zero. The unemployed *cannot* pay." Saunders suggested that programs might accept "sweat equity" (that is, working at the program in exchange for program services), an approach recommended by a number of State standards. Oliver Williams, who studies batterer intervention with African Americans, expressed concern that financial issues are used disingenuously to exclude low-income men from interventions. Williams observed, "If it's a survival issue [for the program], O.K., or a fine, O.K., but don't say exclusion [for nonpayment] is for the good of the client." However, program administrators tend to attribute nonpayment to lack of commitment to program goals. "*Any*body can find $5 per week," one program director said, "Stop smoking. Walk instead of taking the bus. Borrow it from a friend. If they can document that it's coming out of food for the children, then we'll talk about it." Wil Avery at Baltimore's House of Ruth equates program fees with fines and points to their deterrent effect: "One man who had completed the program came to me and said, 'You know, I was going to hit my wife, but then I thought of all that money I'd have to pay again, and I stopped. *Then* I thought about all the things you taught us.' "

> "One man who had completed the program came to me and said, 'You know, I was going to hit my wife, but then I thought of all that money I'd have to pay again, and I stopped. Then I thought about all the things you taught us.' "
>
> —Wil Avery, Program Director, House of Ruth, Baltimore

Program directors and probation officers alike suspect that batterers' refusal to pay and claims of economic hardship are often used as an easy way out of batterer intervention. When judges see batterers for failing to register, they may be swayed by stories of economic hardship and delete the condition of program attendance from the sentence. In jurisdictions where no alternative sentences such as community service exist for battering, judges are often reluctant to jail a batterer for inability to pay. In response to the dearth of options for indigent batterers, probation officers in Baltimore's domestic violence intensive supervision unit, the Family Assault Supervision Team or "FAST Unit," were organizing the Batterers Termination Intervention Group to provide free in-house batterer treatment to batterers who were rejected by local programs because of their inability to pay (as well as those terminated for probation violations or considered too dangerous for community- based programs).

Literacy

Although many programs assign homework and readings, all contend that their curriculums can be adapted to suit batterers with poor or no reading and writing skills. For example, Ina Maka, a Native American intervention in Seattle, has assembled a wide selection of simply written articles for batterers and their families. Programs using the Duluth model report assigning homework or reading lessons in pairs. They do not ask for homework to be turned in, only read aloud in group. At the House of Ruth, batterers with low literacy levels are encouraged to draw pictures as their homework assignments and then to "read" from the pictures. Wil Avery noted that this approach is so effective that group leaders are sometimes unaware of who is illiterate until the program evaluation is completed at the end of the course.

With the vocabulary and conceptual complexity of a college-level course, The Compassion Workshop lectures and homework would be challenging to many participants; nonetheless, an assistant group facilitator insists that the material can be made accessible to participants who listen attentively and that assistants are available to read homework to batterers and to review the program content. He warned, however, that “participants who can’t read probably won’t get as much out of the program.” Steven Stosny, originator and director of The Compassion Workshop, argues that the elevated educational tone of the course engages batterers by showing respect for their ability to understand the material and, as they begin to master the somewhat technical terms and concepts, boosts their self-esteem. Stosny noted that he had experimented with simplifying the language in the program’s curriculum but found that clients preferred to be challenged.

Culturally Competent Interventions: Addressing Race, Ethnicity, and Subculture

Minorities have been discouraged from using mainstream social service agencies by racially or culturally insensitive service provider attitudes and practices.[14] As a result, minorities often turn for help to informal support networks such as family and friends, churches, or community-based social service providers of the same race or ethnicity (many of which are overwhelmed with requests for assistance or ill- equipped to deal with domestic violence). Oliver Williams argues that batterer interventions must become “culturally competent” to retain minority referrals and improve minority participation. A culturally competent intervention draws on the strengths of the culture, whether it is spirituality, a value placed on the family, or communal social systems. The intervention also addresses the weaknesses, such as alcoholism, harsh child discipline, and gender roles, that condone wife-abuse. Culturally competent programs have been developed for African Americans, Latinos (with a distinction drawn between merely bilingual programs and bicultural programs), Haitians, Asians, Native Americans, and recent immigrants.

Williams defines cultural competence according to two criteria, *organizational behavior* and *cultural program efforts*. Organizational behavior consists of “activities an organization undertakes to prepare itself to work with a culturally diverse client population,”[15] such as:

- providing staff with literature concerning effective service delivery to minorities;
- training staff in distinguishing three approaches to serving minorities—beginning with culturally destructive approaches, moving to colorblind

approaches, and finally achieving culturally competent delivery of services;
- seeking qualified consultants for conducting staff training if necessary; and
- engaging in self-evaluation and the active implementation of program changes to achieve cultural competence.[16]

Cultural program efforts are "those activities that not only demonstrate organizational preparedness to work with culturally different clients, but also demonstrate a willingness to work with them,"[17] such as outreach activities to:

- educate the community about the program and its goals;
- show interest in and support for the minority community generally;
- encourage the minority community to utilize batterer treatment services; and
- offer treatment that is sensitive to the needs of the population being served.

> "[Culturally competent programs] not only demonstrate organizationalpreparedness to work with culturally different clients, but also demonstrate a willingness to work with them."
>
> — Oliver Williams, Associate Professor, University of Minnesota Graduate School of Social Work

Oliver Williams argues that the focus on diversity in batterer interventions may be seen as falling along a continuum:

- *Colorblind* interventions believe that focusing on racial or ethnic differences is inappropriate for batterer interventions, that "differences don't make a difference."
- *Healthy heterogeneous* interventions value diversity but operate in a multicultural or multiracial environment.
- *Culturally specific milieu* refers to interventions whose participants are predominantly from one culture or race, so that no special efforts are judged necessary to ensure open discussion of culture or race-specific issues.
- *Culturally focused* interventions pay deliberate attention to the historical or contemporary experiences of a particular cultural or racial group. Cultural identity is defined and linked to behavior.
- *Culturally centered* interventions place a particular race or ethnicity's culture and values at the center of the treatment. Attention is given to culturally significant rituals.

Tailoring interventions to the needs and values of specific racial, ethnic, or subcultural groups is consistent with the feminist/social learning perspective. If battering is in large part the result of learned experiences and cultural attitudes toward the roles of men and women, then treatment should take the nature of those experiences and cultural expectations into account. The feminist model, used by the majority of interventions, takes into account *one* social factor related to battering—sexism—but other social factors may also promote violence. For example, Williams argues that the environment of violence and poverty in which many African American men are raised fosters an association between manhood and violence.[18] Treatment is more effective, he argues, if battering is not isolated from relevant psychological and social realities of membership in a minority group, such as cultural self-hatred, displacement of anger, "blackon-black violence," suicide, drug abuse, and cultural codes, including the urge to respond physically if someone appears to be disrespectful.

Some African American batterers mandated to a program may bring resentment against the criminal justice system, which has to be addressed before the participants can be receptive to modifying their behavior. The fact that men of color are more likely to be arrested and convicted than white male batterers, especially middle-class white batterers, cannot be allowed to obscure the fact that the African American batterers need to change their behavior. However, while the feelings aroused by the racism they have experienced can be a barrier to effective treatment, once a program acknowledges and deals with those feelings, it can also provide a springboard for helping participants to understand the powerlessness and oppression victims experience.

Attempts to modify batterer behavior should also build on the positive values and strengths of minority cultures. For example, Oliver Williams contends that telling African American men "You are hurting this woman, and that is why you should stop" alone will not have as much impact as also saying "You are hurting your community." Facilitators of minority and immigrant groups said that deep concern about children and the family was a hook used to engage court- mandated batterers in treatment. Betty Williams Watson, cofacilitator of an African American men's group at Family Services of Seattle, noted that Father's Day was an emotionally charged time for the men in her group. After participants resurrected anger and hurt at having been abandoned by their fathers, Watson redirected their attention to the similar behavior they were inflicting on their own sons and daughters: by being violent, they were being excluded from the home, effectively abandoning their children.[19]

Another example of recognizing social realities but building on subcultural strengths is provided by a program for Asian immigrants. Programs emphasize that while wife abuse may have been acceptable behavior in their country of origin, they need to obey the laws of their new home. According to a Vietnamese counselor, as children and wives assimilate, husbands may resort to violence to retain control and authority in the family. The counselor reasons with the men that they, too, have adopted new ways, such as dressing and behaving more informally at work. As immigrants, he points out, they value change and adaptation. In short, the men are not being left out of their family's acculturation; the family is growing and changing together.

Groups in which members of a minority culture predominate can create unusually strong feelings of solidarity, allowing members to provide support to each other (as well as to challenge each other) during and after meetings. The rituals the group observes to bring the participants closer and to build trust may vary from culture to culture. For example, a Latino batterer group begins and ends meetings by sharing food; a Native American program uses a sweat lodge and other rituals devoted to healing and cleansing.

In sum, culturally competent interventions have three methods of enhancing the "one-size-fits-all" approach:

- recognizing and working with the social and psychological realities of participants without allowing these realities to become an excuse for abuse;
- capitalizing on cultural strengths and values—such as communality, a belief in family, and spirituality—to promote the change process; and
- decreasing the isolation or discrimination that minority batterers may feel in a culturally heterogeneous group (see below).

The following sections discuss how batterer interventions have been modified to accommodate race, ethnicity, sexual orientation, and gender.

Batterer Programs for Men of African Descent

Two types of programs that serve men of African descent were visited for this book:

- programs that provide the option to join an all African American batterer group; and
- programs that provide only integrated groups.

Among the programs that provided only integrated groups, some were too small, or the percentage of minority clients too few, to support a separate racial group. By contrast, the House of Ruth in Baltimore, whose clientele is predominantly African American, chose an integrated group structure on the grounds that to focus on race or any other issue that is batterer-specific, such as psychological background or socioeconomic class, distracts from the central issue of addressing the violent behavior. For example, group leaders at the House of Ruth observe that the Duluth curriculum's "Power and Control Wheel" (see exhibit 1-1) cuts across all racial or ethnic identities and religious beliefs. John Miller, an African American group facilitator, summed up their viewpoint as follows: "Different cultural backgrounds are no barrier in group. In fact, diversity is a plus because the topic has nothing to do with socioeconomic or race issues. Our exit interviews with program graduates emphasize the importance of learning from the other men—regardless of their race or backgrounds." In his experience, the men in group benefited from seeing the common elements of abusive behavior across all cultures and socioeconomic classes. According to Miller, the presence of batterers from different races, cultures, and social classes in group was a great leveler that demonstrated that no group was exempt from abusing women and that allowed no group to feel superior to any other.

While the House of Ruth's approach is theoretically very different from the culturally competent approaches Oliver Williams advocates, in practice the contrast is not so stark. The batterer group observed for this book was 80 percent African American and was facilitated by an African American woman and man. Although no issues relating to race or African American culture were raised by the men or the facilitators, group facilitators and the program director provided numerous examples of ways in which the material is changed to better suit African American culture when appropriate. Program director Wil Avery, who is African American and a church deacon, emphasized that his understanding of African American culture and southern culture allows him to present the Duluth curriculum in a context that has relevance to African Americans. The House of Ruth is also involved in outreach efforts to the minority community, a step toward cultural competence recommended by Williams.

> "Different cultural backgrounds are no barrier in group. In fact, diversity is a plus because the topic has nothing to do with socioeconomic or race issues. Our exit interviews with program graduates emphasize the importance of learning from the other men—regardless of their race or backgrounds."
>
> — John Miller, Group Facilitator, House of Ruth, Baltimore

Sunya Faloyan, cofounder of the Empowerment Project, a partnership in Charlotte, North Carolina, holds the opposite view: "In mixed groups men can talk about cultural differences as a way to avoid identifying with the other men in group and escape responsibility." Chuck Turner, an African American group educator at EMERGE, where African American groups are available after the initial eight-week orientation, agrees: "An African American group allows men to focus on what *they* did instead of social injustice or racism. It also removes attitudinal obstacles for African American men, such as negative 'self-talk' about the orientation of a white counselor." Turner gave an example of how an African American group can enhance program participation: "One twenty-three-year-old African American man who served three years in jail for drugs was talkative but clownish in [the mixed race] intake group. In the ongoing African American group, he opened up and talked more seriously about gang activity—he was capable of a better discussion." Betty Williams Watson, cofacilitator of the African American men's group at Family Services of Seattle, noted that she has instant credibility with an African American group but that she still needs to address the issue of racism before they can focus on violence: "The men say to me, 'How dare you betray us? Don't you know about racism? You know how we've been treated, what the system has done to us.' I say, 'Yes, but you're beating up women.' "

> "The men say to me, 'How dare you betray us? Don't you know about racism? You know how we've been treated, what the system has done to us. ' I say, 'Yes, but you're beating up women.' "
>
> — Betty Williams Watson, Cofacilitator, African American Men's Group, Family Services of Seattle

Sunya Faloyan gave the example of a mixed group in North Carolina, facilitated by African Americans, in which African Americans were both ridiculed and feared: "The black men in the group were laborers and usually came dressed informally. One night a black man came dressed in a suit; the facilitator and the white batterers ridiculed him, laughing and saying 'You must think you're really *big*.' As long as [the African Americans] were laughing it was all right, but when they got serious it was very threatening to whites." Faloyan explained, "Society is accustomed to seeing black men act as comics or holding a lower position in society. According to society, this is a comfortable role for black men. Whenever black men are seen as acting out of that role it is seen as a threat by society. Black curriculum is important to African Americans because it enables them to construct their own existence and reality (rather than accept the constructs and limitations placed on them by society)."

> "Black curriculum is important to African Americans because it enables them to construct their own existence and reality (rather than accept the constructs and limitations placed on them by society)."
>
> —Sunya Faloyan, The Empowerment Project, Charlotte, North Carolina

Because of their concerns that racism can obstruct batterer treatment, Faloyan and cofounder Radhia Jaabar have developed a still-evolving specialized curriculum for men of African descent, the Kinship Journey. The central themes of the curriculum are that violence against one's partner is violence against oneself (reflecting the traditional African view that men and women are part of one another), spirituality, and the concept of the extended family. The curriculum is structured around Seven Pathways: personhood; family; tradition; black masculinity; collective consciousness; grief, anger, and trust; and spirituality. The men in group supply much of the content under each heading, and the struggle to define each heading leads to discussion. The Kinship Journey also makes use of the Duluth curriculum's videos and role-playing. Jaaber, a consultant to the National Training Project in Minnesota, which markets the Duluth curriculum, is currently piloting the Kinship Journey curriculum around the country.

> "An African American group allows men to focus on what they did instead of social injustice or racism. It also removes attitudinal obstacles for African American men, such as negative 'self- talk' about the orientation of a white counselor."
>
> — Chuck Turner, African American Group Counselor, EMERGE, Cambridge

Outreach to the African American community can be a slow and frustrating process. Watson points out that "the sense of community is stronger among African Americans, but community support for batterers works against treatment because the community is often tolerant of or turns a blind eye to battering." As a consultant for the Breaking the Silence program, a domestic violence awareness program for African American communities, Watson invited 25 churches, which she considers to be the "lifeblood of the community," to a training session on domestic violence issues. While parishioners from 20 churches came, most of them were women and few were ministers. Watson has encountered hostility from the religious community for raising the issue of domestic violence: "One minister told me, 'All our families are happy and sound. You don't come here.' " In her own church, however, Watson is making some headway, posting information in the men's and women's restrooms and in the church foyer and displaying domestic violence awareness materials, such as drawings from children with fathers who batter, letters from batterers to victims, and pictures of a batterer being arrested.

Asian Batterer Groups: Issues for Recent Immigrants

EMERGE in Cambridge, Massachusetts, The Domestic Abuse Intervention Service (DAIS), in Des Moines, Iowa, and the Refugee Women's Alliance in Seattle offer specialized groups for Asian batterers, most of whom are recent immigrants from Cambodia or Vietnam. Unlike other batterer interventions, counseling for Asian immigrants either begins with individual counseling because of cultural barriers to speaking openly in a group, or is entirely one-on- one. For example, at EMERGE, Cambodian batterers are counseled individually at first and then moved into small groups of three or four men once the counselor has established trust that he would not humiliate the man in front of his peers. The Vietnamese counselor at EMERGE works with men individually to avoid humiliating them in Boston's tight-knit Vietnamese community. At DAIS, one multilingual Vietnamese counsels most Asian batterers individually because of similar concerns regarding privacy and humiliation (although he does run a small Laotian group). By contrast, at Seattle's Refugee Women's Alliance, five groups of Asian and other immigrant batterers have been counseled using a complicated system of interpreters. One group, composed of one Cambodian and nine Vietnamese, was conducted in English in order to accommodate the American cofacilitator; another group, composed of five Vietnamese, one Russian, two English-speaking Filipinos, and two English-speaking Laotians, was conducted in English with interpreters for the Russians and Vietnamese. The counselor, Minh-Phuong La Nguyen, claims that family and community roles are similar across Southeast Asia, so the group approach, although slow and difficult with interpreters, works for most clients.

Program directors emphasized the importance of having a native speaker facilitate Asian batterer groups. Counselors who can anticipate and address a client's cultural assumptions are better equipped than American-born counselors to work with Asian batterers. There was a clear consensus among counselors working with Asian immigrants that this population could not participate effectively in the standard Duluth-style intervention because of a number of cultural and psychological characteristics common to many of them, especially an aversion to group work and an abhorrence of confrontation.

Respected Counselors Become "Elders"

Counselors noted the importance of securing and keeping the client's respect; they advised counselors of Asian batterers to be formal and firm in their initial dealings with clients. Once a tone of respect is established, Asian immigrant batterers uniformly regard counselors—who in the programs visited for this book were all Asian immigrants themselves—as "elders" who have assumed the authority figure role of uncles or grandfathers left behind. Counselors also represent the force of the American legal system and serve both as models of assimilation and as experts on American laws, beliefs, and customs. Asian counselors noted that, with the loss of their elders, most recent immigrants have lost their sense of community, making it incumbent on counselors to rebuild their sense of community and collective conscience. As a result, Asian counselors report a much higher personal involvement in the lives of their clients than ordinary group leaders would exercise: counselors explore batterers' experiences as political detainees or victims of torture, discuss pressing personal concerns such as family members left behind in Asia against their will or problems with child rearing and discipline, and even assist with solving practical problems such as filing taxes and registering cars.

Domestic Problems Are Regarded as a Private Matter

According to the Asian counselors, throughout Southeast Asia, domestic abuse is regarded as a private matter not to be discussed in public and also as socially acceptable behavior. Minh-Phuong La Nguyen notes that in Vietnam the community either ignored domestic violence or regarded it as a source of humor. Some Asian batterers have enormous difficulty accepting that these behaviors are illegal in the United States; according to Peter Oeur, a Cambodian counselor at EMERGE, 90 percent of the men he counsels do not understand the concept of emotional or sexual abuse. Furthermore, because it was legal in Cambodia for a man to take two or three wives, Oeur says, American notions of gender equality are difficult for both husbands and wives to accept. At DAIS, the counselor tells the batterers that there is no shame in getting help from outside the family because there is nowhere else to turn, given their loss of the extended family that served as an important support system in their home country. In their home country, the wife was expected to stay at home and run the household; in America, the counselor insists, both parents often have to work to raise a family, so there is no shame in the wife having contact with people outside the family.

Confrontation Is Culturally Inappropriate

All Asian counselors interviewed for this book had evolved a similar nonconfrontational, Socratic method of counseling Asian batterers that relies heavily on metaphors, parables, and analogies, allowing the men to distance the discussion from themselves. Oeur avoids labeling one culture or legal system as "right" and another "wrong," instead comparing "the Cambodian way and the American way," with special emphasis on the importance of human equality. He asks batterers what they think is right, leading with questions like, "Do you think your wife is happy?" Similarly, Dinh Pham, EMERGE counselor to Vietnamese batterers, asks the men, "How do you think domestic violence affects your children?" Phuong describes the situation of a hypothetical wife in an abusive relationship and asks the men, "How would you feel?" After five to eight weeks, Oeur may confront a client who is still blaming the victim or denying abuse, but he is careful to build a strong relationship with the client first.

Women and Children Assimilate More Easily

All four counselors noted that Asian clients feel powerless and threatened by the more rapid assimilation of their wives and children. Phuong reported that his Asian clients say, "I came here, I lost everything, my wife changed. My wife is into new things. I slap her a little. She calls the police." In response, he reminds them of American laws and values and gives concrete examples of how the men are changing too. Several counselors reported building on their clients' desires to learn how to cope with their children's new behaviors to keep them in counseling and build more rapport; some clients still attend EMERGE voluntarily after 40 weeks in order to learn nonviolent parenting skills.

> "My Asian clients say, 'I came here, I lost everything, my wife changed. My wife is into new things. I slap her a little. She calls the police.' I tell them 'It's not O.K. here. We are trying for equality.' "
>
> — Minh-Phuong La Nguyen, Domestic Violence Treatment Coordinator, Refugee Women's Alliance, Seattle

Police Are Feared and Distrusted

Many immigrants arriving from Asia have lived under repressive regimes or have experienced persecution by the police or the military. As a result, many are fearful of contact with the criminal justice system. The impact of this fear on batterer treatment is twofold: the batterer may feel that the arrest was unjustified, but he is nonetheless likely to comply with the court sentence in order to avoid any further contact. Asian counselors reported generally low attrition from treatment. One man reported that following his arrest he was "scared to death. I told myself, 'I'll never do this again. I'd rather run away from my wife than get rearrested,' " even though he still thought that there was nothing wrong with domestic violence.

Latino or Spanish-Speaking Batterer Groups

EMERGE and DAIS both offer Spanish language groups for batterers. In Seattle, Spanish-speaking probationers are generally referred to a neighborhood-based counseling service, Consejo Counseling. Providers of Spanish language and homogeneously grouped Latino batterer interventions raise two issues in this regard.

Latinos who Speak Spanish Represent Diverse Nationalities and Cultures

Although they share a common language, the range of dialects, accents, and cultural norms attributable to Spanish speakers in America is extremely broad. Efforts to make a batterer intervention curriculum relevant to Spanish-speaking Latinos can flounder on the question of which culture to portray. For example, EMERGE's four batterer groups were led by a Nicaraguan and included Panamanians, Dominicans, Mexicans, Uraguayans, and American- born Spanish speakers. Oswaldo Montoya of EMERGE explained that beyond language, his clients share their identity as immigrants, economic instability, and low literacy in their native language. While advocates of ethnically sensitive interventions recommend that the group leader's nationality be the same as that of the participants, as a practical matter this is often not feasible. For example, in Des Moines, because of a lack of qualified native speakers, DAIS hired a white female counselor who is fluent in Spanish but is not a native speaker. In Denver, the demand for bilingual workers has made it economically impossible for AMEND to hire appropriate staff, despite an out-of-state search. The short supply of culturally compatible facilitators is a serious issue for Latino batterer interventions, since the true focus of the specialized curriculum is culture, rather than language.

Latino Values Vary According to Age

Counselors reported a cultural gap between young male Latinos and older Latino men. Young Latino men were considered by counselors to be less family-oriented, more dependent on male friends who portray positive ties with women as a weakness, and more violent. Montoya reported that the older men in group were critical of the younger men's preoccupation with friends over family. He noted that many of the younger batterers displayed limited moral development—for example, more interest in not getting caught than in giving up the violence.

Strategies that programs use with Latino groups include:

- discussing the batterer' s distortion of the concept of "machismo," which originally meant "he who tenderly cares for his family," and the glorification of abusive behavior as an expression of manhood, especially to other men;
- challenging ownership of the partner by, among other techniques, requiring the batterer to call her by her first name instead of "my wife" (a technique common to many mainstream interventions);
- countering excuses for battering based on cultural practices in their native country by letting the group know that they understand the batterer' s perspective, that they too grew up with the same system, but that battering is illegal in this country; and
- spending more time discussing and learning to understand the complicated family ties of clients, some of whom have had two or three marriages or cohabitations, have children from different unions, or have children and family living in other countries.

Native American Approaches to Batterer Intervention

Only one jurisdiction visited for the book had a batterer program based on Native American traditional practices and beliefs. Ina Maka (United Indians of All Tribes Foundation) in Seattle uses a holistic family preservation model (one that provides child protection, victim services, and sexual abuse counseling as well as batterer intervention) combined with Native American practices such as family counseling by kias ("grandmas" who provide home-based support and advice to struggling families), sweat lodges, and smudging (a cleansing ritual). Ina Maka also uses case management, individual therapy, education (including GED classes), job assistance, parenting classes, art therapy, and role-playing in its work with batterers. Ina Maka considers victim safety to be the highest priority but places almost equal emphasis on its other work: victim assistance, sexual abuse therapy for both victims and batterers, child welfare, and drug and alcohol abuse therapy. To Ina Maka, each of these emphases is critical to family preservation.

Although their program is designed to serve Native Americans, it includes white, African American, and recent immigrant batterers because in Seattle batterers may choose which intervention they wish to attend from an approved list provided by probation. Dan Brewer, a group facilitator, commented that although groups are integrated racially and culturally, he has no difficulty addressing issues of race and oppression: "If they say the system isn't fair, we agree. But we say, 'There are no accidents; there's a part you played to get you here.' " Brewer tries to keep the focus on the batterer and his behavior without discounting the cultural context: "We'll talk about the genocide of Native American people, and draw parallels to slavery; both are colonialism. We'll talk about, 'What did it do to the family?' But we are very careful to keep people off pulpits. We are after knowledge and understanding, not blame. Why are Mom and Dad and Grandpa and Grandma the way they are? That happened. Now, what are we going to do about it?"

> "We'll talk about the genocide of Native American people, and draw parallels to slavery; both are colonialism. We'll talk about, 'What did it do to the family?' But we are very careful to keep people off pulpits. We are after knowledge and understanding, not blame. Why are Mom and Dad and Grandpa and Grandma the way they are? That happened. Now, what are we going to do about it?"
>
> — Dan Brewer, Group Facilitator, Ina Maka, Seattle

Following an extensive daylong intake evaluation that includes a detailed history of abuse in the current relationship and the family of origin, psychological assessment, and drug and alcohol screening, batterers participate in a three-part, 42-week program.

- *Phase I* (12 weeks) focuses on anger management, violent behavior, and feelings associated with domestic violence.
- *Phase II* (24 weeks) treats core issues related to family violence (e.g., power, control, and belief systems).
- *Phase III* (6 biweekly sessions) provides aftercare and support in mixed gender groups.

Sexual abuse is a major topic or personal problem for batterers in treatment at Ina Maka: all the female batterers enrolled in the program's first female group were victims of sexual abuse (see below, "Heterosexual Female Batterers"). Male batterers who were victims of sexual abuse are excused from program fees and may be targeted for individual counseling. Each batterer is required to meet with a therapist individually once a month to discuss issues he or she may not be talking about in group. Like Asian counselors, group leaders at Ina Maka take a less confrontational approach with batterers. According to Arlene Red Oak, case manager and group facilitator, "It's O.K. for them to be in denial. They want to work toward having healthy families." Although Ina Maka uses a family systems model, it stops short of couples counseling, telling victims who request therapy together, "No, you'd kill each other." Although program facilitators report that illiteracy is not a problem, program materials are geared to low literacy levels.

Gay and Lesbian Batterer Intervention

Batterer intervention for gays and lesbians is still in its infancy, and its development suffers in part from efforts by practitioners and academics to place gay and lesbian battering behaviors into a familiar theoretical framework. For example, Donald Dutton and others contend that the very existence of battering in lesbian relationships disproves the feminist theory that domestic violence is gender-based.[20] Some feminist practitioners who run groups for lesbian batterers respond that male and female roles underpin even same- sex intimate violence. Other theorists argue that in same-sex relationships, hierarchies based on cultural identity derived from class and race may replace gender as the focus of dominant and power-seeking behaviors. Still others argue for the need to take into account personality characteristics as well as societal influences. Perhaps as a result of this lack of theoretical consensus, services for gay and lesbian batterers have been slow to develop. Another factor delaying the development of services among homosexuals is the considerable reluctance to have the problem of partner violence revealed to the public; many feel the problem should be handled within the gay community lest it contribute to negative stereotypes.

A number of differences between homosexual and heterosexual batterers have treatment implications. For example, more homosexual batterers, especially lesbians, are self-referred because they are unhappy with their own behavior and its consequences. In part, lesbian batterers' readiness to recognize that their violence is a problem they must change may result from their socialization as females; physical violence conflicts with the stereotypical female sex role. According to treatment providers, women are more anxious to improve the quality of their intimate relationships. Disclosure of psychological and family issues is also easier for women. In general, women are more likely than men to seek therapy for any issue. The facilitator of a "women defendants" group (a term used to denote women charged with battering men) said that, unlike the men's group she facilitates, women are eager to participate and volunteer to remain in the group after their court mandate ends.

Several providers of services to lesbian batterers believe that these women find intimacy threatening because of childhood molestation, so they lash out with violence as a defense against closeness. Indeed, Morgaine Wilder, facilitater of lesbian batterer groups in Berkeley, California, says that over 70 percent of the women she treats are victims of childhood sexual abuse.[21] For these women, in addition to stopping the violence, the program must also treat the trauma. Some providers of batterer interventions to lesbians feel that this underlying issue must be treated in individual therapy.

As with racial minorities, the question arises whether there should be separate groups for homosexual batterers. Negative experiences that are similar to problems faced by minority men were reported for lesbians placed in heterosexual male batterer groups: although lesbians can "do the work," they are unable to be open and trusting in the group or to form the peer bonds that allow group members to challenge and support each other. Some gay male batterers can succeed in heterosexual batterer groups if the program is supportive, makes the theoretical connections between homophobia and sexism, and considers it part of the program mission to address homophobia. However, many gay men do not feel comfortable in heterosexual batterer groups, and the task of confronting homophobia may distract facilitators from the central issue of the men's violence.

Heterosexual Female Batterers

Batterer interventions for heterosexual female batterers (who are frequently referred to as "female defendants" by practitioners because of the large proportion of self-defending and angry victims in this classification) are still relatively rare (see appendix D.5, "Assessment Questionnaire for Female Offenders "), but all the jurisdictions visited for this book recognized the need for special programming for female batterers. Tina Busey, director of the Court-Referred Women's Program at Counseling Services in Denver has, over the last 12 years, formulated a specialized program to serve this difficult population most effectively.[22] Busey has identified four types of female batterers:

- *Self-Defending Victims.* These women have multiple injuries, a history of victimization, and have been threatened with injury or murder if they attempt to leave the relationship. The partners of self-defending victims typically have minorinjuries, such as scratches or bites.[23] Police failure to identify the primary physical aggressor properly at the time of the arrest—or the belief that they are required to arrest both parties—brings these victims into the criminal justice system.
- *Mutually Combatant Women.* Approximately 2 to 3 percent of female defendants arrested for battering are in relationships in which both partners attempt to inflict injury equally on the other, but neither party has ever been threatened with murder or sexual abuse.

- *Primary Physical Aggressors.* Approximately 2 percent of women arrested for domestic violence are the primary physical aggressors. In these cases, there are injuries to the man and none to the woman, and the man has been threatened with injury or murder if he attempts to end the relationship.[24]
- *Angry Victims.* Angry victims have been abused in the current relationship and in other relationships as adults. Angry victims begin fighting back and do not wish to be victims again.

Busey attributes the frequency with which police arrest self- defending victims to the sometimes confusing behaviors a victim may display to police. For example, the victim may feel safe to express her own anger after the police have arrived, or the victim may express anger toward the police because the justice system failed to protect her in the past. Victims suffering from post-traumatic stress disorder (PTSD) may have angry outbursts or take aggressive postures— such as picking up a knife—which they feel are necessary in order to survive.[25] Hamberger and Potente's research in Wisconsin shares this conclusion: "Research with the community sample of domestically violent [women] indicated most were motivated by a need to defend themselves from their partner's assaults, or are retaliating for previous beatings."[26] Hamberger and Potente conclude that domestic violence by women is fundamentally different from violence committed by men and therefore requires a different intervention model.

Busey's model of intervention for female defendants at Counseling Services includes working with female defendants on the following areas:

- safety plans;
- lethality checklists;
- family of origin (exposure to violence);
- the cycle of violence;
- victimization/revictimization;
- post-traumatic stress disorder;
- anger and stress management;
- substance abuse treatment, if appropriate;
- parenting;
- women's socialization; and
- healthy adult relationships.[27]

Busey recommends that this treatment be conducted either individually or in same-sex groups. She does not recommend couples therapy for female defendants, both because it may escalate the conflict and because it is prohibited by the Colorado Standards for Service Provision to Battered Women.

COUNTERING THE SPECIALIZED PROGRAMMING TREND: THE COMPASSION WORKSHOP

One new cognitive behavioral intervention based on attachment theory challenges the trend toward increased specialization in batterer intervention. The Compassion Workshop of Prince George's County, Maryland, founded by psychologist Steven Stosny, locates the origin of battering and child abuse in the abuser's use of anger to avoid feeling the more painful emotions of shame or distress, which the abuser may experience as being disregarded, devalued, rejected, powerless, unlovable, unimportant, accused, guilty, or unfit for contact. Stosny labels these painful emotions "core hurts." He employs a cognitive restructuring technique called HEALS (HEALS is an acronym for the steps of the cognitive restructuring approach: Healing, Explain to yourself, Apply self-compassion, Love yourself, Solve) to short-circuit the anger batterers feel in order to smother these more painful feelings before it develops, replacing the anger with compassion for oneself and one's partner or child (see exhibit 4-2). According to Stosny, abusive behavior begins with inappropriate reactions to a perceived emotional threat posed by the victim: "I have never met a dominant, controlling attachment abuser who did not feel that he was reacting to some form of manipulation, domination, and control by the victim; they inevitably feel manipulated by their own guilt."[28] Stosny postulates that if the abuser can learn to feel worthy of support and love ("self-compassion") even in difficult situations, this lays the groundwork for feeling positive emotions of attachment toward others, such as trust, intimacy, and commitment.

The Compassion Workshop is a didactic, future-oriented, training program consisting of 12 two-hour sessions and 43 homework assignments. During the first 6 sessions, clients do not share their experiences in class, only in their homework. Stosny reasons, "Given the number of personality disorders among abusers, 'sharing experience' tends to involve complaining, arguing, and confrontation, until clients learn to say what they need to say to get out of treatment, at which point their reflexive manipulation grows more subtle."[29] During this period, clients also sign agreements to be nonviolent and not to address any "hot issues" at home. Clients are also given instruction concerning time-outs and asked to formulate safety plans to use until they are fully trained in the HEALS method. The first six weeks of instruction focus on the development of internal skills, such as emotional regulation (including the concept that controlling others cannot satisfy one's emotional needs), self-empowerment, and building self-esteem. The second six weeks focus on applying these skills to relationship issues, such as avoiding power struggles, developing relationship skills (e.g., regulating fear of abandonment and fear of engulfment, closeness and distance, resentment and intimacy), and creating plans for the future. At the final session, participants read aloud their "healing letters" in which they apologize to all their victims and acknowledge the destructiveness of their past behaviors, outline the steps of their recovery, and list what they need to do to continue their recovery. The letters are intended both as an acknowledgement of past abuse and as a relapse prevention tool to review during vulnerable periods. By postponing the batterer' s admission of violence to the end of the program, Stosny claims that the letters are composed voluntarily, without compulsion.

The program uses two short films, *Shadows of the Heart* and *Compassion*. The first film, which shows domestic violence through the eyes of a five-year-old who feels responsible for his mother's victimization, is used to break down resistance to treatment and to stimulate a feeling of compassion among clients. Clients are asked to focus on how they could help the child; the compassionate feelings evoked by the film are then used as an example to show that compassion is a more positive emotion than anger and is more likely to build self- esteem. The second film depicts how compassionate behavior can create a greater sense of personal power than violence.

Advantages and Criticisms of the Compassion Workshop Approach

A pilot study, using random assignment of court-ordered spouse abusers to the Compassion Workshop and to five other batterer programs in Maryland and Virginia (all of which used some form of the feminist power and control model), found that, based on victim reports, 87 percent of Compassion Workshop participants were violence free (no pushing, shoving, grabbing) at the end of one year, compared with 41 percent of the comparison group participants. Seventy-one percent of the Compassion Workshop participants were reported to have avoided any verbal aggression, while only 25 percent of the comparison group were no longer verbally abusive. One-year follow-up data on 161 court-ordered men and women produced similar results: 87 percent of the Compassion Workshop participants were violence free and 76 percent were not verbally abusive.[30] The results have raised concerns in the field because they are based on a small sample and because the outcome data rely solely on victim reports (not on arrest data). Because a large percentage of abusers are no longer in a relationship with their original victim during and after treatment, the success rates based on victim reports are likely to be inflated; arrest data would help to provide a fuller—but still not complete—picture of batterer behavior. Nonetheless, this design flaw (reliance on victim reports) is common to both the Compassion Workshop data and those of the comparison programs, so it cannot account for the discrepancy in success rates between the two.

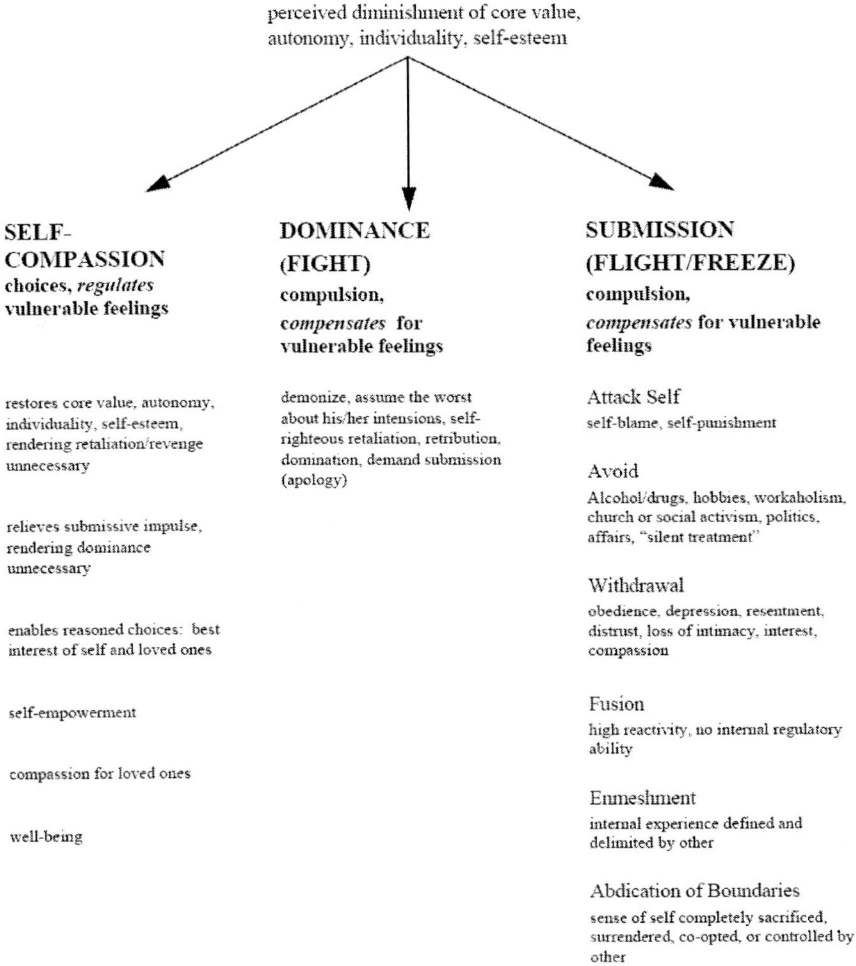

Source: Steven Stosny, "Treating Attachment Abuse: The Compassion Workshop," in *Treating Abusiveness*, ed. Donald Dutton, New York: Guilford, 1996.

Exhibit 4-2. Compassion Workshop: Various Responses to Internal Injury Inflicted by Attachment Figures.

The Compassion Workshop session observed for this book covered problem-solving strategies, symptoms of post-traumatic stress disorder (PTSD) in victims (including why partners should not misinterpret PTSD symptoms as a further rejection), and healthy ways to regulate intimacy in a relationship. There was some group discussion focusing on recent situations in which clients had used skills from the program to avoid violence. Although the presentation of program concepts was at a college level—and the clients included an immigrant with limited English as well as working-class whites and African Americans—most of the clients appeared to be engaged by the material and all were respectful of the group facilitators and each other. (Stosny reports a program completion rate of 77 percent.) In contrast to most other groups observed for this book, which were typically all-male and cofacilitated by a professional male/ female counseling team, this was a mixed gender group cofacilitated by Stosny and a volunteer couple (a former batterer who is a graduate of the Compassion Workshop and his wife and former victim, whose role it is to provide the victim's perspective on the material). A victim who was voluntarily attending the same group as her estranged husband commented that the program had helped her to heal herself and rebuild self-esteem. She found the format nonthreatening and appeared at ease in the presence of the mandated clients. The most marked difference in the Compassion Workshop group setting as compared to others observed for this book was the absence of confrontation, hostility, denial, or "side-tracking" by the clients.

Compassion Workshop is controversial because it includes male and female heterosexual batterers, gay and lesbian batterers, victims, and child abusers in the same program; allows abusers to postpone admission of abuse; allows passive participation; avoids confrontation; downplays the sociological context of abuse (such as sexism or racism); and uses a short treatment period (at a time when treatment for longer than a year is becoming a goal for many practitioners). Nonetheless, further evaluation is warranted to determine whether the low recidivism rates reported by victims are supported by arrest data. It is also important to determine whether the Compassion Workshop model can be effectively facilitated by other trained group leaders, not only by Stosny himself.

Conclusion

The search for effective batterer interventions has led researchers and practitioners alike to look beyond a "one-sizefits-all" approach. The innovations discussed in this chapter should not be regarded as mutually exclusive alternatives; instead, specialized approaches may be seen as refinements of practice that can work together to improve program retention and effectiveness. For example, criminal-justicebased typologies—focusing on previous offenses and arrests, substance abuse histories, and basic demographic data—show promise as a tool for judges, prosecutors, and probation officers to assess risk and assign batterers appropriate sentences, including incarceration, intensive probation, or participation in programs specializing in high-risk offenders. Programs accepting high-risk offenders may benefit from intake assessments that include psychological evaluations to enable them to couple psychological or substance abuse counseling with their standard curriculum. All programs may be able to improve program retention and decrease resistance to treatment by adopting culturally sensitive approaches that accommodate differences in race, ethnicity, gender, sexual orientation, and socioeconomic status. Finally, recent research in the area of batterer typology, which points to severe personality disorders in a quarter of the batterer population, may encourage practitioners to be more open to the combined use of educational and psychotherapeutic models with some batterers.[31] As the notion that all batterers are the same—and should receive the same intervention—gives way to research that argues for a multiplicity of batterer profiles, practitioners from all theoretical camps need to reconsider the notion that only one intervention approach can be valid. Finally, because it is not yet conclusive which—if any—of the current approaches are effective in deterring battering, State standards and guidelines need to provide a safe framework for testing innovative intervention strategies as well as scope for the development and implementation of specialized batterer interventions such as those discussed in this chapter.

REFERENCES

[1] In 1988, Hamberger and Hastings published a review of clinical studies of batterers, which concluded that more effective interventions can be designed by integrating biological and psychological factors. The same year, Mary Russell also published a literature review concluding that treatment decisions should be made on the basis of typologies determined by psychopathology, severity, and context of violence. Hamberger, K. L. and J. E. Hastings, "Personality Characteristics of Spouse Abusers: A Controlled Comparison," *Violence and Victims*, 3 (1988): 31–48; Russell, M., "Wife Assault Theory, Research, and Treatment: A Literature Review," *Journal of Family Violence*, 3 (3) (1988): 193–208.

[2] Gondolf, E.W. and J. Hannekenn, "The Gender Warrior: Reformed Batterers on Abuse, Treatment, and Change," *Journal of Family Violence*, 2 (2), (1987): 177–191.

[3] Gondolf, E., "Multi-Site Evaluation of Batterer Intervention Systems: A Summary of Preliminary Findings," Working Paper, Mid-Atlantic Addiction Training Institute, October 24, 1996.

[4] Holtzworth-Munroe, A. and G. L. Stuart, "Typology of Male Batterers: Three Subtypes and the Differences Among Them," *Psychological Bulletin*, 116 (3), (1994): 476–497. Browne,K.,D.G. Saunders, andK.M. Staecker, "Process-Psychodynamic Groups for Men Who Batter: Description of a Brief Treatment Model," University of Michigan, January 26, 1996.

[5] Dutton, D. and S. Golant, *The Batterer: A Psychological Profile*, New York: Basic Books, 1995.

[6] Hamberger and Hastings, "Personality Characteristics of Spouse Abusers."

[7] Goldkamp, J.S., "The Role of Drug and Alcohol Abuse in Domestic Violence and Its Treatment: Dade County's Domestic Violence Court Experiment," Final Report, Philadelphia: Crime and Justice Research Institute, June 1996.
[8] Goldkamp, "The Role of Drug and Alcohol Abuse in Domestic Violence."
[9] Gondolf, "Multi-Site Evaluation of Batterer Intervention Systems," 4.
[10] Goldkamp, "The Role of Drug and Alcohol Abuse in Domestic Violence," 202.
[11] Straus, M., R. Gelles, and S. Steinmetz, *Behind Closed Doors: Violence in the American Family,* New York: Anchor/Doubleday, 1980.
[12] Interview with Edward Gondolf, October 22, 1996. Preliminary results from Gondolf' s four-site study found that African Americans were 13 percent more likely to drop out of treatment by three months.
[13] Williams, O., "Ethnically Sensitive Practice to Enhance Treatment Participation of African American Men Who Batter," *Families in Society: The Journal of Contemporary Human Services,* (1992): 588–595.
[14] Williams, O. and L. Becker, "Domestic Partner Abuse Treatment Programs and Cultural Competence: The Results of a National Survey," *Violence and Victims*, 9 (3) (1994): 287–296.
[15] Ibid., 289.
[16] Ibid.
[17] Ibid.
[18] Williams, "Ethnically Sensitive Practice."
[19] Cultural traits discussed in this chapter may also be prevalent among nonminority batterers; however, program staff interviewed for this report emphasized these topics in the context of minority intervention.
[20] Dutton, D., "Patriarchy and Wife Assault: The Ecological Fallacy," *Violence and Victims,* 9 (2) (1994): 167– 182.
[21] Morgaine Wilder speaking at the Preconference Institute on Lesbian and Gay Domestic Violence, National Lesbian and Gay Health Conference, Seattle, Washington, August 31, 1996.
[22] Busey, T., "Treatment of Women Defendants," *The Catalyst* (Spring 1993): 3–4; Busey, T., "Women Defendants and Reactive Survival Syndrome," *The Catalyst* (Winter 1993): 6–7.
[23] Sue, H., "Women as Defendants," Applied Group Research, University of Denver, May 22, 1989, cited in T. Busey, "Women Defendants and Reactive Survival Syndrome."
[24] Busey, "Women Defendants and Reactive Survival Syndrome," 6.
[25] Ibid.

[26] Hamberger, K.L. and T. Potente, "Counseling Heterosexual Women Arrested for Domestic Violence: Implication for Theory and Practice," *Violence and Victims*, 9 (2)(1994): 125–137.

[27] Busey, "Treatment of Women Defendants."

[28] Stosny, S., "Treating Attachment Abuse: The Compassion Workshop," in *TreatingAbusiveness*, ed. D. Dutton, New York: Guilford, 1996.

[29] Ibid.

[30] Ibid.

[31] Gondolf, "Multi-Site Evaluation of Batterer Intervention Systems"; Saunders, D., "Feminist-CognitiveBehavioral and Process-Psychodynamic Treatments for Men Who Batter: Interaction of Abuser Traits and Treatment Models," Draft, University of Michigan, January 26, 1996.

Chapter 5

CRIMINAL JUSTICE RESPONSE

KEY POINTS

- Batterer intervention programs alone cannot be expected to deter domestic violence; strong, coordinated criminal justice support is also needed.
- The combined impact of arrest, incarceration, adjudication, and probation supervision may send a stronger message to the batterer about the seriousness of his behavior than what is taught in a batterer program.
- Criminal justice personnel can take actions at all points in the criminal justice system to reinforce the message that battering is a crime and to support the efforts of batterer programs:

1. Expedite Domestic Violence Cases. Adopt policies to expedite batterers' trial dates, sentencing, probation contact, and batterer program intake.
2. Use Specialized Units and Centralized Dockets. Specialized domestic violence prosecution and probation units, and centralized court dockets for battering cases and restraining orders improve services to victims and better coordinate batterer prosecution, sentencing, and supervision.
3. Gather Broad-Based Offender Information Quickly. Create a system to gather complete defendant information for prosecutors and judges, including previous arrests and convictions (for both domestic violence and other crimes), substance abuse, child welfare contacts, and victim information.

4. *Take Advantage of Culturally Competent or Specialized Interventions.* Maximize effective use of batterer programming by seeking appropriate interventions for batterers who are indigent, high-risk, female, mentally ill, or incarcerated.
5. *Coordinate Batterer Intervention with Substance Abuse Treatment.* In cases where the batterer has an alcohol or drug abuse problem, courts should mandate treatment as well as batterer intervention. Probation officers should intensively monitor batterers' compliance with substance abuse treatment through weekly urine testing.
6. *Be Alert to the Risks to Children in Domestically Abusive Households.* Judges and probation officers should be alert to the danger posed by domestic violence to children (even to children who are not themselves physically abused) and coordinate with child protective services and programs that specialize in domestically abusive families to ensure that batterers' children are safe and are receiving appropriate services.
7. *Create a Continuum of Supports and Protection for Victims.* Victim advocates should be provided to monitor victim safety and to assist victims with the criminal justice system from the time of the assault through trial and/or probation. Victim advocates attached to probation units are particularly important in monitoring the safety of women whose batterers are sentenced to a batterer program.
8. *Encourage Interagency Cooperation.* Organize formal coordinating committees of probation officers, prosecutors, battered women's advocates, child protection workers and batterer intervention providers to discuss batterer referral and monitoring policies regularly.

- State standards are needed to deter inexperienced or unethical counselors but may inadvertently stifle innovation.
- Probation supervision is central to criminal justice policy concerning battering and cooperation with batterer interventions.

Batterer intervention programs are only one link in a chain of criminal justice responses to battering. To be effective, not only batterer intervention programming but all links in the chain must be strong. Andrew Klein, chief probation officer for the Quincy, Massachusetts, District Court argues:

> [T]reatment programs alone are rarely enough— many provide only a small part of what is needed to stop serious batterers. To be effective, these programs must operate within the broader context of a comprehensive intervention effort. Treatment really begins with the issuance of a restraining

> order or arrest for domestic violence and continues with successful prosecution and significant, enforced sanctions. Tough monitoring is also necessary. . . .[1]

Coordinated criminal justice efforts are particularly important in combatting domestic violence because victims of domestic abuse can be endangered by any breakdown in communication, failure of training, or lack of follow-through by criminal justice agencies, batterer interventions, or victim advocates and liaisons. The opposite is also true: an efficient, consistent criminal justice response to battering can reinforce the message of batterer programs and motivate batterers to comply with treatment. Sid Hoover, supervisor of Seattle's Municipal Probation Domestic Violence Unit, speculates that most batterers sentenced to probation comply with court orders to attend batterer programs:

> . . . as a result of what the criminal justice system has already shown them before they came in our door—in other words: "I got arrested, I got court orders out against me, I can lose my family and my house, I'm responsible, and I have to do something to change." They're not going to wait until they walk in [probation's] door to realize that, they're going to realize it the first night they're in jail.

Compliance with probation conditions is a threshold issue affecting program outcomes: to be effective, batterer programs must enroll clients and maintain client cooperation. Klein emphasizes the importance of the criminal justice context of batterer intervention when he writes, "When it comes to changing batterers, we are usually talking about forced treatment."[2]

This chapter examines steps the criminal justice system can take to enhance the efficacy of batterer intervention. The discussion, based on interviews with criminal justice and program personnel at five sites (see chapter 3, "Pioneers in Batterer Intervention"), is divided into three sections:

- Section one provides an overview of the principal features of a coordinated systemwide response to battering (from arrest to prosecution, sentencing, program referral, and monitoring by probation or parole) (see the box "Key Components of an Integrated Criminal Justice Response to Battering") and then discusses key systemwide practices that may contribute to—or impede—batterer intervention efficacy.

> "[T]reatment programs alone are rarely enough—many provide only a small part of what is needed to stop serious batterers. To be effective, these

programs must operate within the broader context of a comprehensive intervention effort. Treatment really begins with the issuance of a restraining order or arrest for domestic violence and continues with successful prosecution and significant, enforced sanctions. Tough monitoring is also necessary. . . ."

— Andrew Klein, Chief Probation Officer, Quincy, Massachusetts, District Court Model Domestic Abuse Program

- *Section two* provides an in-depth discussion of issues of particular interest to *probation officers* who coordinate and oversee batterer participation in programs and a discussion of probation services at the five sites.
- *Section three* discusses ways in which criminal justice agencies can cooperate and collaborate with batterer interventions.

KEY COMPONENTS OF AN INTEGRATED CRIMINAL JUSTICE RESPONSE TO BATTERING

Batterer intervention programs are unlikely to change offender behavior without the support and cooperation of the criminal justice system. Supportive system responses include coordination among agencies, the use of victim advocates throughout the system, the designation of special units or individuals responsible for handling battering cases, and the provision of appropriate training for personnel concerning domestic violence issues and procedures.[3]

Law enforcement officers need training to increase their sensitivity to the needs of victims and to investigate allegations of domestic violence thoroughly, including filing reports of calls where no arrests were made. Law enforcement officers need to be able to:

- identify the primary aggressor, including understanding the effects of post-traumatic stress disorder and issues concerning same-sex couples (see box, "Determining the Primary Physical Aggressor");
- execute a proarrest or mandatory arrest policy;
- gather evidence at the scene, including photographs and statements that may be important to the prosecution if the witness does not wish to press charges; and

(Continued).

- arrange for a temporary restraining or no-contact order.

In addition, law enforcement officers need to enforce bench warrants issued for batterers who have not reported to probation or whose probation has been revoked for program noncompliance.

Pretrial screening for offenders charged with domestic-violence-related offenses needs to ensure that batterers are not released on their own recognizance or on bail before arraignment. Pretrial services personnel need to gather as much background data as possible for the prosecutor and judge, including history of prior arrests, convictions, domestic violence arrests and convictions, any previous batterer intervention, and substance abuse.

Selected prosecutors should specialize in domestic violence cases. They need adequate support from police, probation officers, and victim advocates to be able to follow through on domestic abuse cases and to pursue the volume of cases generated by a proarrest policy or a mandatory arrest statute.

Prosecutors need to:

- *pursue cases without victim testimony, if necessary,* so that victims do not need to confront their batterers to use the criminal justice system;
- *use a vertical prosecution model* to increase victim cooperation and prosecutor familiarity with each case;
- *keep offender files* containing information concerning previous arrests and convictions, substance abuse history, child protective services contact, reports from probation, and recorded statements made by the defendant to the court (e.g., "I couldn't register for batterer treatment because my grandmother died");
- *make use of victim advocates* (see below) both to assist in case preparation and to reduce the victim's anxiety during prosecution;
- *pursue probation revocations* in domestic violence cases with the same urgency as the original case, since a revocation hearing indicates renewed danger to the victim; and
- request batterer intervention program participation as a condition of probation or other sentence.

(Continued).

System-based victim advocates should be available to victims at all stages of the criminal justice process. Advocates attached to specialized police, prosecutor, and probation units need to:

- *establish contact with the victim* as quickly as possible (some now accompany police to the scene of the complaint);
- *explain the criminal justice system* to the victim;
- *gather evidence* for police and prosecutors
- assist the victim with safety planning and provide service referrals;
- notify victims of key offender events (such as termination from program) and other imminent threats to their safety;
- assist probation officers by monitoring batterer compliance with sentencing conditions through victim reports; and
- assist victims to testify in court at trial and probation revocation hearings.

Advocates from different departments and agencies need to coordinate their services, so that victims are not "dumped" following prosecution and so that multiple service referrals are not made.

Judges, preferably assigned to centralized special domestic violence dockets, need to be willing to issue meaningful and appropriate sentences—including jail time, mandatory participation in batterer intervention programs, participation in substance abuse treatment, and fines or community service, depending on the circumstances of the case. Courts need to process domestic violence cases quickly and require prompt enrollment in a batterer program and immediate contact with probation, if these are terms of a batterer's sentence. Judges should also respond forcefully, with graduated sanctions, to reports from probation and program staff that a batterer is not abiding by the terms of his sentence, including failure to comply with the rules of the batterer program. Judges also need to be familiar with State standards for batterer programs (where they exist) to guide them in the sentencing of batterers.

Finally, judges need to be alert to the co-occurrence of domestic violence and child abuse, and the dangers posed to children who witness domestic violence. Judges should coordinate batterer intervention with child protective services programming where appropriate and familiarize themselves with new programming targeting batterers who also abuse children in their care.

(Continued).

Probation officers, organized in specialized domestic violence units with reduced caseloads, need to provide intensive probation supervision. They also need to understand the issues surrounding domestic violence, batterer interventions, and emerging batterer typologies in order to supervise and monitor batterers effectively, including ensuring that they comply with their sentences. Probation officers also need to:

- prepare thorough presentencing reports on batterers (see below);
- obtain information on batterers sentenced to probation in a timely manner and issue warrants for batterers who do not report to probation;
- develop assessment tools or referral policies to assist in assigning batterers to appropriate batterer programs;
- *provide intensive supervision* for all batterers;
- *develop resources* for supervising batterers who are not accepted by or are not appropriate for mainstream batterer interventions; and
- *assess batterer drug and alcohol abuse and closely monitor batterer sobriety* with random drug and alcohol screening, when appropriate.

Finally, probation officers can take the lead in establishing at least monthly meetings between batterer intervention service providers and probation officers to discuss difficult cases and other issues of mutual concern (see p. 95, "Local Domestic Violence Coordinating Committees").

To assist criminal justice personnel, *batterer programs* need to:

- provide regular reports to probation and the courts, tracking who has enrolled, offender cooperation with program requirements, sobriety, and sentence compliance;
- have contact with advocates for the victims of their clients and provide timely notification to the victim and probation—or any other appropriate agency—if a new threat to victim safety arises;
- meet regularly with representatives of the domestic violence probation and prosecution units to discuss topics of mutual concern (see p. 94, "Collaboration among Community Partners"); and
- meet regularly with representatives of independent battered women's programs to discuss topics of mutual concern

Criminal Justice System Issues Affecting Batterer Intervention

A number of systemwide issues have an indirect but serious impact on the efficacy of batterer intervention.

Enrollment in a Batterer Intervention Should Occur Quickly

Depending on State-level speedy trial laws and the backlogs faced by local courts, a batterer who chooses to take his case to trial may extend the period between arrest and sentencing to three months or longer. Probation officers and prosecutors suggest that even under ideal circumstances the time between sentencing and program enrollment would on average be six weeks. In reality, however, several months may be consumed because of program overcrowding, fixed program intake dates, client resistance and claims of indigence, and additional hearings to reorder uncooperative offenders to programs or to extend the period allowed for compliance. Gondolf found that some men entered programs two years after arrest. According to a Seattle probation officer, 89 percent of probationers miss the first six-week deadline to enroll in a batterer program; at that point they are scheduled for a hearing—usually three weeks away—when they are likely to be given another month to comply. If they continue to fail to comply, probation officers may shorten the time between violation and court date, but many batterers are still able to postpone program participation for many months.

While many offenders are slow to enroll in court-ordered programs, many others never show up at all. In 1994–1995, 350 of the 753 men referred to House of Ruth in Baltimore failed to appear for intake. Possible explanations include inability to pay, arrests for other crimes, flight from the jurisdiction, or neglect in the vast caseloads of general probation (intensive probation is available only for the most serious domestic violence offenders). In Des Moines, probation officers report that approximately one-third of all batterers ordered to probation and batterer intervention never report for supervision or program intake. Probation officers notify the court of the violation and a bench warrant is issued; however, arrests are rare because of staffing shortages. In 1996, local police received a small grant to pay officers overtime to enforce warrants against batterers. The goal of the initiative is to rearrest half of the 800 batterers who failed to comply with their court orders in the last year (including batterers who failed the program as well as those who never reported to probation).

Pittsburgh's Domestic Abuse Counseling Center (DACC): Short-term Programming with Strong Criminal Justice and Community Links

DACC is a nonprofit program offering batterer intervention at 15 sites in Western Pennsylvania. DACC uses an innovative combination of batterer counseling, broad-based community education, and coordinated community response featuring collaborative efforts with social service agencies, the criminal justice system, battered women's agencies, and health organizations (including substance abuse and mental health providers). DACC's approach is notable for several features:

- in-court intake personnel who facilitate batterer enrollment within two weeks of arrest and schedule program orientation within three weeks of arrest (see exhibit 5-1, "Domestic Abuse Counseling Center (DACC) Timeline/Flowchart");
- a diversion program monitored directly by the court at regular intervals (three mandatory court reviews in four months; see exhibit 5-1);
- a short-term cognitive behavioral intervention (16 weekly 90-minute sessions);
- a pilot program offering an intensive intervention (three meetings per week) for high-risk or repeat offenders who are not appropriate for entry into the general program. Offenders remain in the intensive program until they display appropriate attitudes and behaviors for entry into the regular program;
- dual tracking of batterers with substance abuse or mental health issues. DACC provides case management and monitoring for batterers participating in substance abuse or mental health counseling;
- a specialized intervention group for law enforcement officers; and
- a court liaison who provides information, consultation, and case review for the Domestic Violence Court to expedite proceedings and ensure appropriate court action.

DACC was chosen for a multisite evaluation sponsored by the Centers for Disease Control, which is still under way. A 1993–1994 evaluation found that program participants were nonviolent for at least six months following the program, and half the victims reported feeling "very safe" at the six-month follow- up.

Whatever the causes, by allowing slow compliance and noncompliance with court-ordered batterer intervention, the criminal justice system not only creates an appearance of unconcern for the crime—which contradicts program messages that battering is both illegal and socially unacceptable—but may also endanger the victim. Furthermore, delays in program participation may also limit the deterrent benefit of participating in batterer programs. Commenting on the preliminary results of his evaluation of four batterer interventions, Edward Gondolf speculated that speed of enrollment in treatment might, upon further evaluation, predict recidivism better than the type of criminal justice referral (pretrial diversion versus conviction), program length, or program content.[4]

Communities with a centralized domestic violence docket and a limited number of intervention providers may be able to *schedule program intake onsite at the time of sentencing.* The Domestic Abuse Counseling Center in Pittsburgh (DACC) reduced the time lost between sentencing and program enrollment by instituting program registration at the courthouse (see exhibit 5-1). Program Director Wil Avery at House of Ruth estimated it would require approximately $30,000 per year to fund court-based intake staff because facilitators and other program staff currently perform intake on a part-time basis on weekends; however, the cost of instituting such a change would be nominal for programs with full-time intake personnel, which could establish a satellite office at the courthouse.

Reducing the time between sentencing and contact with probation also helps to expedite program referral. In Baltimore, offenders are simultaneously ordered to report to central intake at probation and parole and to enroll in a batterer program. However, if the batterer disobeys both orders, three months elapse before central intake begins to write letters to the batterer's last address; during this period, neither probation nor House of Ruth is aware that the batterer has been referred to them by the courts. By contrast, other jurisdictions impose stricter and shorter limits on the time a batterer is permitted to wait before reporting to the domestic violence probation unit. For example, probationers participating in a diversion program in Denver (which requires batterers to enter a guilty plea in order to participate) are given a week to report to the program's treatment provider. If they fail to report after a month, their probation is revoked and their conviction entered.

Probation officers and program directors note that simple procedures, such as *faxing program staff the lists of probationers referred to a specific program,* can help overburdened probation officers by making it possible for programs to track who is supposed to have registered and notify probation when particular offenders have not enrolled. However, in many jurisdictions, program referral practices that give probationers a wide choice of programs to attend make this kind of control difficult. The standard approach in many communities, allowing the batterer to choose his own intervention from a list of approved providers, may work against prompt enrollment and make the job of probation officers more difficult. A more efficient approach might be to allow probation officers to assign batterers to a specific program (taking into account the probationer's neighborhood, special needs, and financial capabilities). According to probation officer Dexter Shipman in Colorado's 18th Judicial District, "We found through experience that if you give [batterers] two or three programs to choose from— some would even ask for the entire list—they spend two or three months shopping around to find which program is a dollar cheaper or seems to fit their schedule perfectly. So we stopped doing that and now we make specific referrals."

> "We found through experience that if you give [batterers]two orthreeprograms to choosefrom— some would even ask for the entire list— they spend two or three months shopping around to find which program is a dollar cheaper or seems to fit their schedule perfectly. So we stopped doing that and now we make specific referrals."
>
> —Dexter Shipman, Probation Officer, 18th Judicial District, Colorado

Centralization Improves Service Delivery

A centralized docket for domestic violence cases, used by the Quincy District Court in Massachusetts, presents a number of advantages for all criminal justice agencies that handle domestic violence cases, especially as domestic violence cases are increasingly handled by dedicated domestic violence units or by individuals with reduced and specialized caseloads.

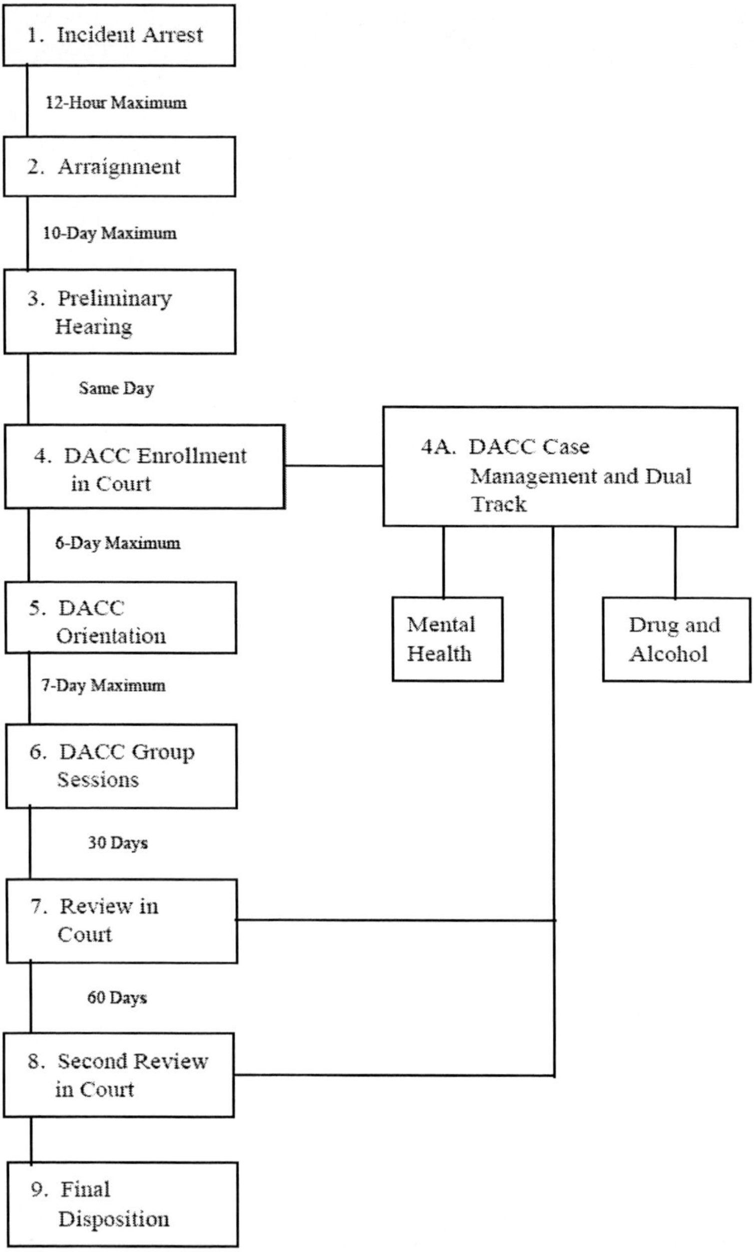

Source: Program Materials, DACC, Pittsburgh, PA, 1996.

Exhibit 5-1. Domestic Abuse Counseling Center (DACC) Batterer Enrollment and Intervention Timeline/Flowchart.

- Prosecutors who specialize in domestic violence cases need not waste time traveling from court to court to try cases. In Baltimore, where the prosecution of domestic violence cases is decentralized, municipal domestic violence prosecutor Ronnie Young is able to serve only five of nine police districts. The rest are served by line prosecutors. Following the planned creation of a centralized docket, Young, along with additional staff, expects to serve all nine police districts and to prosecute all batteries, stalkings, and violations of temporary restraining orders at one location.
- *Probation* units located near or in the courthouse with the domestic violence docket can receive immediate referrals from the court. One program reported that as soon as batterers are sentenced, they are told, "Now walk down that hall and report to probation before you leave."
- *Judges* using specialized dockets not only become expert on domestic violence issues but are also more likely to note the repeat offender or the offender who continues to avoid complying with the terms of his sentence.
- *Court-based victim advocates* (whether working with prosecutors or probation officers) need a centralized, secure facility in or near the court to provide support and services for victims who plan to testify. Beth Ledoux, a victim advocate who worked in both the prosecutor office and probation department of the Quincy District Court, emphasizes the need for a secure passage for victims to the courtroom. When her office was moved away from the courthouse and housed with probation several blocks away, Ledoux left herjob because she felt it would be too dangerous for victims to go for counseling to the same office as batterers and to travel unprotected between the office and the court for revocation hearings.

Determining the Primary Physical Aggressor: A Knotty Issue for Law Enforcement

Counselors and victim advocates express concern that some batterers referred to programs—mostly women and homosexuals—have been improperly identified as the primary aggressor. Because studies have found that the majority of women arrested for battering are so-called "self-defending victims" (see chapter 4, "Current Trends in Batterer Intervention"), the proper identification of the primary physical aggressor is extremely important in order to avoid both revictimizing these women and wasting criminal justice resources.

Similarly, advocates for battered gays and lesbians caution police not to assume that the physically larger partner is always the primary aggressor; as with other couples, care must be taken to question the couple and any witnesses closely before making an arrest. It is equally important for police officers to avoid dual arrests, which may not only involve arresting innocent parties but also make it impossible to prosecute anybody. Victim advocates note that mistaken identification of the primary aggressor may occur at the scene because bruises caused by battering may take hours to appear, whereas some signs of defensive violence, such as scratching or biting, are immediately apparent. Advocates also emphasize the importance of determining if there has been a history of abusive incidents—or a recent escalation of abuse—which may have led the victim to react fearfully and more violently to a perceived or real threat. In some instances, police may find a chaotic scene where it is not readily apparent which party is the perpetrator and which is the victim. For example, victims may feel safe to express anger against the batterer in the presence of police, thereby giving the impression they are the perpetrators, or may even verbally abuse the police. Linda Ferry, supervisor of the Domestic Violence Unit in Denver's City Prosecutor's office, cautions police not to be provoked into arresting both parties by an angry victim's disrespectful conduct: "As much as police may get satisfaction from [arresting both parties], not 'shutting up' is not criminal"—or indicative of who the batterer is. One technique to avoid dual arrests is to distinguish between the initial aggressor and the person who has been most severely injured as a result of the violence. In addition, Ferry tells officers to get as much information as possible at the time of the arrest because, "as uncooperative as somebody might seem at the scene, they're going to be worse later." Before taking statements officers need to separate the parties, making sure that both are out of eyesight and earshot of each other. In instances where both parties exhibit signs of injury, officers should consider the possibility of self-defense and examine the relative level of injury or force involved.

Sheri Yeates, domestic violence prosecutor in King County (Seattle), raises another issue related to centralization of services: neighboring jurisdictions may find it more efficient to contract with one authority to provide services. According to Yeates:

> Parts of the Municipality of Bellevue are incorporated, and then there are regions—literally like fingers in and out—that are still unincorporated. So you might live on one side of the street and the City would respond, and on the other side of the street King County would respond. . . . [Bellevue] is

contracting with [the County] to provide services because it is more beneficial to clients who are moving back and forth. Victims [from both the County and the City] will have the same advocate.

Prosecutors and Judges Need Accurate and Complete Defendant Information

Prosecutors, judges, and probation officers need a system for accessing relevant defendant information, including previous arrests (for both domestic-violence-related and nondomestic violence offenses, especially those involving assault), substance abuse history, civil cases and restraining order information, involvement with child protective services, and any previous experience with batterer intervention, to make proper decisions concerning plea bargains, sentencing, and bail.

Linda Ferry, supervisor of the Domestic Violence Unit and Diversion Program in Denver's City Attorney's Office, describes its method of data collection:

> In this unit, victim advocates *intervene* immediately, before the case goes to first arraignment, to try to determine if there's a pattern of abuse that's gone on—reported or not. We try to garner whatever information we can from the victim regarding the situation and the defendant. . . . We have the cooperation of probation in that effort—they have a form with the defendant's State criminal history on it. We also look up everything that's in the City files, and we get a pretty good profile.

Prompt data collection is important in Denver, because approximately one-third of batterers either plead guilty at first arraignment and are sentenced to immediate probation or plead "not guilty" and are given the opportunity to participate in a diversion program for first-time offenders with no criminal record. The diversion program offers a deferred judgment for one year, and defendants are expected to plead guilty at the next arraignment if they are accepted for it. The defendant can also have the case set for trial. However, because domestic violence defendants are not eligible for bail until they come before a judge, Ferry knows that the batterer will not be released until arraignment and that arraignment will not be scheduled until the next day— sufficient time to contact the victim and collect defendant data. Further screening of candidates for program diversion is done by an in-house probation officer for the program, which operates out of the prosecutor's office. At the initial interview with the probation officer, diversion candidates sometimes reveal a criminal record or simply display an uncooperative attitude that may disqualify them from diversion. In this program, batterers who plead guilty but do not qualify for either immediate probation or the diversion program—those who have a significant history of domestic violence or who are already on probation—are referred to probation for a presentence interview for further information collection and are likely to receive jail time in addition to extended probation.

> "We try to garner whatever information we can from the victim regarding the situation and the defendant. . . . We have the cooperation of probation in that effort—they have a form with the defendant's State criminal history on it. We also look up everything that's in the City files, and we get a pretty good profile."
>
> — Linda Ferry, Supervisor, Domestic Violence Unit, Denver City Attorney's Office

Loss of information—or failure to obtain complete information about batterers—can have serious consequences for both victims and batterer programs. Batterers whose behavior has resulted in police calls to the home, or who have been arrested but never convicted, may be treated as "first-time offenders," offered diversion, or released without bond or a restraining order if proper research has not been conducted.

Intervention Is Needed for All Batterers

Jurisdictions need to develop program options for the full range of batterers, not only low-risk male heterosexual batterers who are amenable to standard treatment. Many program providers and probation officers voiced concern that only a fraction of convicted batterers ever entered interventions. For example, among the five sites examined in this study, only Denver has batterer interventions geared explicitly to high-risk batterers. As a result, high-risk batterers—along with those who are incarcerated, psychologically disturbed, female, gay, non-English speaking, indigent, or merely uncooperative—often fall through the cracks. Probation should work with local intervention providers to develop sentencing options for different categories of batterers that include intervention.

In Baltimore, probation officers are exploring the possibility of providing in-house batterer groups for high-risk batterers and uncooperative batterers who have been terminated by local programs. According to Suzanne Sigona, director of Probation for Denver County, "Obviously, everyone needs treatment. Even if they've served time in jail, if they haven't received treatment we haven't really gotten anywhere.

We've made the public happy because [punishment] seems better to them [than treatment], but we haven't addressed the [underlying] issue."

> "Obviously, everyone needs treatment. Even if they've served time in jail, if they haven't received treatment we haven't really gotten anywhere. We've made the public happy because [punishment] seems better to them [than treatment], but we haven't addressed the [underlying] issue."
> — Suzanne Sigona, Director of Probation, Denver County

As sentencing and program options for a fuller range of batterers are developed, assessment tools to assist probation and the courts in assigning batterers to appropriate interventions must also be developed. Both the criminal justice-based assessment of offender risk and amenability to intervention developed by Goldkamp from his study of the Dade County Domestic Violence Court and the more detailed assessment tool used by probation in Denver's 18th Judicial District to assign batterers to risk categories suggest ways in which meaningful assessments can be made quickly with basic defendant information (see chapter 4, "Current Trends in Batterer Intervention," for a full discussion of these assessment tools).

Diversion Sends the Wrong Message

In the 1970's the United States Civil Rights Commission drew attention to the negative symbolism evoked by diverting battering cases. Today there is little controversy on this point; California recently banned the diversion of domestic violence cases.[5] In another State, in a jurisdiction where diversion is used, a guilty plea is a prerequisite for participation. Because fewer than 5 percent of cases are resolved in that manner, 95 percent of batterers are effectively excluded from program participation. As a result, batterers most likely to qualify for these "creamof-the-crop" diversion programs are better educated, middle-class professionals who accept treatment, rather than take their case to trial, in the hope of avoiding a criminal record. While diversions such as these may make sense in terms of efficient case disposition, Quincy probation chief Andrew Klein cautions, "Actions speak louder than words—diversion says battering is trivial." Other experts caution that a wide range of sentencing arrangements are swept together under the rubric of "diversion" and that some of these arrangements provide access to swift program enrollment while maintaining batterer accountability (see box, "Pittsburgh's Domestic Abuse Counseling Center," p. 85).

State Service Provider Standards Help Control Abuses but May Block Program Diversity

In 1996, 28 States and the District of Columbia had developed standards or guidelines governing programs or individuals providing batterer intervention. Another 13 States were in the process of developing standards or guidelines (see exhibit 5-2, "Information Matrix on Interventions for Batterers," and appendix A, "State Standards Matrix"). While their requirements and enforceability vary widely, most of these guidelines are designed to institutionalize current norms among mainstream batterer interventions (see chapter 3, "Pioneers in Batterer Intervention").

Most practitioners in the field welcome these controls as a deterrent to inexperienced or unethical counselors who might provide treatment without proper preparation—substance abuse counselors without domestic violence expertise, for example, who have clients that are also court- ordered batterers.

Standards and guidelines may also regulate program providers who use unconventional techniques (such as short-term programs or anger management counseling) or approaches that many consider to be dangerous to victims, such as couples counseling (see chapter 2, "The Causes of Domestic Violence").

While controls are appropriate in a field where program malfeasance may jeopardize victim safety, too little is known about the efficacy of current interventions to create standards that stifle innovation. For example, in Iowa, where State standards mandate use of the Duluth curriculum, a special exception was needed to permit Des Moines criminal justice and program staff to explore the use of a different curriculum with high-risk batterers.

Local networks of program providers and criminal justice agencies that are still in the process of developing State standards need to make a conscious effort not to stifle thoughtful attempts at innovation (as opposed to reckless disregard for accepted practices). For example, The Compassion Workshop operates in Maryland, where guidelines are still being developed, but would not be eligible for certification in many States because of the brevity of the treatment model, mixed-gender treatment groups, and nontraditional program curriculum. The program founder, Steven Stosny, is working with the committee responsible for developing standards to create a format under which his

program could operate, but he is encountering resistance among mainstream program providers to his proposal that the standards should evolve based on quasi-experimental, independent program evaluations. For example, if program evaluations showed that shorter programs—such as The Compassion Workshop—prevent recidivism as effectively as longer ones, then (according to his proposal) requirements stipulating longer treatment periods would be removed from the standards. In North Carolina, another State where standards are still under development, the Empowerment Project was not given referrals by the local court, and was thus effectively shut down, because of controversy surrounding its use of exclusively African American batterer groups and its African culture-based curriculum. The Empowerment Project has survived by shifting its efforts to training program staff in other States, but its experience illustrates that even informal constraints on practice by peers and the criminal justice system may effectively foreclose the development of new approaches to batterer intervention.

Ideally, standards should be crafted to foster innovation while providing safeguards for victims. For example, State and local boards could provide oversight for and evaluation of newly proposed interventions and integrate research findings into their required or recommended practice models. Furthermore, better evaluation of existing programming would allow standards to focus on performance-based outcomes, rather than stipulating content.

The implementation of State standards may be fraught with controversy. In Colorado, licensed professionals who do not want further requirements imposed on their practices actively oppose the training required by the standards. Some probation officers in the State express concern that standards result in a "cookie cutter" approach to batterer intervention when recent research points to the need for a diversity of approaches, increased assessment, and specialized intervention strategies. They note, however, that having no standards would be more dangerous than having overly restrictive ones. Colorado's standards are implemented by local boards in the 22 judicial districts. According to the Colorado Coalition Against Domestic Violence, two boards have been completely inactive, three districts have only one provider each—inadequate for their caseloads—and three other districts have no certified batterer intervention providers. Local boards have been sued in several districts and threatened with lawsuits in eight others because the enabling statute empowers them to certify programs but is unclear about their decertification authority.

Fear of liability and disagreements among treatment providers concerning needed credentials has limited the boards' effectiveness. In short, the adoption of standards can be a complex undertaking that may accelerate the debate surrounding batterer intervention rather than end it.

THE KEY ROLE OF PROBATION: BATTERER SUPERVISION

Probation officers are the most critical link between the criminal justice system and batterer interventions. At the five sites visited for this study, some, if not all, batterers on probation were selected for intensive supervision by specialized probation units or designated officers because officers in general probation supervision are often too overburdened to provide any meaningful supervision of batterers. However, while officers in specialized units can do a better job, many still feel concerned that their caseload prevents them from offering all the services and supervision they believe are necessary. According to Sid Hoover, supervisor of Seattle's Municipal Domestic Violence Probation Unit, "We're doing it as skimpy as you can imagine. You've got about 180–190 clients, so you've got 150 on a face-to-face supervision, and you've got 21 working days to see them all and deal with all their noncompliance and all their crazy stuff—that's not very many minutes per guy. If we tried to get involved with victim service the way we feel it should be done it would dilute [our efforts] so much that we would be opened up to liability."

With the permission of the court, Hoover had enlisted a volunteer to provide notifications and counseling to the 1,100 victims of his unit's probationers, but after extensive training, the volunteer quit without explanation. Hoover, speculating that "it would be asking too much emotionally" for a volunteer to provide this service, has decided to wait for funding for a paid victim advocate.

> "We're doing it as skimpy as you can imagine. You've got about 180–190 clients, so you've got 150 on a face-to-face supervision, and you've got 21 working days to see them all and deal with all their noncompliance and all their crazy stuff— that's not very many minutes per guy. If we tried to get involved with victim service the way we feel it should be done it would dilute [our efforts] so much that we would be opened up to liability."
>
> — Sid Hoover, Supervisor, Domestic Violence Probation Unit, Seattle

In Baltimore, prosecutors decide which batterers are referred to the Family Assault Supervision Team (FAST) and which are sent to general probation. In the FAST Unit, each probation officer supervises an average of 43 cases, for a total of 316—less than a third of all battering cases sent to probation. These reduced caseloads allow officers to work closely with victims, many of whom are illiterate and need special advocacy to help them assert their rights with criminal justice agencies. The FAST unit is able to process a warrant within 24 hours for probationers who are in violation of their sentences and to maintain weekly contact with House of Ruth to monitor batterers' progress in the program. One of the major problems probation officers face in Baltimore is how to intervene with sociopathic, extremely violent, female, or indigent probationers who are refused by the two programs in the city. One officer observed that 50 percent of her caseload was "too violent or scary" for local interventions. Faced with a lack of local programming, the FAST unit is researching how it might provide in-house batterer intervention for probationers who are terminated from House of Ruth or are not appropriate for community- based programs. FAST Field Supervisor Peggy Araya saw the planned in-house groups as "positive reinforcement that domestic violence is a crime" and a way to ensure that all batterers received some form of intervention.

In Colorado's 18th Judicial District outside of Denver, more than 90 percent of battering cases are misdemeanors and, as a result, had never received any supervision until the chief of probation decided *some* form of supervision was necessary for victim safety. The chief utilized the Deputy Probation Officer Program—a corps of 45 volunteers—to help supervise these low-risk batterers. In addition to the volunteers, who maintain small caseloads, a staff officer supervises all high-risk probationers (approximately 150 cases): a staff coordinator monitors the volunteers and screens batterers; a victim advocate attempts to contact all victims; and a consultant psychologist performs batterer risk assessment (see chapter 4, "Current Trends in Batterer Intervention," for a detailed description of the assessment tool used). The 18th Judicial District has had very positive experiences with using volunteers.

The Quincy District Court Probation Department is part of an integrated, comprehensive approach to domestic violence that emphasizes coordination among criminal justice agencies, batterer programs, substance abuse treatment programs, social services, victim advocates, and the community.[6] Key probation department policies include:

- preparation of thorough presentencing reports urging judges to impose strict probation conditions;
- establishment of the court—and the probation officer as a representative of the court—as the authority regulating the batterer' s relationship with the victim;
- maximum intensity supervision that may include weekly batterer program meetings, four weekly alcohol or substance abuse self-help meetings, one addiction counseling session, one face-to-face meeting with their probation officer, and one weekly alcohol or drug test, with the goal of almost daily contact with the probationer;

- strict monitoring of batterer program and substance abuse treatment compliance, with "compliance" requiring active participation; and
- utilization of the rules of evidence governing probation proceedings that permit hearsay testimony (for example, allowing the responding police officer to testify in lieu of the victim concerning reports of new abusive incidents), have a lower standard of proof, and place less emphasis on the accused's right to confront witnesses than the rules pertaining to criminal trials.[7]

The principal characteristics that distinguish the Quincy Probation Department from others visited for this book were its emphasis on maximum intensity probation and its focus on substance abuse as a factor that exacerbates batterer recidivism. Andrew Klein emphasized that weekly urine or alcohol tests were so important that the department would pay for them if the batterer failed to do so. Until recently, the Quincy Probation Department had a grant- funded victim advocate who assisted victims to testify at probation hearings, provided referrals, and assisted batterer programs and probation officers with victim information. However, as mentioned previously, when the probation department offices were moved to a location where victims visiting the probation-based advocate might encounter their batterers, the advocate quit her work on the grounds that she might endanger the victims.

Collaboration among Community Partners

Richard Tolman has argued that the greatest contribution batterer programs make may not be their work with individual offenders but rather their ability to bring together major actors in the criminal justice and community service sectors to work cooperatively to reduce domestic violence. In his view, cooperative efforts among criminal justice agencies, batterer interventions, victim advocates, battered women's agencies, and the community are likely to produce more significant reductions in battering than any single unit or program. Tolman also believes that much of what is important in changing social attitudes toward domestic violence lies in the coordinated and consistent messages criminal justice agencies send through their interactions with victims and batterers and in criminal justice agencies' cooperative work with community groups, schools, and batterer interventions. In this view, changing the behavior of individual batterers is only part of the larger policy objective of deterring everyone from battering their partners.

Jonathan Cohen, assistant director of the Batterers Intervention Project in New City, New York, takes this line of reasoning further. Cohen advises communities without batterer intervention programs to focus first on creating a coordinated community response to battering by involving criminal justice agencies, battered women's agencies, mental health and medical institutions, schools, businesses, religious organizations, child protective services, the media, and social service agencies. According to Cohen:

> Once you realize that coordinated community response is the level at which men's violence can be changed or stopped, it's easier to let go of one's investment in individual men changing [the aim of most batterer programs].

From a criminal justice perspective, individual change in batterers is a legitimate and important goal; however, Cohen's point—that battering may be better deterred by coordinated social and criminal justice policies than by work with individual batterers—is an important one and highlights the need to maintain a broad view of domestic violence policy while fine-tuning specific departmental policies affecting batterer programs.

This section describes formal and informal collaborations between criminal justice agencies program staff and community partners that include:

- informal monthly meetings between batterer intervention providers and probation staff;
- local task forces that coordinate and monitor citywide or regional domestic violence policies, including batterer intervention operation; and
- Statewide committees to formulate State-level standards for batterer programs and other domestic violence policies.

Informal Cooperation between Probation and Program Staff

A common form of collaboration is the informal monthly meeting between probation officers and program providers intended to provide a forum for the discussion of issues of mutual concern and to encourage communication and cooperation between criminal justice personnel and program providers. Seattle's Domestic Violence Intervention Committee (DVIC) is chaired by the chief probation officer and initially included both batterer program providers and victim advocates. These meetings between probation and program providers were especially important because they facilitated communication with a large number of treatment providers at once. In addition to meeting with their own service providers, the probation office was planning to meet with other domestic violence committees in neighboring jurisdictions at least quarterly to exchange information. Much of DVIC's work focuses on building communication among the various service providers who come into contact with batterers and their victims. For example, DVIC sponsored a conference to encourage information exchange between battered women's advocates and batterer program providers. A battered women's advocate praised the conference for providing a new perspective for advocates, saying, "It was a different language to them—one they'd never heard before. [Previously] it was hard [for us] to understand what batterer treatment providers deal with."

Discussion at one DVIC meeting focused on plans to offer a training session on batterer intervention for substance dependency providers and issues related to batterers and substance abuse. The implementation of State standards for batterer programs was also discussed, as well as plans to lobby for changes or refinements in the standards. Other topics included plans for a future meeting to focus on intervention issues relating to African Americans and plans to begin offering batterer programs for incarcerated batterers.

Local Domestic Violence Coordinating Committees

A number of communities have city- or county-level committees charged with coordinating domestic violence policy between criminal justice agencies and the social service sector. Some of these committees are policymaking bodies, while others provide a forum for exchanging information on new domestic violence procedures or programs. In some States, State standards empower local committees to certify batterer program providers.

Since 1985, the Mayor's Domestic Violence Coordinating Committee (DVCC) in Baltimore has been monitoring and coordinating the criminal justice and community response to domestic violence. The DVCC, chaired by Judge Mary Ellen Rinehardt, administrative judge for the District Court for Baltimore City, includes representatives from the local batterer intervention, probation and parole officers, law enforcement personnel, pretrial release services staff, the chief prosecutor of the State's Attorney's domestic violence unit, and a policy director from the Mayor's office. The group's central accomplishment has been to draft and continuously update the "Baltimore City Domestic Violence Policies and Procedures," guidelines that are intended to ensure that 1) domestic violence is treated as a crime, 2) the offender is held responsible, and 3) the victim is protected. Ongoing tasks of the committee include:

- adopting a uniform definition of domestic violence;
- developing a system for tracking and monitoring cases;
- developing and coordinating specialized units;
- developing and coordinating training programs;
- strengthening agency policies and procedures; and
- coordinating effort between the criminal justice system and batterer program providers.[8]

State-Level Domestic Violence Committees and Task Forces

State-level committees and task forces on domestic violence address policy issues such as how to raise funding for batterer intervention or special criminal justice units from taxes and fines, the centralization of funding for domestic violence services, and legal reforms needed to provide services to victims or hold batterers accountable. State committees are also often charged with developing drafts of standards or guidelines for the certification of batterer programs.

In Maryland, the State Standards Committee, with representatives from local criminal justice agencies, children and family services, batterer programs, and victim services agencies, discussed policy issues of general interest and together considered possible solutions to common problems. Among the topics discussed were the needs of victims who are dually diagnosed (those with substance abuse and mental health issues); enforcement of child support payments due to victims within 30 days (so that the family is not evicted); problems with the funding of children's services; dangers posed by visitation rights granted to divorced batterers; lack of funding sources for batterer programs; and the growth of national organizations that provide private defense council to accused batterers and child abusers. A subcommittee working on a draft proposal for State standards for batterer intervention presented key issues to be discussed at a full session devoted to the topic.

Conclusion

The criminal justice response to domestic violence is critical to batterer programs because interventions rely on the criminal justice support to add force to their work. The examples of probation supervision at five sites illustrate that there are many ways to approach batterer supervision. Nevertheless, probation officers in all the jurisdictions emphasized the need for:

- maintaining intensive supervision of batterers;
- developing programming options for all batterers; and
- cultivating good communication with program providers.

All the examples of cooperation discussed above contribute positively to the work of batterer interventions, but the informal meetings between batterer program providers and probation officers offer the greatest single opportunity for solving local issues affecting batterer intervention. These groups should serve as a resource for city- and State-level groups that are looking for guidance in developing local protocols or State-level standards.

References

[1] Klein, A., Editorial, National Bulletin on Domestic Violence Prevention, 2 (5) (May 1996): 1.

[2] Ibid.

[3] For a detailed description of an integrated criminal justice response to domestic violence, see Gelb, A., The Quincy Court Model Domestic Abuse Program Manual, Swampscott, MA: Production Specilaties, n.d. (See chapter 6, "Sources of Help and Information," for availability.)

[4] Interview with Edward Gondolf, October 22, 1996.

[5] Klein, A., Editorial, National Bulletin on Domestic Violence Prevention, 2 (4) (April 1996): 2.

[6] See Gelb, The Quincy Court Model Domestic Abuse Program Manual.

[7] Ibid.

[8] "Baltimore City Domestic Violence Policies and Procedures," Manual, revised 1995: 3

Chapter 6

SOURCES OF HELP AND INFORMATION

KEY POINTS

The numerous sources of additional information on batterer interventions include:

- organizations;
- reference services;
- State agencies;
- literature; and
- individual practitioners.

A number of resources are available to batterer intervention program staff and criminal justice professionals who work with batterer programs. This chapter includes:

- sources of batterer intervention training and materials;
- a listing of materials and information on battering and batterer intervention written from a criminal justice perspective;
- national organizations concerned with domestic violence that can assist criminal justice personnel and batterer intervention providers with information, training, technical assistance, or referrals;
- a directory of State coalitions on domestic violence;

- a list identifying agencies and individuals that are responsible for formulating, approving, or implementing State batterer intervention standards or guidelines;
- a list of individuals willing to share their expertise in batterer intervention, specialized interventions, and criminal justice links to batterer programs; and
- a selected bibliography, organized by topic, highlighting standard texts, new publications of interest, and key program materials.

Batterer Intervention Training and Materials

The following organizations provide training for batterer intervention personnel.

National Training Project
Duluth Domestic Abuse Training Project 206 W. Fourth Street
Duluth, MN 55806
(218) 722-2781, ext. 111
Training by the National Training Project is required for programs that wish to use the Duluth curriculum. Contact Tina Olsen, National Training Project Coordinator.

EMERGE: Counseling and Education to Stop Domestic Violence
2380 Massachusetts Avenue, Suite 101
Cambridge, MA 02140
(617) 547-9879
(617) 547-0904 (fax)
EMERGE offers four services that may be of use to practitioners:

- a four-day intensive course for counseling men who batter, which is offered several times a year and is approved for continuing education credits for social workers and alcohol counselors;
- publications on batterer intervention and working with specialized batterer populations, some of them in Spanish, which may be purchased by mail;
- information concerning an educational curriculum for adolescents available from the Dating Violence Intervention Project, an EMERGE partner; and

- a two-day intensive course for counseling adolescent batterers, offered several times per year and also approved for continuing education credits for social workers and alcohol counselors.

National Training Institute Batterers Intervention Project South Main Street
New City, New York 10956
(914) 634-5729
(914) 634-7839 (fax)
Contact: Phyllis Frank, Ph.D.

The National Training Institute provides technical assistance and professional training based on an educational approach. It provides training in all aspects of the New York State model but will tailor training to the needs of agencies from different States.

The Empowerment Project
2722 Bancroft Street
Charlotte, NC 28206
(704) 372-8878/344-9311
Contacts: Sunya Faloyan and Radhia Jaaber, cofounders

The Empowerment Project has developed a still evolving curriculum to address batterers of African descent. Program development consulting is available.

Criminal Justice Materials and Information

The following resources may assist criminal justice professionals in formulating a coordinated response to battering and in assessing batterers who are mandated to interventions.

Quincy District Court Model Domestic Violence Response Materials
Quincy Court/Polaroid Information Service P.O. Box 100
Penfield, NY 14516-9958
(800) 662-8337, ext. 62

The Quincy Court Model Domestic Abuse Program is an award-winning project that has been recognized as a national model by the National Council of

Juvenile and Family Court Judges and replicated throughout Massachusetts. Polaroid is a corporate sponsor for the production of the following informational materials and product catalogs:

- Quincy Domestic Violence Community Response Guide
- Quincy Domestic Violence Probation Response Guide
- Quincy Domestic Violence Police Response Guide
- Domestic Violence Use of Photography Overview
- Law Enforcement Product Catalog
- Law Enforcement Curriculum Guide
- Instant Evidence Domestic Violence Edition
- Kidcare Event Guide

National Criminal Justice Reference Service (NCJRS)
P.O. Box 6000
Rockville, MD 20849-6000
(800) 851-3420
E-mail: askncjrs@ncjrs_aspensys.com

NCJRS, a service sponsored by the National Institute of Justice, provides access to free government publications (including a number of those listed in the Selected Bibliography) and assistance with criminal justice research.

Criminal Justice Manuals and Videos
(800) 932-4632
The Pennsylvania Coalition Against Domestic Violence (PCADV) offers a number of criminal justice resources, including manuals, instructional videos, pamphlets, and posters. The following manuals relate to batterer intervention:

- Accountability: Program Standards for Batterer Intervention Services ($15)
- Safety for Women: Monitoring Batterers' Programs ($25/$15 for domestic violenceprograms)
- Confronting Domestic Violence: Effective Police Response ($15)
- Prosecuting Domestic Violence Crimes: A Training Guide ($35)
- Seeking Justice: Legal Advocacy Principles and Practice ($50/$40 for domestic violence programs)
- Domestic Violence Protection Orders Handbook ($15)

Domestic Violence Behavioral Checklist

Michael Lindsay and Frank Robinson have developed a copyrighted page-long checklist to assist probation officers with batterer risk assessment. For information contact:

Frank Robinson, Ph.D.
Department of Probation
18th Judicial District
1610 Littleton Boulevard Littleton,
CO 80120
(303) 794-4890

NATIONAL ORGANIZATIONS CONCERNED WITH DOMESTIC VIOLENCE

The following national organizations provide current information concerning battering, batterer intervention, and legal issues related to battering.

Battered Women's Justice Project:
(800) 903-0111

The project provides training, technical assistance, and resources through a partnership of three nationally recognized organizations. After dialing the central "800" number, callers may choose from three extensions:

- Extension #1: Domestic Abuse Intervention Project

Addresses the criminal justice sytsem's response to domestic violence, including the development of batterer programs.

(612) 824-8768 (TDD)
(612) 824-8965 (fax)

- Extension #2: Pennsylvania Coalition Against Domestic Violence

Addresses civil court access and legal representation issues of battered women. Provides comprehensive information, resources, policy development, and technical assistance designed to prevent domestic violence and to enhance community response.

(717) 671-4767
(717) 671-5542 (fax)

- Extension #3: National Clearinghouse for the Defense of Battered Women

Addresses battered women's self-defense issues.
(215) 351-0010
(215) 351-0779 (fax)

Center for the Prevention of Sexual and Domestic Violence
936 North 34th Street, Suite 200
Seattle, WA 98103
(206) 634-1903
(206)634-0115 (fax)

Provides training and educational materials (articles, videos) to the religious community on sexual abuse and domestic violence.

Health Resource Center on Domestic Violence
Family Violence Prevention Fund
383 Rhode Island Street, Suite 304
San Francisco, CA 94103-5133
(800) 313-1310
(415) 252-8991 (fax)

Provides specialized information packets designed to strengthen the health care response to domestic violence, as well as technical assistance and library services to support training and program development.

Resource Center on Child Custody and Child Protection
National Center for Juvenile and Family Court Judges
(NCJFCJ)
P.O. Box 8970
Reno, NV 89507
(800) 527-3223
(702) 784-6160 (fax)

Provides information, consultation, technical assistance, and legal research related to child protection and custody issues within the context of domestic violence.

National Clearinghouse on Marital and Date Rape
2325 Oak Street
Berkeley, CA 94708
(510) 524-1582

Provides fee-based phone consultations ($30 per year for organizations / $15 per year for individuals, plus hourly rate) offering research assistance, referral to marital rape experts, information concerning State rape laws. Speakers bureau of marital or date rape survivors. Information packet including State law chart, bibliography, and statistics, $10, prepaid.

National Coalition Against Domestic Violence
P.O. Box 18749
Denver, CO 80218
(303) 839-1852
(303) 831-9251 (fax)
Provides statistics, articles, and research assistance on domestic violence.

State Coalitions on Domestic Violence

The following coalitions may be contacted for information about local batterer interventions, shelters, and community coalitions concerned with domestic violence. In addition, many coalitions are involved with the development of batterer intervention standards or guidelines in their States.

Alabama Coalition Against Domestic Violence
P.O. Box 4762
Montgomery, AL 36101
(334) 832-4842
(334) 832-4803 (fax)

Alaska Network on Domestic Violence and Sexual Assault
130 Seward Street, Room 501
Juneau, AK 99801
(907) 586-3650
(907) 463-4493 (fax)

Arkansas Coalition Against Domestic Violence
#1 Sheriff Lane, Suite C
LittleRock,AR72114
(501) 812-0571
(501) 371-0450 (fax)

California Alliance Against Domestic Violence
619 Thirteenth Street, Suite I
Modesto, CA 95354
(209) 524-1888
(209) 524-0616 (fax)

Colorado Domestic Violence Coalition
P.O. Box 18902
Denver, CO 80218
(303) 831-9632
(303) 832-7067 (fax)

Connecticut Coalition Against Domestic Violence
135 Broad Street
Hartford, CT 06105
(860) 524-5890
(860) 249-1408 (fax)

D.C. Coalition Against Domestic Violence
P.O. Box 76069
Washington, DC 20013
(202) 783-5332
(202) 387-5684 (fax)

Delaware Coalition Against Domestic Violence
P.O. Box 847
Wilmington, DE 19899
(302) 658-2958
(302) 658-5049 (fax)

Florida Coalition Against Domestic Violence
1535 C-5 Killearn Center Boulevard
Tallahassee, FL 32308
(800) 500-1119
(904) 668-6862
(904) 668-0364 (fax)

Georgia Advocates for Battered Women and Children
250 Georgia Avenue, S.E., Suite 308
Atlanta, GA 30312
(800) 643-1212
(404) 524-3847
(404) 524-5959 (fax)

Hawaii State Coalition Against Domestic Violence
98-939 Moanalua Road
Aiea, HI 96701-5012
(808) 486-5072
(808) 486-5169 (fax)

Iowa Coalition Against Domestic Violence
1540 High Street, Suite 100
Des Moines, IA 50309-3 123
(800) 942-0333 (515) 244-8028 (515) 244-7417 (fax)

Idaho Coalition Against Sexual and Domestic Violence
200 North Fourth Street, Suite 10-K
Boise, ID 83702
(208) 384-0419
(208) 331-0687 (fax)

Illinois Coalition Against Domestic Violence
730 East Vine Street, Suite 109
Springfield, IL 62703
(217) 789-2830
(217) 789-1939 (fax)

Indiana Coalition Against Domestic Violence
2511 East 46th Street, Suite N-3
Indianapolis, IN 46205
(800) 332-7385 (317) 543-3908
(317) 568-4045 (fax)

Kansas Coalition Against Sexual and Domestic Violence
820 S.E. Quincy, Suite 416
Topeka, KS 66612
(913) 232-9784
(913) 232-9937 (fax)

Kentucky Domestic Violence Association
P.O. Box 356
Frankfort, KY 40602
(502) 875-4132
(502) 875-4268 (fax)

Louisiana Coalition Against Domestic Violence
P.O. Box 3053
Hammond, LA 70404-3053
(504) 542-4446
(504) 542-6561 (fax)

Maine Coalition for Family Crisis Services
128 Main Street
Bangor, ME 04401
(207) 941-1194
(207) 941-2327 (fax)

Maryland Network Against Domestic Violence
11501 Georgia Avenue, Suite 403
Silver Spring, MD 20902-1955
(800) MD-HELPS
(301) 942-0900
(301) 929-2589 (fax)

Massachusetts Coalition of Battered Women's Service Groups/Jane Doe Safety Fund
14 Beacon Street, Suite 507
Boston, MA 02108
(617) 248-0922
(617) 248-0902 (fax)

Michigan Coalition Against Domestic Violence
P.O. Box 16009
Lansing, MI 48901
(517) 484-2924
(517) 372-0024 (fax)

Minnesota Coalition for Battered Women
450 North Syndicate Street, Suite 122
St. Paul, MN 55104
(800) 646-0994 (in 612 Area Code)
(573) 646-6177
(573) 646-1527 (fax)

Missouri Coalition Against Domestic Violence
331 Madison Street
Jefferson City, MO 65101
(314) 634-4161
(314) 636-3728 (fax)

Mississippi State Coalition Against Domestic Violence
P.O. Box 4703
Jackson, MS 39296-4703
(800) 898-3234 (601) 981-9196
(601) 982-7372 (fax)

Montana Coalition Against Domestic Violence
P.O. Box 633
Helena, MT 59624
(406) 443-7794
(406) 449-8193 (fax)

Nebraska Domestic Violence and Sexual Assault Coalition
315 South Ninth #18
Lincoln, NE 68508-2253
(800) 876-6238 (402) 476-6256

Nevada Network Against Domestic Violence
2100 Capurro Way, Suite E
Sparks, NV 89431
(800) 500-1556
(702) 358-1171
(702) 358-0546 (fax)

New Hampshire Coalition Against Domestic and Sexual Violence
P.O. Box 353
Concord, NH 03302-0353
(800) 852-3388
(603) 224-8893
(603) 228-6096 (fax)

New Jersey Coalition for Battered Women
2620 Whitehorse/Hamilton Square Road
Trenton, NJ 08690
For Battered Lesbians: (800) 224-0211 (in NJ only)
(609) 584-8107
(609) 584-9750 (fax)

New Mexico State Coalition Against Domestic Violence
P.O. Box 25363 Albuquerque, NM 87125
(800) 773-3645 (in NM only)
(505) 246-9240 (505) 246-9434 (fax)

New York State Coalition Against Domestic Violence
79 Central Avenue
Albany, NY 12206
(800) 942-6906
(518) 432-4864
(518) 432-4864 (fax)

North Carolina Coalition Against Domestic Violence
P.O. Box 51875
Durham, NC 27717
(919) 956-9124 (919) 682-1449 (fax)

North Dakota Council on Abused Women's Services State Networking Office
418 East Rosser Avenue, Suite 320
Bismarck, ND 58501 (800)472-2911 (in ND only)
(701) 255-6240
(701) 255-1904 (fax)

Ohio Domestic Violence Network
4041 North High Street, Suite 101
Columbus, OH 43214
(800) 934-9840
(614) 784-0023
(614) 784-0033 (fax)

Oklahoma Coalition Against Domestic Violence and Sexual Assault
2200 North Classen Blvd, Suite 610
Oklahoma City, OK 73801
(800) 522-9054
(405) 557-1210
(405) 557-1296 (fax)

Oregon Coalition Against Domestic and Sexual Violence
520 Northwest Davis Street, Suite 310
Portland, OR 97204
(503) 223-7411
(503) 223-7490 (fax)

Pennsylvania Coalition Against Domestic Violence/ National Resource Center on Domestic Violence
6440 Flank Drive, Suite 1300
Harrisburg, PA 17 112-2778
(800) 932-4632
(717) 545-6400
(717) 545-9456 (fax)

Rhode Island Coalition Against Domestic Violence
422 Post Road, Suite 104
Warwick, RI 02888
(800) 494-8100
(401) 467-9940
(401) 467-9943 (fax)

South Carolina Coalition Against Domestic Violence & Sexual Assault
P.O. Box 7776
Columbia, SC 29202-7776
(800) 260-9293
(803) 750-1222
(803) 750-1246 (fax)

South Dakota Coalition Against Domestic Violence and Sexual Assault
P.O. Box 141 Pierre, SD 57401
(800) 572-9196
(605) 945-0869 (605) 945-0870 (fax)

Tennessee Task Force Against Domestic Violence
P.O. Box 120972
Nashville, TN 37212
(800) 356-6767
(615) 386-9406
(615) 383-2967 (fax)

Texas Council on Family Violence
8701 North Mopac Expressway, Suite 450
Austin, TX 78759
(512) 794-1133
(512) 794-1199 (fax)

Domestic Violence Advisory Council (Utah)
120 North 200 West
Salt Lake City, UT 84145
897-LINK
538-4100
(801) 538-3993 (fax)

Vermont Network Against Domestic Violence and Sexual Assault
P.O. Box 405 Montpelier, VT 05601
(802) 223-1302
(802) 223-6943 (fax)

Virginians Against Domestic Violence
2850 Sandy Bay Road, Suite 101
Williamsburg, VA 23185
(800) 838-VADV
(804) 221-0990
(804) 229-1553 (fax)

Washington State Coalition Against Domestic Violence
2101 Fourth Avenue East, Suite 103
Olympia, WA 98506
(800) 562-6025
(360) 352-4029
(360) 352-4078 (fax)

West Virginia Coalition Against Domestic Violence
P.O. Box 85
181B Main Street
Sutton, WV 2660 1-0085
(304) 765-2250
(304) 765-5071 (fax)

Wisconsin Coalition Against Domestic Violence
1400 East Washington Avenue, Suite 232
Madison, WI 53703
(608) 255-0539
(608) 255-3560 (fax)

Wyoming Coalition Against Domestic Violence and Sexual Assault
341 East E. Street, Suite 135A
Pinedale, WY 82601
(800) 990-3877
(307) 367-4296
(307) 235-4796 (fax)

INFORMATION CONCERNING STATE AND LOCAL STANDARDS AND GUIDELINES ON BATTERER INTERVENTION

The chart on pages 104–107 provides contact names, addresses, and telephone numbers for organizations and offices involved in administering or developing batterer intervention standards and guidelines. The information in appendix A, "State Standards Matrix," was current as of November 1996.

INDIVIDUALS

The matrix on pages 108–109 identifies individuals who have agreed to respond to telephone calls for technical assistance with batterer interventions or criminal justice linkages to batterer interventions. These individuals represent members of the project advisory board or individuals interviewed in the preparation of this book.

SELECTED BIBLIOGRAPHY

General Information

Campbell, J.C., ed. Assessing Dangerousness: Violence by Sexual Offenders, Batterers, and Child Abusers. Thousand Oaks, CA: Sage Publications, 1995.
Dutton, D. and S. Golant. The Batterer: A Psychological Profile. New York: Basic Books, 1995.
Edelson, J. and R.M. Tolman, Intervention for Men Who Batter: An Ecological Approach. Newbury Park, CA; Sage Publications, 1992.

Gelles, R. and D.R. Loseke. Current Controversies on Family Violence. Newbury Park, CA: Sage Publications, 1993.

Pence, E. and M. Paymar, Education Groups for Men Who Batter: The Duluth Model. New York: Springer, 1993.

Sirles, E.A., S. Lipchik, and K. Kowalski. "A Consumer's Perspective on Domestic Violence Interventions." Journal of Family Violence, 8(3) (1993): 267.

Stosny, S. "Treating Attachment Abuse: The Compassion Workshop." In Treating Abusiveness, ed. Donald Dutton. New York: Guilford, 1996.

Straus, M., R. Gelles, and S. Steinmetz. Behind Closed Doors: Violence in the American Family. New York: Doubleday, 1980.

Straus, M. and R. Gelles, eds. Physical Violence in American Families: Risk Factors and Adaptions to Violence in 8,145 Families. New Brunswick, NJ: Transaction Publishers, 1990.

Yllo, K. and M. Bograd. Feminist Perspectives on Wife Abuse. Newbury Park, CA: Sage Publications, 1988.

Resources for Practitioners

Adams, D., L. Bancroft, T. German, and C. Sousa. Program Manual: First State Groups for Men Who Batter. Quincy, MA: EMERGE, 1992.

Davies, J. Using Safety Planning As an Approach to Woman-Defined Advocacy. Legal Aid Society of Hartford County, CT, 1994.

Ganley, A. "Understanding Domestic Violence." InImproving the Health Care Response to Domestic Violence: A Resource Manual for Health Care Providers. Harrisburg, PA: Family Violence Prevention Fund and the Pennsylvania Coalition Against Domestic Violence, n.d.

Massachusetts Coalition ofBattered Women Service Groups. For Shelter and Beyond: Ending Violence Against Women and Their Children, 2d ed. Boston: Massachusetts Coalition of Battered Women Service Groups, n.d.

Sousa, C., L. Bancroft, and T. German. "Preventing Teen Dating Violence: A Three Session Curriculum for Teaching Adolescents." Cambridge, MA: Dating Violence Intervention Project, n.d.

State of Iowa. Final Report of the Supreme Court Task Force on Courts' and Communities' Response to Domestic Abuse. State of Iowa, submitted to the Supreme Court of Iowa, August 1994.

Criminal Justice Issues

Buzawa, E. and C. Buzawa. Do Arrests and Restraining Orders Work? Thousand Oaks, CA: Sage Publications, 1996.

Buzawa, E. and C. Buzawa. Domestic Violence, The Criminal Justice Response, 2d ed. Thousand Oaks, CA: Sage Publications, 1996.

Hamberger, K.L. andJ.E. Hastings. "Court-Mandated Treatment of Men Who Assault Their Partner: Issues, Controversies, and Outcomes." In Legal Responses to Wife Assault, ed. N. Z. Hilton, Newbury Park, CA: Sage Publications, 1993: 188–229.

James, N. "Domestic Violence: A History of Arrest Policies and a Survey of Modern Laws." Family Law Quarterly, 28 (3) (1994): 509–515.

Rosenfeld, B.D. "Court-Ordered Treatment of Spouse Abuse." Clinical Psychology Review, 12 (1992): 205–226.

Syers, M. and J. Edelson. "The Combined Effects of Coordinated Criminal Justice Intervention in Woman Abuse." Journal of Interpersonal Violence, 7: 490–502.

Specialized Populations and Intervention Strategies

Browne, K., D.G. Saunders, and K.M. Staecker. "ProcessPsychodynamic Groups for Men Who Batter: Description of a Brief Treatment Model." Unpublished Manuscript, University of Michigan, January 26, 1996.

Busey, T. "Treatment of Women Defendants." The Catalyst (Spring 1993): 3–4.

Busey, T. "Women Defendants and Reactive Survival Syndrome." The Catalyst (Winter 1993): 6–7.

Coleman, V.E. "The Relation Between Personality and Perpetration of Violence." Violence and Victims, 9 (2) (1994): 141.

Dutton, D. "Trauma Symptoms and PTSD-like Profiles in Perpetrators of Intimate Abuse." Journal of Traumatic Stress, 8(2) (1995): 299–3 16.

Hamberger, K.L. and T. Potente. "Counseling Heterosexual Women Arrested for Domestic Violence: Implication for Theory and Practice." Violence and Victims, 9 (2) (1994): 125–137.

Holtzworth-Munroe, A. and G.L. Stuart. "Typology of Male Batterers: Three Subtypes and the Differences Among Them." Psychological Bulletin, 116 (3) (1994): 476–497.

Goldkamp, J.S. "The Role of Drug and Alcohol Abuse in Domestic Violence and Its Treatment: Dade County's Domestic Violence Court Experiment," Final Report. Philadelphia: Crime and Justice Research Institute, June 1996.

Island, D. and P. Letellier. Men Who Beat the Men Who Love Them: Battered Gay Men and Domestic Violence. New York: Harrington Park Press, n.d.

Saunders, D. "Husbands Who Assault: Multiple Profiles Requiring Multiple Responses." In Legal Responses to Wife Assault, ed. N.Z. Hilton, Newbury Park, CA: Sage Publications, 1993.

Saunders, D. "A Typology of Men Who Batter: Three Types Derived from a Cluster Analysis." American Journal of Orthopsychiatry, 62 (2) (1992): 264–275.

Williams, O. "Ethnically Sensitive Practice to Enhance Treatment Participation of African American Men Who Batter." Families in Society: The Journal of Contemporary Human Services (1992): 588–595.

Williams, O. and R.L. Becker. "Domestic Partner Abuse Treatment Programs and Cultural Competence: The Results of a National Survey." Violence and Victims, 9 (3) (1994): 287–296.

Government Publications Related to Domestic Violence

Bureau of Justice Statistics. Domestic Violence: Violence Between Intimates, Selected Findings. Washington, DC: U.S. Department of Justice, November 1994. (NCJ- 149259)

Fein, R.A., B. Vossekuil, and G. Holden. "Threat Assessment: An Approach to Prevent Targeted Violence." Research in Action Series. Washington, DC: National Institute of Justice, September 1995.

Hofford, M. and A. Harrell. Family Violence: Interventions for the Justice System, Program Brief. Washington, DC: Bureau of Justice Assistance, October 1993. (NCJ-144532)

Langhan, P.A. and C.A. Innes. Preventing Domestic Violence Against Women. Washington, DC: U.S. Department of Justice, Bureau of Justice Statistics, 1986.

National Institute of Justice. Domestic Violence, Stalking, and Anti-Stalking Legislation, An Annual Report to Congress under the Violence Against Women Act. Washington, DC: U.S. Department of Justice, April 1996.

Program Evaluation

Chen, H., C. Bersani, S.C. Myers, and R. Denton. "Evaluating the Effectiveness of a Court-Sponsored Abuser Treatment Program." Journal of Family Violence, 4 (1989): 309–322.

Davis, R.C. and B.G. Taylor. "Does Batterer Treatment Reduce Violence? A Synthesis of the Literature." Victim Services Research, New York, NY. Unpublished Manuscript, July1997.

Davis,R.C. andB.G. Taylor. "AProactiveResponseto Family Violence: The Results of a Randomized Experiment." Criminology,35 (2) (1997): 307–333.

Dobash, R., R.E. Dobash, K. Cavanagh, and R. Lewis. "Re- Education Programs for Violent Men—An Evaluation." Research Findings, 46 (1996): 1–4.

Dutton, D.G. "The Outcome of Court-Mandated Treatment for Wife Assault: A Quasi-Experimental Evaluation." Violence and Victims, 1(3) (1986): 163–175.

Edelson, J.L. and M. Syers. "Relative Effectiveness of Group Treatments for Men Who Batter." Social Work Research and Abstracts (June 1990): 10–17.

Gondolf, E.. "Batterer Intervention: What We Know and What We Need to Know." Paper presented at the Violence Against Women Strategic Planning Meeting, sponsored by the National Institute of Justice, Washington, DC, March 31, 1995.

Gondolf, E. "Multi-Site Evaluation of Batterer Intervention Systems: A Summary of Preliminary findings." Working Paper, Mid-Atlantic Addiction Training Institute, October 24, 1996.

Hamberger, K.L. and J.E. Hastings. "Recidivism Following Spouse Abuse Abatement Counseling: Treatment Program Implications." Violence and Victims, 5 (3) (1990): 157–170.

Harrell, A. Evaluation of Court Ordered Treatment for Domestic Violence Offenders, Final Report. Washington, DC: The Urban Institute, October 1991.

Palmer, S.E., R.A. Brown, and M.E. Barrera. "Group Treatment Program for Abusive Husbands: Long-Term Evaluation." American Journal of Orthopsychiatry, 62(2) (1992): 276–283.

Saunders, D.G. "Interventions for Men Who Batter: Do We Know What Works? In Session: Psychotherapy in Practice, 2 (3) (1996): 8 1–93.

APPENDIX A.
STATE STANDARDS MATRIX

APPENDIX A. 1

Alabama
Alaska
Arizona
Arkansas
California, Los Angeles County
California, San Diego County
Colorado
Connecticut
District of Columbia (D.C.)
Delaware
Florida

Information Matrix on Interventions for Batterers

	Status of Standards or Guidelines	Certifying Agency	Intervals for Certification/Fee
Alabama	guidelines & standards for membership to Alabama Association of Violence Intervention Programs standards for member agencies operating Family Violence Intervention programs, draft as of May 10, 1996	Alabama Association of Violence Intervention Programs	3 years; renewal application must be submitted at least 90 days prior to expiration
Alaska	standards for programs approved by the Council on Domestic Violence and Sexual Assault, working w/ Department of Corrections to incorporate Council on Domestic Violence and Sexual Assault's approved standards	Council on Domestic Violence and Sexual Assault, Department of Public Safety	every 2 years
Arizona	none	_	_
Arkansas	none	_	_
California, Los Angeles County	standards (by county)	County Departments of Probation and Parole	initial application of $250 per site; annual renewal fee of $250 per site required in July each year
California, San Diego County	standards (by county)	Treatment Evaluation and Monitoring Committee on behalf of Probation Department, District Attorney's and City Attorney's Domestic Violence Units	reevaluations required every 2 years unless earlier reevaluation needed as result of complaint or violation of standards
Colorado	standards	local Certification Board - appointed pursuant to Section 18-6-802, 8B C.R.S. (1988 Supp.)	programs must perform at satisfactory level or subject to conditional certification; failure to comply w/ conditions w/in timeframe is grounds for decertification
Connecticut	none	_	_

Information Matrix on Interventions for Batterers (Continued)

	Status of Standards or Guidelines	Certifying Agency	Intervals for Certification/Fee
D.C.	standards*	–	–
Delaware	protocol of standards in development (draft)	n/a	no current certification process but recommend one be implemented; if none adopted, standards should provide measure
Florida	standards	Department of Corrections	$300 per applicant, $100 per assessor; annual monitoring visits will determine continuation of certification

Key: SA = Substance Abuse;
MH = Mental Health;
Psych. Eval. = Psychiatric Evaluation;
*Text not yet available.

Information Matrix on Interventions for Batterers (Continued)

STATE	Court Contact/ Referrals	Length of Treatment	Screening Criteria
Alabama	written notice to courts of perpetrator noncompliance; whenever action to limit/deny admission to program, or revoke/refuse certification renewal, written notice made to referring courts, probation officers and Alabama Coalition Against Domestic Violence	minimum of 24 hours, each session not less than 2 hours in length	history of abuse/violence, alcohol/drug abuse, criminal history, mental illness; problems w/ parenting; family history; lethality
Alaska	open communication & working relationships w/ court system, probation, law enforcement	minimum of 24 wks w/ wkly group participation; monitor for recidivism of abuse for period of not less than 12 months following completion of program	assess batterer violence profile; SA issues; psych. eval.; police records, legal pleadings, court orders, victim interview; lethality assessment
Arizona	–	–	–
Arkansas	–	–	–
California, Los Angeles County	written referrals from probation, courts permitting enrollment; provide to probation/courts progress reports every 3 mos. or as ordered; immediate reports if program finds defendant unsuitable; proof of enrollment w/in 30 days of conviction	complete no fewer than 52 wkly group sessions within 15 months - meet for min. 2 hrs w/ no more than 10 minutes for breaks	assess socioeconomic situation; family/community background; education; criminal, medical, vocational, SA histories; age; current offense; treatment history; motivation to recover; lethality; history of violence

Information Matrix on Interventions for Batterers (Continued)

STATE	Court Contact/ Referrals	Length of Treatment	Screening Criteria
California, San Diego County	if probation granted, or execution or imposition of sentence is suspended, defendant must complete program; notification of disposition/plan to referral source - Probation Officer, Prosecuting District Attorney, Prosecuting City Attorney	minimum of one year w/ minimum of 30 sessions - one session weekly for first 24 weeks, one session monthly for last 6 months	initial intake evaluation - SA, profile of violent behavior, psych. eval., assessment of potential to harm, medical history, social/psychological/cultural history
Colorado	court-ordered referrals; notification to probation department/supervisory authority of termination/completion of program	minimum of 36 sessions meeting weekly but can be reduced to 24 weekly sessions at discretion of program provider	intake evaluation - SA, violence profile, psych. eval., medical history, assess power/control issues, social/psych/cultural history
Connecticut	–	–	–
D.C.	–	–	–
Delaware	volunteered for program, court-ordered, referred from other agency	16 sessions over 20 wk period or 24 sessions over 30 wks; each session min. of 1 hr - preferred length 90 minutes - 2hrs	SA, MH, learning capacity evaluation; history of violence; lethality assessment; assess other abusive behavior
Florida	court, self, and employer referral	24 group sessions completed within at least 32 weeks - each session will be 1.5 hrs for a total of 36 hrs	intake assessment and orientation; SA, MH, and mental capacity evaluated

Key: SA = Substance Abuse;
MH = Mental Health;
Psych. Eval. = Psychiatric Evaluation;
*Text not yet available.

Information Matrix on Interventions for Batterers (Continued)

STATE	Additional Treatment/Referrals	Staff Education/Training	Staffing Requirements
Alabama	referrals made for SA treatment; admission delayed in case of mental instability; additional treatment may be necessary but cannot replace family violence intervention	experience working w/ perpetrators; supervisors/consultants min. MA/MS in counseling, social work, psych, related field; personnel w/ at least 3 yrs exp. w/ victims & perpetrators; person w/ 2 yrs group facilitation; 24 hrs training intervention program	violence free; drug free; no criminal convictions; reflect ethnic & linguistic minorities within community
Alaska	referral to appropriate treatment program for SA - may be prior to, or concurrent w/ participation in batterer program	supervisory staff - training/1 yr experience working w/ victims & perpetrators; trained in male role belief system, impact of racism, sexism, homophobia; min 40 hrs training on domestic violence by local victim advocacy program	violence free for min. 3 yrs; no felony convictions; no convictions for drug use/misdemeanor assault; ability to work in multicultural environment
Arizona	_	_	_
Arkansas	_	_	_

Information Matrix on Interventions for Batterers (Continued)

STATE	Additional Treatment/Referrals	Staff Education/Training	Staffing Requirements
California, Los Angeles County	concurrent SA treatment/detoxification if needed	knowledge of spousal, child, sexual, & SA; knowledge of subjects w/in curriculum; ability to confront batterers; cultural/ethnic sensitivity training	nonsexist, respectful attitudes/actions; agency authorization to facilitate groups; avoid violence, use of drugs, intimate relationships w/ clients, sexual harassment, conflicts of interest
California, San Diego County	referrals determined by Treatment Evaluation and Monitoring Committee, SA treatment not a substitute for domestic violence treatment	Licensed: Master's/Doctorate degree in human service clinical field. Unlicensed: attend 24 hrs in-service training, develop intervention skills; demonstrate minimum of 24 hrs formal domestic violence training in programs approved by Committee (yearly)	meet standards outlined by professional groups w/ which affiliated; violence free; free of criminal convictions; no SA; do not maintain sexist/victim blaming attitudes; follow standards outlined in *Tarasoff* v. *Board of Regents* and other related rulings
Colorado	referrals to SA treatment but not substitution for intervention; separate sessions but content may be combined	entry - BA/BS human srvc. area, total 155- 169 hrs domestic violence/counseling related areas; counselors - 800 hrs direct client contact, 200 hrs in certified prgm w/in 6 mos.; supervisor - additional 3+ yrs exp., licensed; all - 24 hrs continuing educ.	should reflect diversity of community; meet standards outlined by affiliated professional groups; violence free; free of criminal convictions; no substance abuse; do not maintain sexist/victim blaming attitudes; report suspected abuse & danger to victim
Connecticut	–	–	–

Information Matrix on Interventions for Batterers (Continued)

STATE	Additional Treatment/Referrals	Staff Education/Training	Staffing Requirements
D.C.	_	_	_
Delaware	recommendations made for SA intervention; SA/MH treatment not ordered or provided in lieu of domestic violence treatment but may be concurrent if conducted on outpatient basis	facilitators w/ BA/BS, supervisors w/ MA/MS social sciences/srvcs.; 104 hrs experience w/in 6 months.; 40 hrs victim-centered training; 40 hrs batterer intervention training; 4 hrs court hearings on domestic violence; 12 hrs continuing educ. annually	violence free; free of recent criminal convictions; do not perpetuate sexist attitudes; refrain from victim-blaming; do not abuse drugs/alcohol
Florida	individual concurrent counseling allowed for diagnosed psychiatric disorder; SA or MH treatment not provided in place of intervention - concurrent on outpatient basis	facilitators - BA/BS or 2 yrs exp., 78 hrs direct contact w/in 6 mos, 40 hrs victim-centered training; trainees - 27 hrs approved intervention & 4 hrs drug abuse training, 4 hrs riding w/ law enforcement/4 hrs court visit; 12 hrs continuing educ. yrly	criminal background check; drug-free; compliance w/ sexual harassment policy; violence free

Key: SA = Substance Abuse;
MH = Mental Health;
Psych. Eval. = Psychiatric Evaluation;
*Text not yet available.

Information Matrix on Interventions for Batterers (Continued)

STATE	Structure	Prescribed Curriculum	Prohibited Methods/ Theories
Alabama	group processing approach using education, intervention; minimum of 2 facilitators (prefer male & female), average of 15 members	identify, discuss, confront, change abusive behavior & effects from violence; confront excuses; discuss anger & ways to manage it; non-cooperative/abusive communication & ways to change; identify cultural/social influences which contrib. to abuse/violence	couples/marital counseling or mediation; individualized intervention not recognized modality; any methods that place responsibility for perpetrator behavior on victim
Alaska	educational group format - "homework" outside of group sessions; confrontation as part of counseling model; cofacilitation - recommend male & female, one facilitator may be from the victim advocate program	dynamics of domestic violence - power/control, consequences of abuse/violence, belief systems supporting domestic violence, alternatives to violence/abuse; taking responsibility; prohibition of victim blaming; role of sexism, stereotypes; partnership	couples/relationship counseling inappropriate until minimum 6 months free of violence/coercion
Arizona	–	–	–
Arkansas	–	–	–

Information Matrix on Interventions for Batterers (Continued)

STATE	Structure	Prescribed Curriculum	Prohibited Methods/ Theories
California, Los Angeles County	same gender group sessions w/ 15 persons or less (may grow to 20 persons only if there is a cofacilitator; group discussion & lecture supplemented w/ group interaction)	gender roles; socialization; nature of violence; dynamics of power & control; effects of abuse on children/others; confront victim blaming, sexism, dehumanizing; accountability; alternatives to violence	couples & family counseling
California, San Diego County	group treatment - providers decide if open or closed; range from minimum of 4 to maximum of 12 batterers; individual treatment for those who are actively psychotic	patterns of/cycle of violence, family patterns, time-outs, myths & beliefs on provocation, control plan, tactics of power and control, anger management and aggressive behavior, stress management, sex role socialization, conflict resolution, communication	approach/practice which blames, intimidates, endangers victim; ventilation, punching pillows, hitting w/ batakas (foam bats); couples or family therapy only after prescribed treatment completed
Colorado	group therapy - maximum of 12 participants; up to program if open or closed	psychoeducational - definition of cycle/violence, time-outs, provocation, methods of control, anger/stress management, sex role training, conflict resolution, communication, taking responsibility, attitudes toward opposite sex, effects of violence	blaming/endangering victim; ventilation techniques; couples, family therapy only appropriate after victim safety ensured

Information Matrix on Interventions for Batterers (Continued)

STATE	Structure	Prescribed Curriculum	Prohibited Methods/ Theories
Connecticut	–	–	–
D.C.	–	–	–
Delaware	psychoeducational - separate groups for adults & adolescents, of same gender; individual counseling recommended based on ongoing assessment; maximum 10-15 members per 1 facilitator, no more than 20 per 2 facilitators (may be 1 male, 1 female)	responsibility; define domestic violence; cycle of violence; behavior & cues; communication/articulation of feelings; problem-solving; conflict resolution; stress management; self-esteem; stereotypes; support systems; sociocultural basis	couples, marriage, family therapy prior to batterer assessment; male dominance; misuse of systems theory - blaming victim; violence as addiction; fair fighting techniques
Florida	maximum group size is 15 per one facilitator w/ no more than 24 group members per two facilitators; may be co- facilitated by a male and female but not mandatory; groups are open (accepting new members on ongoing basis); groups must be same gender	take responsibility; define; erase myths; cycle of violence; identify behavior/cues, communicate; improve problem-solving, conflict resolution, stress management, self-esteem; challenge stereotypes; improve support systems; explore social/cultural basis	those who blame/intimidate/ endanger victim, require victim participation; couple, marriage or family therapy prohibited during psychoeducational phase; psychodynamic intervention; anger management; communication enhancement; systems theory

Key: SA = Substance Abuse;
MH = Mental Health;
Psych. Eval. = Psychiatric Evaluation;
*Text not yet available.
*Text not yet available

Information Matrix on Interventions for Batterers (Continued)

STATE	Contact w/ Victim	Fee for Service
Alabama	work cooperatively w/ victims/family violence programs; develop safety plan w/ victims; ensure victim awareness of available resources	client's financial responsibility - must define payment policy including provisions for indigent clients; may charge intake/evaluation separate from services; may charge separate fee per session; may negotiate deferred payment/partial payment plans
Alaska	regular safety checks, refer all victims to local victim advocacy agency, notify of batterer progress, gather information for lethality assessment	batterers required to pay fee - nonpayment by clients results in noncompliance status; fee determined on sliding scale as long as scale reflects comprehensive level of service
Arizona	–	–
Arkansas	–	–
California, Los Angeles County	inform that defendant in program, victim resource information available	sliding fee schedule - defendants not blocked from attending for failure to pay but may be returned to court for violation hearing
California, San Diego County	develop safety and protection plan in consideration of victim's unique circumstances - giving victim information, procedures, steps, alternative actions in order to maximize safety and protection	all clients must pay fee - on a sliding scale
Colorado	coordination between defendant and victim therapists highly recommended w/in laws of confidentiality; crisis management - for victim safety, contact through victim advocate or therapist if possible	accepted into program regardless of ability to pay - sliding scale

Information Matrix on Interventions for Batterers (Continued)

STATE	Contact w/ Victim	Fee for Service
Connecticut	–	–
D.C.	–	–
Delaware	develop safety plan - regular contact (victim liaison should be of same gender as victim), offer referrals/assistance, inform of batterer status in group, report threats of violence	fee for services (including initial assessment) no matter how minimal should be assessed
Florida	victim contact by providers required; victim's prerogative to participate; contact intended to show that someone has concern for victim and those affected, and does not blame the victim for the violence	based on sliding scale - suggested that programs assess wkly fees from $5 to $50 based on participant ability to pay; mandated one-time fee of $30 to be assessed on each court-ordered program participant

Key: SA = Substance Abuse;
MH = Mental Health;
Psych. Eval. = Psychiatric Evaluation;
*Text not yet available.

APPENDIX A.2

Georgia
Hawaii
Iowa
Idaho
Illinois
Indiana
Kansas
Kentucky
Louisiana
Maine
Maryland
Massachusetts

Information Matrix on Interventions for Batterers

STATE	Status of Standards or Guidelines	Certifying Agency	Intervals for Certification/Fee
Georgia	recommended protocol, not State-mandated	no certification but monitored by network of local domestic violence programs; letter of recommendation from local domestic violence program for families	n/a
Hawaii	standards, not State-mandated (draft in final review)	none to date	n/a
Iowa	standards	Department of Corrections	2 year accreditation; no fee mentioned; if below standards, given timeframe to bring deficiencies into compliance
Idaho	minimum guidelines, not State-mandated	–	–
Illinois	standards	Department of Public Aid	compliance packages reviewed & if passed, placed on list, renewal dates/procedures explained only after passing
Indiana	protocol, by county	Office of the Prosecuting Attorney, Marion County	no certification - group counseling w/ programs approved by the diversion coordinator
Kansas	none	–	–
Kentucky	standards*	Department of MH	–

Information Matrix on Interventions for Batterers (Continued)

STATE	Status of Standards or Guidelines	Certifying Agency	Intervals for Certification/Fee
Louisiana	minimum standards (not State-mandated - voluntary) released October 1996	–	–
Maine	minimum standards in development 4th draft, September 13, 1996	Department of Public Safety - on temporary basis until final standards adopted	(no specific information given)
Maryland	in development	–	–
Massachusetts	standards	Department of Public Health	valid for 2 years; renewal application must be submitted no later than 60 days prior to expiration

Key: SA = Substance Abuse;
MH = Mental Health;
Psych. Eval. = Psychiatric Evaluation;
*Text not yet available.

Information Matrix on Interventions for Batterers (Continued)

STATE	Court Contact/ Referrals	Length of Treatment	Screening Criteria
Georgia	program should not be in lieu of criminal punishment	at least 6 months	SA, admission of perpetration of domestic violence, desire to change
Hawaii	establish working relationship w/ courts, esp. probation and family service departments, and local police departments	attend no fewer than 40 hours - individual sessions no less than 1.5 hrs long	intake evaluation no longer than 8 sessions (component of total 40 hr program) - evaluate for SA, mental illness
Iowa	courts, correctional institutions or Judicial District Dept. of Correctional Services; institutional counselors; voluntary participants or from other referral source	Duluth Curriculum of 24 weekly sessions (recommended), minimum of 16 session model w/ 2 sessions on each theme	intake evaluation - SA, compatibility to program (can turn away batterer), history of violence/abuse, MH problems
Idaho	–	–	–
Illinois	expected that providers accept majority of court referrals (as conditions of sentencing rather than diversion)	recommend 16 weeks - at least 32 hours of intervention (may include individual counseling but emphasis should be on group)	intake evaluation - background on family, relationships, criminal history, use of violence/abusive behavior, MH, SA, risk to victim/others
Indiana	referrals made by Prosecutor's Office as "last resort" - full prosecution more appropriate in other cases; diversion coordinator acts as liason between court and service providers for purpose of reporting defendants' participation in batterer groups	6 wk program - only "in cases in which victim and defendant do not have an ongoing relationship"; 26 wk group sessions offered by counseling agencies	intake screen - no mental illness, SA, prior convictions; victim was not pregnant at time of crime; victim does not object - only means of victim cooperation; no previous attacks w/in previous 12 months
Kansas	–	–	–

Information Matrix on Interventions for Batterers (Continued)

STATE	Court Contact/ Referrals	Length of Treatment	Screening Criteria
Kentucky	–	–	–
Louisiana	–	–	–
Maine	referred to programs by the courts; program involvement w/ local law enforcement, judicial system, health & human services, schools; programs report status of participant to court/probation	48 wks, weekly sessions at least 90 minutes long	evaluate history of SA, psychiatric illness, infliction of abuse, police reports; degree of possessiveness of victim; access to weapons
Maryland	–	–	–
Massachusetts	must report noncompliance to court, report SA problem to Probation Officer and court, progress reports made to court to determine probation status	80 hours, w/ individual sessions of 1.5 - 2 hours; intake session shall be no longer than 8 sessions and considered a component of the total 80 hours	intake evaluation - family history, history of SA, psychiatric illness, infliction of abuse/violence, police reports, possession/access to weapons, degree of possessiveness toward victim, lethality

Key: SA = Substance Abuse;
MH = Mental Health;
Psych. Eval. = Psychiatric Evaluation;
*Text not yet available.

Information Matrix on Interventions for Batterers (Continued)

STATE	Additional Treatment/Referrals	Staff Education/Training	Staffing Requirements
Georgia	should not replace or interfere w/ addressing abusive behavior; referrals made for additional treatment	instructors working >20 hrs wk must complete 40 hrs orientation before working unsupervised; staff working <20 hrs wk must complete 20 hrs orientation; ongoing training/supervision by domestic violence experts	–
Hawaii	treatment for SA or other problems may be deemed necessary for total treatment but must not replace treatment for domestic violence	Master's/Doctorate human services clinical field w/ 1 yr experience as therapist w/ supervision; Bachelor's w/ 3 yrs experience in case management/group therapy w/ supervision; receive minimum of 50 hrs training; 24 hrs continuing education in counseling	violence free, no violence or criminal convictions for minimum of 5 yrs; do not perpetuate sexist/victim-blaming attitudes; do not abuse drugs/alcohol; staff composition should reflect diversity of community served
Iowa	SA addressed prior to or in conjunction w/ batterer treatment, referrals made to other agencies, cannot be substituted for batterer program	facilitators must complete training (20 hrs) on dynamics of domestic violence, overview of Duluth Model; observe minimum of 3 batterer classes; train on conducting intake interviews (optional); local ongoing training as program needs develop	selection based on understanding of domestic violence issues; involvement from local coalition & domestic violence project
Idaho	–	–	–

Information Matrix on Interventions for Batterers (Continued)

STATE	Additional Treatment/Referrals	Staff Education/Training	Staffing Requirements
Illinois	SA addressed prior to/in conjunction with programming; referrals to other agencies should be initiated; additional treatment should not be substituted for batterer program	training on domestic violence, legal issues, facilitation skills, batterer characteristics, victim safety/sensitivity, assessment/intake skills; staff receive support from battered women's program; inexperienced staff have intensive supervision	meet standards outlined by affiliated professional groups; violence free; do not perpetuate victim-blaming, sexism, racism, homophobia, classism; report all allegations of abuse
Indiana	providers must submit written recommendation to the court; providers should be prepared to continue to monitor secondary participation; SA treatment will carry on in conjunction w/ batterer treatment (unless inpatient treatment is necessary)	should have minimum of 2 years experience in area of domestic violence or meet standards outlined by professional groups	safety is first priority, violence free
Kansas	–	–	–
Kentucky	–	–	–
Louisiana	–	–	–
Maine	(to be developed)	programs shall adopt curriculum of training for all staff & volunteers; plan for ongoing staff development (more training information to be developed)	violence free, no history of domestic violence/abuse unless director satisfied (completed program & violence free for 3 yrs, or 7 yrs if did not complete program)

Information Matrix on Interventions for Batterers (Continued)

STATE	Additional Treatment/Referrals	Staff Education/Training	Staffing Requirements
Maryland	–	–	–
Massachusetts	additional treatment not to replace intervention for domestic violence; referrals made to outside agencies or serviced within program	experience w/ domestic violence perpetrators; supervisors - 3 yrs/more grp. facilitation, clinical experience; all have min. 24 hrs DPH domestic violence training; leaders observe at least 6 group sessions; ongoing training on sexism, racism, homophobia	violence free; training on how to interview/assess people for intervention work; substance free; no criminal record; orientation to acquaint w/ program; reflect ethnic, linguistic makeup of community served

Key: SA = Substance Abuse;
MH = Mental Health;
Psych. Eval. = Psychiatric Evaluation;
*Text not yet available.

Information Matrix on Interventions for Batterers (Continued)

STATE	Structure	Prescribed Curriculum	Prohibited Methods/ Theories
Georgia	group/classroom format to provide accountability and confrontation	focus on immediate behavioral change, nature of/effects of domestic violence, develop safety planning, nonviolent conflict resolution, communication, community service, change, contribution - Duluth Model	traditional therapy for batterers - stress management, anger control, insight therapy, couples therapy
Hawaii	group educational sessions - suggested maximum of 15 same-sex participants	identification, confrontation, change of abusive behavior; effects of violence; confrontation of excuses; learning cooperative/nonabusive communication; identification of cultural/social influences	initial couples/family counseling; blaming victim; lessening batterer responsibility; stand-alone treatment - anger management, systems theory, addiction counseling, containment, de-escalation
Iowa	single sex, heterosexual, group education, cofacilitated by male/female teams	focus on responsibility for violence and use of power and control, Duluth Men's Education Program Model, support groups should not be organized in lieu of education groups	traditional couples/family therapy not most appropriate treatment
Idaho	–	–	–
Illinois	groups are primary format, w/ male- female cofacilitation; individualized plans to meet participant needs	definitions of abuse, safety planning, attitude and belief changes, skill development for nonabusive behavior, social change - taking responsibility to change social environment/community	traditional couples and family therapy inappropriate as primary intervention - joint intervention may be referred only as means to help couples work out other issues and not for treatment of battering

Information Matrix on Interventions for Batterers (Continued)

STATE	Structure	Prescribed Curriculum	Prohibited Methods/ Theories
Indiana	group treatment - single-sex; individual counseling only available in conjunction with the educational group	education around provocation, cycle of violence, SA (or make referrals to agencies)	–
Kansas	–	–	–
Kentucky	–	–	–
Louisiana	–	–	–
Maine	designed for men who batter women & her children; male & female cofacilitators	accountability for abusive behavior	–
Maryland	–	–	–
Massachusetts	group educational sessions - maximum of 15 same-gender participants	change of abusive and controlling behaviors; discussion of effects of violence/abuse on victims and others; confrontation of excuses; practice of cooperative, nonabusive communication; identification of social/cultural influences contributing to abuse	couple/conjoint counseling inappropriate initially; causality in past; communication enhancement, anger management, systems theory, violence as addiction, family therapy, containment, de-escalation, poor impulse control, psychopathology, fair fighting

Key: SA = Substance Abuse;
MH = Mental Health;
Psych. Eval. = Psychiatric Evaluation;
*Text not yet available.

Information Matrix on Interventions for Batterers (Continued)

STATE	Contact w/ Victim	Fee for Service
Georgia	contact w/ shelters and coalitions, contact if victim in imminent danger	sliding scale
Hawaii	–	sliding scale
Iowa	attempt to contact - explore safety issues, options available, referral to domestic violence project for shelter and legal advocacy; inform of batterer status	fee scale established by Judicial District Department of Correctional Services, batterers may perform community service in lieu of full payment but should pay nominal fee for programming
Idaho	–	–
Illinois	collaboration w/ domestic violence programs, warn victim of potential danger, determine safety of victim, assess batterers abusive behavior, link to victim services, develop safety plan	payment for service except for those unable to pay, based on sliding scale or alternative system established by service provider
Indiana	open channels of communication w/ victims, support groups in which victim is participating, law enforcement, social service providers; routinely contact to verify victim safety; victims able to address court with own sentencing recommendations	$75 diversion fee ($50 diversion + $25 user fee) for all accepted into program plus counseling costs. Flat $150 for defendants who participate in 6-wk program. 26-wk sessions charged on sliding scale based on income.
Kansas	–	–
Kentucky	–	–
Louisiana	–	–

Information Matrix on Interventions for Batterers (Continued)

STATE	Contact w/ Victim	Fee for Service
Maine	only in consultation w/ battered women's program;should not seek information from partner; should contact to warn of danger to victim, to inform of batterer participation & how to get more information, to encourage use of local domestic violence services	program may charge fee - sliding scale, victims should not be expected to pay, batterer pays, community service may be required in lieu of fee when batterer cannot pay, probation officer notified if failure to pay
Maryland	–	–
Massachusetts	confidential interview - provide information on program, update on client status, history of abuse/violence, limitations of confidentiality, SA, homicide/suicide attempts/ideations, history of mental illness/treatment, increase victim safety	all clients pay - programs may charge up to $3500 per client, may charge intake and evaluation separately from intervention services, may charge group sessions on sliding scale, may negotiate deferred payment schedule or partial payment

Key: SA = Substance Abuse;
MH = Mental Health;
Psych. Eval. = Psychiatric Evaluation;
*Text not yet available.

APPENDIX A.3

Michigan, Wayne County
Minnesota
Missouri
Mississippi
Montana
Nebraska
Nevada
New Hampshire
New Jersey
New Mexico
New York
North Carolina
North Dakota
Ohio
Oklahoma
Oregon
Pennsylvania

Information Matrix on Interventions for Batterers

STATE	Status of Standards or Guidelines	Certifying Agency	Intervals for Certification/Fee
Michigan, Wayne County	standards (not State-mandated)	Department of Probation and Parole	certification process not specified
Minnesota	none, currently developing suggestions for programming in Twin Cities	–	–
Missouri	standards, draft in process	Department of Probation and Parole	–
Mississippi	none	–	–
Montana	none (preliminary discussions and information gathering)	–	–
Nebraska	in development	–	–
Nevada	none	–	–
New Hampshire	none	–	–
New Jersey	standards for provider certification, not batterer programs	New Jersey Association of Domestic Violence Professionals	term not specified; $250, fee reduction possible
New Mexico	in development	–	–
New York	guidelines, draft as of 3/96	Office for the Prevention of Domestic Violence (OPDV)	duration of program certification determined by OPDV; intervention programs pay cost of monitoring process
North Carolina	in development (no draft yet)	–	–

Information Matrix on Interventions for Batterers (Continued)

STATE	Court Contact/ Referrals	Length of Treatment	Screening Criteria
North Dakota	draft as of March 1, 1996 (non-mandatory guidelines)	Division of Parole and Probation	
Ohio	standards (recommended)	Ohio Domestic Violence Network	
Oklahoma	standards for State-funded programs*	–	–
Oregon	protocols*	–	–
Pennsylvania	standards (recommended)	Pennsylvania Coalition Against Domestic Violence, intervention programs monitored by domestic violence programs & advocates	intervention program pays monitoring fees

Key: SA = Substance Abuse;
MH = Mental Health;
Psych. Eval. = Psychiatric Evaluation;
*Text not yet available.

Information Matrix on Interventions for Batterers (Continued)

STATE	Court Contact/ Referrals	Length of Treatment	Screening Criteria
Michigan, Wayne County	referred as condition of probation	39 hrs spread over no less than 26 weekly sessions	all batterers provided service regardless of race, gender, ethnicity, sexual preference, physical/mental disability; evaluation of criminal, SA, MH histories, potential lethality
Minnesota	–	–	–
Missouri	–	–	–
Mississippi	–	–	–
Montana	–	–	–
Nebraska	–	–	–
Nevada	–	–	–
New Hampshire	–	–	–
New Jersey	must have knowledge of laws and court system	not specified	no discrimination, reasonable fees must be charged; SA assessment
New Mexico	–	–	–

Information Matrix on Interventions for Batterers (Continued)

STATE	Court Contact/ Referrals	Length of Treatment	Screening Criteria
New York	information exchange, progress reports	no specific program length recommended; longer participation allows for more exposure to material presented in educational groups; court-mandated referrals (min. participation of 1-3 yrs) send stronger message that battering is a crime	assessment - background on violence and abuse; option to screen out applicants w/ severe MH problems or extensive criminal assault record; SA; potential lethality
North Carolina	–	–	–
North Dakota	provide courts, probation/parole, other referral agencies w/ information; obtain court orders & treatment records; submit participant progress reports; document incidents	minimum of 24 wkly sessions - averaging 2 hrs; option of extending participant membership indefinitely based on treatment outcomes	intake must include referral source, violence history, criminal record, lethality assessment, abuse/violence inventory, mental status exam, drug/alcohol screening, medical/psychological/drug evaluation (as necessary)
Ohio	accountable to criminal justice system by actively communicating w/ probation, courts	–	lethality assessment on first contact with batterer, emotional & behavioral assessment, history of and current emotional, behavioral, SA problems; age appropriate mental status exam; social and legal assessment

Information Matrix on Interventions for Batterers (Continued)

STATE	Court Contact/ Referrals	Length of Treatment	Screening Criteria
Oklahoma	–	–	–
Oregon	–	–	–
Pennsylvania	program responsible to justice system - report status of participant, warn of risks to victim, provide training/technical assistance to justice system; court-mandated participants are subject to formal contract w/ court	29 sessions (includes 8 phase one workshops - 1 hr weekly; 3 individual conferences; 18 phase two groups - 2 hrs weekly)	determined by individual program; readiness for intervention; psychological pathology; previous intervention opportunities; criminal, drug, MH history; history of abuse, violence, target of abuse, threats, depression; lethality

Key: SA = Substance Abuse;
MH = Mental Health;
Psych. Eval. = Psychiatric Evaluation;
*Text not yet available.

Information Matrix on Interventions for Batterers (Continued)

STATE	Additional Treatment/Referrals	Staff Education/Training	Staffing Requirements
Michigan, Wayne County	SA prior to or in conjunction w/ program - referrals to other agencies but not as substitution for treatment	counselors certified by State; supervisors have 3 yrs experience w/ batterers, victims; supervisor w/ 3 yrs group facilitation experience; each have minimum of 24 hrs training in domestic violence from established treatment provider; ongoing training	meet standards of affiliated professional groups; violence free, no history of domestic violence unless director satisfied w/ completion of treatment & no arrests for minimum of 6 mos; drug free; no criminal record; reflect ethnic/linguistic community
Minnesota	–	–	–
Missouri	–	–	–
Mississippi	–	–	–
Montana	–	–	–
Nebraska	–	–	–
Nevada	–	–	–
New Hampshire	–	–	–
New Jersey	must do substance abuse assessment; refer to other providers as needed	180 hours of training: 168 of core curriculum; and 12 hours of program visits (no batterer programs); continuing education	no prejudice, serve best interest of client, refer as necessary, non-violent lifestyle

Information Matrix on Interventions for Batterers (Continued)

STATE	Additional Treatment/Referrals	Staff Education/Training	Staffing Requirements
New Mexico	–	–	–
New York	SA treatment prior to acceptance to program	supervisors - experienced w/ both victims & perpetrators or supervised by outside domestic violence advocate/staff, w/ 3 yrs experience group facilitation, minimum 40 hrs training by established domestic violence & intervention program, ongoing training	reflect ethnic, linguistic diversity of community; drug free; uphold, model, teach tenets on sexism, racism, classism, homophobia, oppression & impact of violence against women
North Carolina	–	–	–
North Dakota	referrals made to other agencies for specialized treatment following intake - may not be substitute for domestic violence treatment	facilitators - licensed in human service-related field/complete continuing education credits in domestic violence issues; experience w/ victims (min. 1 yr) & perpetrators (min. 50 hrs); training in issues listed in program curriculum	violence free, drug free, no criminal convictions; familiarity w/State laws, law enforcement, probation, prosecution, court policies re: domestic violence; participate in domestic violence task force/coalition
Ohio	MH services arranged, assess and refer for additional services	–	at minimum, possess appropriate professional credentials; reflect cultural/ethnic diversity of community served
Oklahoma	–	–	–
Oregon	–	–	–

Information Matrix on Interventions for Batterers (Continued)

STATE	Additional Treatment/Referrals	Staff Education/Training	Staffing Requirements
Pennsylvania	SA, MH, other treatment appropriate, referrals outside of agency	trained annually on sexism, racism, homophobia & impact on violence; supervisors - experience w/ perpetrators & victims (at least 1 w/3 yrs exp., & 1 w/ 3 yrs facilitation); min. of 40 hrs from both established domestic violence & intervention programs	violence free; free from criminal convictions; drug free; do not perpetuate victim-blaming, sexism, misogyny; open to communication; reflect ethnic/linguistic diversity of community served

Key: SA = Substance Abuse;
MH = Mental Health;
Psych. Eval. = Psychiatric Evaluation;
*Text not yet available.

Information Matrix on Interventions for Batterers (Continued)

STATE	Structure	Prescribed Curriculum	Prohibited Methods/ Theories
Michigan, Wayne County	groups - same-gender, sexuality; repeat offender groups no more than 12; first-time offender groups a maximum of 18	identification, confrontation, and change of abusive behavior; effects on victim and others; cooperation; nonabusive communication; cultural/social influences	fair arguing education; male responsibility; conflict resolution; anger management; couple, family therapies as primary; causality in past; systems theory; containment; de-escalation
Minnesota	–	–	–
Missouri	–	–	–
Mississippi	–	–	–
Montana	–	–	–
Nebraska	–	–	–
Nevada	–	–	–
New Hampshire	–	–	–
New Jersey	certification for individual, group, and family domestic violence counselors	power imbalance between men and women; responsibility for violence, sociological, cultural issues	none specified
New Mexico	–	–	–

Information Matrix on Interventions for Batterers (Continued)

STATE	Structure	Prescribed Curriculum	Prohibited Methods/ Theories
New York	open group accepting new participants no longer than every three weeks, facilitated by minimum of two instructors/facilitators, w/ participants of the same gender	examine belief system; defining abuse & results; understand causes - social/cultural context; examine criminality of actions; teach responsibility for actions; provide information on stopping abuse, on respect, and community response to violence	traditional methods like stress management, anger control, psychotherapy, couples counseling, family therapy, communication skill building, mediation and conflict resolution
North Carolina	_	_	_
North Dakota	group therapy treatment of choice - no more than 10 adult males (gay batterers may enroll if provider determines this appropriate), minimum of 2 facilitators; providers decide if open/closed sessions; individual therapy only under special circumstances	education - dynamics of domestic violence, power control issues, intergenerational patterns, victim issues, legal intervention, skills building, conflict resolution, gender role training, cognitive restructuring; therapy; crisis management	approaches that blame, intimidate, endanger, coerce victim; couples, marriage, family therapy during batterer treatment (only after program completed, violence ends, victim agrees); anger management; addiction counseling defining violence as addiction
Ohio	group sessions preferred; educational component is lecture/presentational style - didactic, limited discussion; psycho- educational/therapeutic modalities have cofacilitation - male/female teams that model egalitarian and mutually empowering roles	based on assessment of client; intervention not defined but should comply w/ regulations of Ohio Counselor & Social Worker Board, Ohio Psychology Board, Ohio Medical Board - practice of education counseling, social work, psychology, medicine	_
Oklahoma	_	_	_

Information Matrix on Interventions for Batterers (Continued)

STATE	Structure	Prescribed Curriculum	Prohibited Methods/ Theories
Oregon	–	–	–
Pennsylvania	short-term educational format or comprehensive intervention initiatives; formal group facilitated by 2 coleaders; individual sessions used to supplement	profeminist (supplement w/ cognitive-behavioral & psychoeducational)-define abuse, cultural supports, examine values facilitating abuse, learning alternatives, teach respect of women, accept consequences, effects of abuse, responsibility plans	Insight Model, Ventilation Model, Interaction Model; couple format rarely appropriate until batterer accepts responsibility for violence

Key: SA = Substance Abuse;
MH = Mental Health;
Psych. Eval. = Psychiatric Evaluation;
*Text not yet available.

Information Matrix on Interventions for Batterers (Continued)

STATE	Contact w/ Victim	Fee for Service
Michigan, Wayne County	duty to warn if perpetrator poses threat	expected to contribute to payment for service
Minnesota	–	–
Missouri	–	–
Mississippi	–	–
Montana	–	–
Nebraska	–	–
Nevada	–	–
New Hampshire	–	–
New Jersey	none specified	n/a
New Mexico	–	–
New York	offer information/referrals to partners & others affected; never seek information from partner; only contact in case of danger to victim, to inform on batterer participation; communicate through domestic abuse advocates	fee structure developed by programs - pay fee whether or not it is court-mandated, sliding scale available for clients who need it, community service may serve in lieu of full payment but must still participate in intervention program
North Carolina	–	–

Information Matrix on Interventions for Batterers (Continued)

STATE	Contact w/ Victim	Fee for Service
North Dakota	work w/ domestic violence programs to assure advocacy, safety planning, other assistance; inform of legal protection/freedom from violence; request batterer history (voluntary); explain program/interface; give referrals; assess lethality; warn of danger	financial support by court for batterer services, fee requirements for participation whether or not court ordered, sliding scale available for indigent clients
Ohio	should refer primary victims to victim programs and refrain from attempting to also work with these clients (excluding contact in context of safety checks or brief contact regarding the intervention plan of the victim's mate)	treatment costs, if any, to be borne by the client
Oklahoma	_	_
Oregon	_	_
Pennsylvania	notify of acceptance/rejection for service; encourage plans for protection; inform of outreach, advocacy, other services, domestic violence programs	batterers responsible for their own education/treatment whether participation is socially or court-mandated

Key: SA = Substance Abuse;
MH = Mental Health;
Psych. Eval. = Psychiatric Evaluation;
*Text not yet available.

APPENDIX A.4

Rhode Island
South Carolina
South Dakota
Tennessee
Texas
Utah
Vermont
Virginia
Washington
West Virginia
Wisconsin

Information Matrix on Interventions for Batterers

STATE	Status of Standards or Guidelines	Certifying Agency	Intervals for Certification/Fee
Rhode Island	in development, draft as of 8/96	Department of Corrections/Adult Probation and Parole	assigned certification for a time period (determined by committee), interim certification pending specified modifications, certification w/held for specified reasons
South Carolina	none	–	–
South Dakota	in development	–	–
Tennessee	in development	–	–
Texas	guidelines (for Texas Battering Intervention and Prevention Project [BIPP] funded programs)	Community Justice Assistance Division, Texas Department of Criminal Justice	certified programs will receive funding if program proposal accepted; monitored by BIPP
Utah	standards (only for Department of Human Services programs)	Department of Human Services	–
Vermont	standards (in process of being ratified)	Department of Corrections	–
Virginia	none	–	–
Washington	standards	Division of Children & Family Services	
West Virginia	nothing State-mandated	–	–

Information Matrix on Interventions for Batterers (Continued)

STATE	Status of Standards or Guidelines	Certifying Agency	Intervals for Certification/Fee
Wisconsin	standards for State-funded domestic abuse batterers treatment grants/contracts	Department of Corrections, using Colorado State model for regional accreditation	–
Wyoming	nothing State-mandated	–	–

Key: SA = Substance Abuse;
MH = Mental Health;
Psych. Eval. = Psychiatric Evaluation;
*Text not yet available.

Information Matrix on Interventions for Batterers (Continued)

STATE	Court Contact/ Referrals	Length of Treatment	Screening Criteria
Rhode Island	court/probation referrals must receive progress reports, must be notified of batterer dismissal immediately	minimum of 29 weeks with a total of at least 40 contact hours, missed sessions must be made up, missing more that 2 consecutive sessions results in dismissal	intake assessment - history of abuse, violence, mental illness, medical history, SA
South Carolina	_	_	_
South Dakota	_	_	_
Tennessee	_	_	_
Texas	develop collaborative relationships w/ criminal justice, judicial system - increase court referrals, refer persons eliminated from program	minimum of 36 hours over minimum of 18 weeks; individual counseling sessions should not be included in the required 36 hours	assess appropriateness for participation - history of violence, thoughts of suicide/homicide, weapons, obsessiveness, rage, depression, SA, sexual abuse, nature of relationships, police reports, referral
Utah	court-ordered into treatment or volunteer; those who do not pass screening referred back to court for alternative disposition; written procedures for notifying courts	sessions provided at least 1 hr/wk for minimum of 12 wks	client interview - determine clinical profile, treatment needs; police records, criminal history, prior treatment records, potential for more violence, profile of violence behavior, mental status

Information Matrix on Interventions for Batterers (Continued)

STATE	Court Contact/ Referrals	Length of Treatment	Screening Criteria
Vermont	refer first-time misdemeanor offenders, allow certain offenders in as part of bail release condition, voluntary participants included (but held accountable as ordered offenders)	26 wks w/ additional time to complete requirements of program capped at 52 wks, meet for 1.5-2 hrs wkly	–
Virginia	–	–	–
Washington	court orders for perpetrator treatment	criteria for completion defined by program; at a minimum, 12 or more months - 26 wkly group sessions, monthly face-to-face contact w/ provider until 12 months up	program authority to accept/reject referrals, assess history of violence, SA, history related to homicide/suicide, lethality, weapons assessment, obsession/dependency on victim, depression, MH, sexual abuse, criminal history, cultural
West Virginia	–	–	–
Wisconsin	report recurrence, threats, violations	–	assess risk/danger, responsibility, dependency, perception of control, history of abuse, arrest record, drug use history, availability of weapons, suicide/homicide ideation, family, MH, financial, educational, social, criminal histories
Wyoming	–	–	–

Key: SA = Substance Abuse;
MH = Mental Health;
Psych. Eval. = Psychiatric Evaluation;
*Text not yet available.

Information Matrix on Interventions for Batterers (Continued)

STATE	Additional Treatment/Referrals	Staff Education/Training	Staffing Requirements
Rhode Island	SA addressed above and beyond batterer intervention by licensed certified agency and shall not substitute for intervention treatment; batterer referred back to probation	facilitator qualifications, training, & supervision to be developed	facilitator qualifications, training, & supervision to be developed
South Carolina	–	–	–
South Dakota	–	–	–
Tennessee	–	–	–
Texas	collaboration w/ SA treatment community, refer to other programs for SA, other programs to meet particular needs	volunteer/paid exp. in domestic violence program, human services, relevant activism or degree in related discipline; staff complete 40 hrs orientation (20 hrs if have previous training w/in 3 yrs) with program laws; min. of 20 hrs/yr staff development	recommends staff that reflects cultural diversity of community
Utah	domestic violence counseling provided conjointly w/ or after other necessary treatment	licensed/consulting physician, psychologist, social worker, nurse, marriage/family therapist; person w/ graduate degree & 1 yr experience; licensed social services worker w/ 3 yrs experience who may cofacilitate	providers must comply w/ Department of Human Services Licensing Standards, Section C-IV, outpatient treatment standards; staff licensed in accordance w/ MH Professional Practice Act (UCA 58-60)

Information Matrix on Interventions for Batterers (Continued)

STATE	Additional Treatment/Referrals	Staff Education/Training	Staffing Requirements
Vermont	participants in need of SA or MH treatment will be referred back to the Department of Corrections for formal assessment - addressed prior to, simultaneously w/, or subsequent to batterer treatment	–	violence free; demonstrate attitude free from victim blaming, sexism, misogyny
Virginia	–	–	–
Washington	other therapies may be concomitant but may not substitute for the perpetrator treatment, referrals made on basis of intake evaluation; program determines prioritization of outside therapy	min. 30 hrs training from established victim & perpetrator program, min. 250 hrs supervised direct contact treatment w/ perpetrators & victims; direct contact - BA/BS or equivalent; supervisors - min. 3 yrs, MA/MS or equivalent	registered/certified MH professionals; free from criminal convictions
West Virginia	–	–	–
Wisconsin	alcohol/other drug abuse treatment cannot substitute for batterer treatment; referrals to appropriate treatment (MH problems) made	entry level - 40 hrs training on domestic violence/perpetrator services; 1 yr group facilitating experience; supervisor - 3 yrs exp./approved by local Community Coordinated Response Team, domestic abuse service; min. 12 hrs continuing education yearly	violence free, have not been perpetrators of violence (unless director believes they are violence free); drug/alcohol free; communicate respect (do not perpetuate sexist, victim-blaming attitudes)
Wyoming	–	–	–

Key: SA = Substance Abuse;
MH = Mental Health;
Psych. Eval. = Psychiatric Evaluation;
*Text not yet available.

Information Matrix on Interventions for Batterers (Continued)

STATE	Structure	Prescribed Curriculum	Prohibited Methods/ Theories
Rhode Island	groups of a maximum of 15, single sex participants led by one male and one female cofacilitator	definition of domestic violence, development of responsibility plan, different forms of abuse, techniques for nonabuse, communication skills, impact on partner/children, parenting, stereotyping, sexual abuse/pornography, relationship to child abuse	control techniques that perpetuate abuse - anger management, ventilation techniques
South Carolina	_	_	_
South Dakota	_	_	_
Tennessee	_	_	_
Texas	group format, single sex, w/out victim participation, ideally no more than 15 participants, recommend male w/ female coleaders	orientation, curriculum approved by TCFV based on cognitive and behavioral treatment principles, interpersonal/re-socialization techniques - nature of domestic violence, safety planning, attitude/belief changes, non-abusive behavior, community service	traditional couples counseling, family therapy, mediation, approaches w/ victim and batterer together
Utah	assessment information used to compile individualized treatment plan	assessment information used to compile individualized treatment plan	couples/family therapy not provided until risk assessment conducted
Vermont	education group/class- 10-15 first-time misdemeanor offenders (although offenders under bail release & volunteers	profeminist model - identify & eliminate violent/controlling behaviors, challenge sexist expectations & attitudes; cognitive-behavioral	those that bring victim into circle of responsibility for violence - causality in past, communication

Information Matrix on Interventions for Batterers (Continued).

STATE	Structure	Prescribed Curriculum	Prohibited Methods/ Theories
Vermont	included), led by 2 facilitators, preferably male and female, open ended; individual attention very limited - reasons must be documented	& psychoeducational models - learning non-violence; violence primary focus of intervention	communication enhancement, anger management, systems theory, addiction counseling, family/couples therapy, containment, de-escalation, poor impulse, psychopathology
Virginia	–	–	–
Washington	weekly group treatment sessions	address belief system which legitimizes/sustains violence; use of power/control over partner; definitions of abuse, battering, domestic violence; accountability for actions; forms of abuse; WA State law; techniques for change, impact of abuse	concomitant marital/family therapy may not be consistent w/ victim safety
West Virginia	–	–	–
Wisconsin	single-sex group run by 2 facilitators	male power/control; sociocultural basis; sexism/gender stereotyping; personal responsibility; domestic violence laws/consequences; identification of abuse, controlling/violent behaviors; drug/alcohol awareness; self-awareness; personal change strategies	couples/family therapy as primary treatment; treatment mandating victim involvement; program oriented toward anger management/psychodynamic; center causality in past; abusers not held accountable
Wyoming	–	–	–

Key: SA = Substance Abuse; MH = Mental Health;
Psych. Eval. = Psychiatric Evaluation; *Text not yet available.

Information Matrix on Interventions for Batterers (Continued)

STATE	Contact w/ Victim	Fee for Service
Rhode Island	in cases of danger to victim, contact must be made, notify in writing of batterer's acceptance/rejection in program, provide information about intervention program and available services	pay for services based on sliding scale and all programs shall accommodate batterers regardless of ability to pay, fees waived in exchange for volunteer service if batterer unable to pay full fee
South Carolina	–	–
South Dakota	–	–
Tennessee	–	–
Texas	inform of program limitations, potential danger/risk, program content, available service and support, develop safety plan	recommended that batterer pay for his services - sliding scale or fee waiver policy, partial scholarships, inability to pay policy, accepting insurance as copayment, attendance policy
Utah	maintain/document cooperative working relationships w/ victims, domestic violence services/programs; gain information about perpetrator; duty to warn statute to protect victim	intended that domestic violence funds be used to pay for treatment; appropriate sliding fee schedule utilized to bill 1st & 3rd party payments prior to billing balance to DFS Domestic Violence Fund
Vermont	–	–
Virginia	–	–

Information Matrix on Interventions for Batterers (Continued)

STATE	Contact w/ Victim	Fee for Service
Washington	protect victim, update on client status, encourage victim to make plans to protect herself and her children, inform victim of services, outreach, and programs; establish cooperation with domestic violence victim programs	client must pay for treatment
West Virginia	–	–
Wisconsin	contact for assessment, monitoring, treatment of batterer; assist in safety plan; provide appropriate legal information, referrals; inform about batterer program; conduct follow-up	expected to contribute to costs - client contribution determined by program
Wyoming	–	–

Key: SA = Substance Abuse;
MH = Mental Health;
Psych. Eval. = Psychiatric Evaluation;
*Text not yet available.

Appendix B. Program Personnel and Criminal Justice Professionals Interviewed for This Book

The following is a partial list of individuals interviewed on site and by telephone for this book. Some interviews were conducted in groups, and only the supervisor is listed below. In addition, some individuals requested anonymity.

Site Interviews

Seattle, Washington

Ron Alexander
Group Leader
Ina Maka
(observation)

Don Berrysmith
Zegree, Ellner and Berrysmith

Dan Brewer
Facilitator
Ina Maka

Lucinda Cervantez
Community Advocate
New Beginnings for Women

Meg Crager
Director
Family Services of Seattle

Seth Ellner
Zegree, Ellner and Berrysmith

Roxanne Roos Finney
Director
Ina Maka

Ann Ganley, Ph.D.
Mental Health Clinic
Seattle V. A. Medical Center

Minh-Phuong La Nguyen
Domestic Violence Treatment Coordinator
Refugee Women's Alliance

Lynne Gordon
Domestic Violence Coordinator
King County Judicial Administration

Hon. Helen Halpert
Seattle Municipal Court
Domestic Violence Docket

Sheila Hargesheimer
Domestic Violence Coordinator
City of Seattle

Sid Hoover
Supervisor
Municipal Probation Domestic Violence Unit

Roland Maiuro, Ph.D.
Director
Harborview Medical Center
University of Washington Medical School

Anna Meyer
Domestic Violence Counselor
Seattle Counseling Service for Sexual Minorities

Arlene Red Oak
Case Manager and Group Leader
Ina Maka

Karen Rosenberg
Legal Advocate
New Beginnings for Women

Greg Routt
Group Leader
Family Services of Seattle

Judith Shoshana
Domestic Violence Unit
City Prosecutor's Office

Betty Williams Watson
Group Leader and Teen Outreach Coordinator
Family Services of Seattle

Joan Zegree
Zegree, Ellner and Berrysmith

Quincy/Cambridge, Massachusetts

David Adams, Ed.D.
Program Director EMERGE

Susan Cayouette, Ed.D.
Clinical Director
EMERGE

Andy Klein, Ph.D.
Chief Probation Officer
Quincy District Court

Oswaldo Montoya
Counselor
EMERGE

Maureen Pasik
Counselor
EMERGE

Dinh Pham
Counselor
EMERGE

Chuck Turner
Training Director
EMERGE

Des Moines, Iowa

Dale Chell
Supervisor
Domestic Abuse Intervention Service
Children and Families of Iowa

Maureen C. Dion
Group Facilitator
Domestic Abuse Intervention Service
Children and Families of Iowa

Hon. Carol S. Egly
Polk County Courthouse

Hon. Cynthia Moisan Polk
County Courthouse

Tam Khac Nguyen
Counselor
Domestic Abuse Intervention Service
Children and Families of Iowa

Joe Quinn
Probation Officer
Polk County Jail

Denver, Colorado

Amy Ambrose
Counselor
AMEND

Mark Barnes
Probation Officer
18th Judicial District

Debbie Buckmaster
Program Coordinator
Victim Advocacy Program
Probation Department
18th Judicial District

Tina Busey
Counselor
AMEND

Christine Collins
Counselor
AMEND

Carol Dewey
Counselor
AMEND

Peter Di Leo
Counselor
AMEND

Linda Ferry
Program Administrator
Domestic Violence Unit City
Attorney's Office

Linda Foote Smith
Probation Department
Denver County Court

Rob Gallup
Executive Director
AMEND

Gary Gibbens
Co-Director
AMEND

Robert McBride
Director
The Third Path

Frank Robinson,
Ph.D. Consultant
Probation Department
18th Judicial District

Dexter Shipman
Probation Officer
18th Judicial District

Suzanne Sigona
Director
Probation Department Denver County Court

Baltimore, Maryland

Peggy Araya
Chief Officer
Family Assault Team
Probation Department
Baltimore City

Wil Avery
Batterer Program Manager
House of Ruth

L. Tracy Brown
Director
Coordinating Council on Criminal Justice
Office of the Mayor
Baltimore City

W. Roland Knapp
Director
Division of Parole and Probation
Baltimore City

John Miller
Facilitator, Batterer Program
House of Ruth

Trish Miller
Facilitator, Batterer Program
House of Ruth

Steven Stosny, Ph.D.
Founder
The Compassion Workshop

Rachel A. Wohl
Director
Attorney General's and Lt. Governor's
Family Violence Council

Roni Young
Director
Domestic Violence Unit
State's Attorney's Office Baltimore City

INTERVIEWED BY TELEPHONE

John Beem
Executive Director
Men Overcoming Violence (MOVE)
San Francisco, California

Don Chaplin
Nonviolence Program Coordinator
Domestic Abuse Intervention Project
Duluth, Minnesota

Jon Cohen
Assistant Director
Batterer Intervention Project
New City, New York

Terrence Crowley
CIE Project Director
Men Stopping Violence
Douglasville, Georgia

Diane Davis
Director of Therapy
Domestic Abuse Project
Minneapolis, Minnesota

Sunya Faloyan
Director and Founder
Empowerment Project
Charlotte, North Carolina

Bob Foster
Director
Domestic Abuse Counseling Center
Pittsburgh, Pennsylvania

Bernadette Gerhardt
State Monitor
Division of Family Services
Olympia, Washington

Kevin Hamberger
Director of Behavioral Science
St. Catherine's Family Practice
Kenosha, Wisconsin

Amy Houghton
Colorado Coalition Against Domestic Violence
Denver, Colorado

Luriline Kahapea
Administrative Assistant and Accountant
Alternatives to Violence
Hilo, Hawaii

Beth Ledoux
(former victim advocate for the Quincy District Court
Department of Probation)
Braintree, Massachusetts

Michael Lindsey
Founder
The Third Path
Arapaho County, Colorado

Sharon Miller
Education Specialist
First Step
Jacksonville, Florida

Cindy Minton
Clinical Social Worker
The Batterer Group
Dayton, Ohio

Wendy Mow-Taira
Director
Alternatives to Violence
Hilo, Hawaii

Toby Myers
Director
PIVOT of Aid to Victims of Domestic Violence (AVDA)
Houston, Texas

Steve Piatt
Director
The Batterer Group
Dayton, Ohio

Antonio Ramirez
Director
ManAlive
San Francisco, California

About the National Institute of Justice

The National Institute of Justice (NIJ), a component of the Office of Justice Programs, is the research agency of the U.S. Department of Justice. Created by the Omnibus Crime Control and Safe Streets Act of 1968, as amended, NIJ is authorized to support research, evaluation, and demonstration programs, development of technology, and both national and international information dissemination. Specific mandates of the Act direct NIJ to:

- Sponsor special projects, and research and development programs, that will improve and strengthen the criminal justice system and reduce or prevent crime.
- Conduct national demonstration projects that employ innovative or promising approaches for improving criminal justice.
- Develop new technologies to fight crime and improve criminal justice.
- Evaluate the effectiveness of criminal justice programs and identify programs that promise to be successful if continued or repeated.
- Recommend actions that can be taken by Federal, State, and local governments as well as by private organizations to improve criminal justice.
- Carry out research on criminal behavior.
- Develop new methods of crime prevention and reduction of crime and delinquency.

In recent years, NIJ has greatly expanded its initiatives, the result of the Violent Crime Control and Law Enforcement Act of 1994 (the Crime Act), partnerships with other Federal agencies and private foundations, advances in technology, and a new international focus. Some examples of these new initiatives:

- New research and evaluation is exploring key issues in community policing, violence against women, sentencing reforms, and specialized courts such as drug courts.
- Dual-use technologies are being developed to support national defense and local law enforcement needs.
- The causes, treatment, and prevention of violence against women and violence within the family are being investigated in cooperation with several agencies of the U.S. Department of Health and Human Services.
- NIJ's links with the international community are being strengthened through membership in the United Nations network of criminological institutes; participation in developing the U.N. Criminal Justice Information Network; initiation of UNOJUST (U.N. Online Justice Clearinghouse), which electronically links the institutes to the U.N. network; and establishment of an NIJ International Center.
- The NIJ-administered criminal justice information clearinghouse, the world's largest, has improved its online capability.

- The Institute's Drug Use Forecasting (DUF) program has been expanded and enhanced. Renamed ADAM (Arrestee Drug Abuse Monitoring), the program will increase the number of drug-testing sites, and its role as a "platform" for studying drug-related crime will grow.
- NIJ's new Crime Mapping Research Center will provide training in computer mapping technology, collect and archive geocoded crime data, and develop analytic software.
- The Institute's program of intramural research has been expanded and enhanced.

The Institute Director, who is appointed by the President and confirmed by the Senate, establishes the Institute's objectives, guided by the priorities of the Office of Justice Programs, the Department of Justice, and the needs of the criminal justice field. The Institute actively solicits the views of criminal justice professionals and researchers in the continuing search for answers that inform public policymaking in crime and justice.

INDEX

A

B

C

F

G

H

I

J

K

L

M

P

Q

R

S

T

W

Y